12/91

P9-CRT-990

WAR IN THE GULF

Turner Publishing, Inc.

ATLANTA

CNN
WAR IN THE GULF

Published by Turner Publishing, Inc.
A Subsidiary of Turner Broadcasting Systems, Inc.
ONE CNN Center
Atlanta, Georgia 30348

R.E. Turner, Chairman of the Board, Turner Broadcasting Systems, Inc.
Tom Johnson, President, CNN

STAFF FOR THIS BOOK

Michael Reagan
Publisher

Charles O. Hyman
Project Director

Norman Polmar
Editor

Thomas B. Allen
F. Clifton Berry
Norman Polmar
Authors

Laura D. Johnston
Senior Editor

Kate Glassner
Designer

Michael Anderson
Picture Editor

Ken Mowry
*Informational Graphics
Designer*

Jerry Litofsky
*Graphics and Production
Director*

James W. Porges
Research Coordinator

Pages 2/3 Flanked by firepower, a U.S. Navy pilot snaps a portrait of himself and two A-7E Corsair attack aircraft during a Gulf War sortie.
JOHN LEENHOUTS / U.S. NAVY

Pages 4/5 A 1,900-pound shell flies from the billowing blast of a 16-inch gun of the U.S. battleship *Wisconsin* (BB-64), off the Kuwaiti coast.
JOE MAHONEY / UPI / BETTMANN

Pages 6/7 A victorious American soldier stands atop an Iraqi tank whose turret has been blown away. Kuwaiti oil wells blaze on the horizon.
PETER TURNLEY / BLACK STAR

Page 9 Masked and draped in anti-chemical gear, French soldiers prepare for Gulf War horrors that never came: poison gas and bacterial warfare.
ABBAS / MAGNUM

Its gun stilled, an Iraqi tank burns before the eyes of the victors, and the war ends after 100 hours of desert fighting.
KENNETH JARECKE /CONTACT

Iraqi soldiers, stripped of arms, become prisoners of war. More than 65,000 Iraqis surrendered and an estimated 100,000 deserted.
KENNETH JARECKE /CONTACT

First Edition
Library of Congress Catalog Number 91-065803

10 9 8 7 6 5 4 3 2 1
ISBN 1-878685-00-7 (hardcover)
ISBN 1-878685-01-5 (paperback)
Distributed by Andrews & McMeel
4900 Main Street
Kansas City, Missouri 64112

Printed and bound in the USA by R.R. Donnelley & Sons.

CONTENTS

Television viewers throughout the world saw the Persian Gulf War while it happened. *War in the Gulf* translates the immediacy of that televised war into the traditional form for recounting events: a book.

The idea for the book came from the Cable News Network, which provided the authors with CNN's eyewitness record of the war. The strength of television news is its imagery; the weakness of television is its fleetingness. Images flash past, reporters' words fade away. To preserve this perishable chronicle, CNN turned to a team of book writers. Their sources included the films and transcripts of CNN war coverage. They have made a narrative of instants of war.

Television coverage of the Persian Gulf War changed the face of war. No longer can war be an event faraway in time and place. Television made war immediate. That is part of the story of the Persian Gulf War. Reporting on the war means reporting about television.

The war, through television, was not something that happened over there, but something that happened now. Viewers in a score of nations saw their loved ones in a war while the war was being fought. American mothers and fathers saw sons and daughters at the moment a desert wind swept through a tent city, at the moment that tracers laced a far-off sky. Iraqis saw a Tomahawk missile skimming the Baghdad skyline—and television viewers simultaneously saw the Iraqis seeing the Tomahawk. These images within images spiraled on and on, each a moment that wiped out distance, leaving only time and feeling.

When a television camera showed a Scud missile hurtling overhead, both the reporter on screen and the viewers throughout the world shared a moment of fear. Leaders, whether in a government office or an air-raid bunker, saw their words and acts appearing on the screen. Then those images produced other images, as reaction followed action, denial followed declaration. When coalition aircraft bombed an Iraqi target, the bombs themselves carried cameras. The bomb's image of the bomb approaching a target became an image passed on to television viewers – and to Saddam Hussein, who was watching his war on television, often waging his war on television.

One television moment of commentary particularly captured the spiraling image-within-image-within-image phenomenon of this war. Benjamin Netanyahu, Israeli deputy foreign minister, was in Jerusalem but also, by television, on CNN's "Larry King Live." Netanyahu was taking calls from viewers around the world while Saddam Hussein was sending Scuds against Israel.

Netanyahu knew that what he was saying as a diplomat was being heard by Saddam Hussein in a bunker somewhere in Iraq, and by leaders in Moscow, in Washington, in London, in Riyadh. Israelis, Netanyahu said, were pacing their lives by television, waking up to TV and going to sleep to TV, seeing their part of the war both by living it and watching it on the screen.

"Television is no longer a spectator," he said. "You know, in physics, in subatomic physics, there's something called the Heisenberg Principle, which basically says that, if you observe a phenomenon, you actually change it. Well, we now have the Heisenberg physics of politics. As you observe a phenomenon with television, instantly you modify it somewhat. And I think that what we have to make sure of is that the truth is not modified, and that it's constantly fed to the leaders and to the publics in the democratic countries."

This book is an attempt to look at that image-filled war, without modifying what happened.

"We're getting starbursts, seeming starbursts," CNN anchorman Bernard Shaw reported on January 16, 1991, when tracer fire, streaking missiles, and bomb explosions lit the Baghdad sky. The coalition's first air attack had begun, and throughout the world people started seeing a war while it happened.

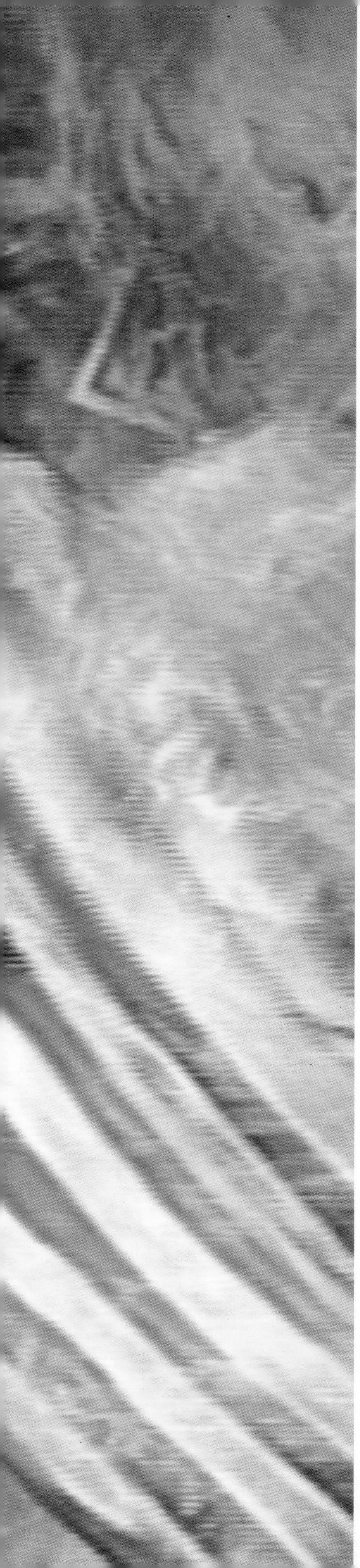

A Troubled Middle East

Writing after World War I, T. E. Lawrence – the legendary Lawrence of Arabia – described Arabs as "a people of spasms, of upheavals, of ideas, the race of the individual genius. . . . Their largest manufacture was of creeds." Implied in his British view of Arabia was the belief that these nomadic geniuses, wandering their seas of sand, needed a bit of imperial organization.

As a British Army lieutenant colonel, Lawrence organized and led Arab guerrilla units fighting against the Turks in World War I. As Lawrence of Arabia, he made a career writing and lecturing about his adventures. He became a symbol of the West's fascination with white-robed Arabs and their exotic desert world.

The British Empire had discovered the Arabs long before Lawrence arrived. The British and French label for the strategic region reflected its place in imperial thinking. It was called the Near East – meaning nearer London and Paris than the Far East. The region was a cultural fountainhead: the birthplace of the alphabet at Sumer; the roots of law in Babylon's Code of Hammurabi; the legendary site of the Garden of Eden in Iraq; the holy land of Judaism, Christianity, and Islam. But Europe saw this crucible of civilization in geopolitical terms, as a crossroad of commerce.

To protect that crossroad, Great Britain had supported the Turk-ruled Ottoman Empire, which for centuries had controlled most Arab lands. The British saw the empire as a force that kept Russia out of the Near East. (The label "Middle East" dates to World War II, when the region was seen, from a

Jordanians burn an American flag, symbol of the U.S.-led coalition forged in response to Iraq's invasion of Kuwait. Jordan's King Hussein gave his open support to Iraq.

CNN

15

global viewpoint, as lying between Europe and the Far East.)

Near the end of the 19th Century, as Arab nationalism began to challenge a weakened Ottoman Empire, the British started dealing directly with emirs, the princely rulers of small Arabian realms. One of the first emirs favored by the British was the sheik of Kuwait. In 1899, the ruling Al-Sabah family put their foreign relations and defense under British protection.

By then, Great Britain was deeply involved in the region. After the opening of the British-financed Suez Canal in 1869, the kingdom of Egypt virtually became part of the British Empire, though the monarchy did not become an official British protectorate until 1914.

Turkey sided with Germany against Great Britain and France in World War I. As a result, the victorious allies forced the Turks from Arab lands and then transformed the region into an assortment of states under British or French control. The carving produced the modern Middle East.

At the same time, the British were dealing with efforts by Jews and Arabs to establish independent states in Palestine. The British and the French long had given leading Arabs assurances of a Palestinian state, but had ignored similar demands from Jews. In 1897, the first World Zionist Congress had vowed "to create for the Jewish people a home in Palestine secured by public law," and influential Zionists, such as Lord Rothschild, worked to get the vow fulfilled.

In 1917, British Foreign Secretary Arthur Balfour, in a letter to Rothschild, said the British government would "view with favour the establishment in Palestine of a national home for the Jewish people." The Balfour Declaration spurred Jewish immigration to Palestine, whose Jewish population rose from 57,000 in 1919, to 152,000 in 1923. The influx fueled Arab opposition, which, at times, turned violent.

Palestine was one of the territories arbitrarily formed from the Ottoman wreckage. Within a few years after World War I, the state-makers of Great Britain and France began creating a Middle East mosaic of nations, which from its inception shimmered with once and future strife.

In Palestine, fighting between Arab and Jewish communities led to proposals in the 1930s that the 1920 British mandate be replaced by two sovereign states, one Arab and the other Jewish. World War II made the Middle East a battleground and overshadowed, temporarily, the Palestinian crisis.

As survivors of the Holocaust began arriving in Palestine after the war, the British mandate expired, and in the vacuum Israel was established in May 1948. Egypt, Iraq, Transjordan, Syria, and Lebanon responded by attacking Israel. About 750,000 Arab Palestinians fled. When armistices ended the war in July 1949, Israel had expanded into Galilee and the Negev.

The area of Palestine, some of which had been designated for an Arab state, was partitioned between Egypt, Jordan (formally Transjordan), and Israel, which occupied about four-fifths of what had been Palestine. Arab nations would not recognize Israel's existence, and Arab-Israeli warfare continued.

Much of the warfare has erupted over disputed territory. Israel seized an Egyptian coastal area, the Gaza Strip, in 1956; it took the West Bank, the Golan Heights, and the Sinai Peninsula in the 1967 Six-Day War. On October 6, 1973, in what became known as the Yom Kippur War, the Egyptian Army stormed across the Suez Canal while Syrian forces attacked in the Golan Heights. Israel soon drove the Syrians across the border and pushed to within 20 miles of Damascus when Jordan sent troops to defend the Syrian capital. The Soviet Union airlifted weapons to the Arabs, and the United States countered with an airlift of arms to Israel. Under pressure from the United States, Egypt and Israel agreed to a cease-fire on October 24.

Peace between Egypt and Israel seemed impossible, but in 1977 a dramatic breakthrough began when Egyptian President Anwar Sadat made a historic visit to Jerusalem to show Egypt's desire for peace. Israeli Prime Minister Menachem Begin then visited Egypt. In the United States, President Jimmy Carter was the host of a summit that drew the two leaders Continued on page 21

THE CHANGING FACE OF THE MIDDLE EAST

Six hundred years of Ottoman rule ended after World War I, when victorious Britain and France divided the Middle East into political spheres of influence. The borders dictated by postwar politics remain largely unchanged today.

SOURCE: KNIGHT-RIDDER TRIBUNE NEWS

MIDDLE EAST LEADERS

IRAQ
Republic of Iraq

**PRESIDENT
SADDAM HUSSEIN**

 Leftists killed the king of Iraq in 1958, launching an era of coup and counter-coup until the Baath Arab Socialist Party took over in 1968, purged the army, and wiped out all political opposition. Baathist strong-arm leader Saddam Hussein took power in 1979 and put down the Kurd's revolt by bombing Kurdish villages. He gained supreme power through a ruthless secret police and a penchant for killing real and suspected rivals.

Stabilized by terror, Iraq prospered. New housing and improved medical services increased Saddam's popularity. He became a hero of the Arab world for his renunciation of the Egyptian peace treaty with Israel and for sharing Iraq's oil wealth with poorer Arab states.

When Saddam went to war against Iran in 1980, the United States "tilted" its support toward Iraq. But the Reagan administration, along with most of the civilized world, condemned Iraq for murdering thousands of Kurds – 5,000 by Amnesty International's estimate – as the Iran-Iraq war was ending in 1988.

169,235 sq. mi. (438,317 sq. km.); pop. 18,074,000. Capital: Baghdad, pop. 3,844,600. People: 95% Muslim, 55% Shiite, 40% Sunni; 75% Arabs, 20-25% Kurds; some Turks. Government: Dictatorship, officially a republic. GNP: $35 billion (1989). Arms: 30.7% of GNP (1985). Total armed forces (1990): 1,000,000 plus reserves.
AP / WIDE WORLD PHOTOS;

IRAN
Islamic Republic of Iran

**PRESIDENT
HASHEMI RAFSANJANI**

 Shah Mohammad Reza Pahlavi succeeded his father in 1941 and assumed full control in 1953. He tried to stave off revolution by liberalizing his rule. But a violent revolt, led by conservative Shiite Muslims, drove him from the "Peacock Throne" in 1979. Militants seized the U.S. Embassy and took 62 Americans hostage.

A fiercely anti-American Shiite leader, the Ayatollah Ruhollah Khomeini, established a theocracy. In Jan. 1981, four months after the Iran-Iraq war began, Iran returned the U.S. hostages. The war continued, with great loss of life on both sides, until Aug. 1988, when Iran accepted a U.N. cease-fire resolution.

Khomeini died in June 1989, and the exporting of religious revolution seemed to die with him. His successor, Hashemi Rafsanjani, called himself a builder and a moderate, raising hope of a change in U.S.-Iranian relations. But the United States continued to maintain a policy that supported Iraq over Iran.

636,296 sq. mi. (1,648,000 sq. km.); pop. 53,867,000. Capital: Tehran, pop. 6,022,000. People: 93% Shiite Muslim; 63% Persian, 19% Turkomans and Baluchis, 3% Kurds, 4% Arabs. Government: Islamic republic, a theocracy of fundamentalists. GNP: $75 billion (1986). Arms: 7.9% of GNP (1985). Total armed forces: 504,000.
JEAN GAUMY / MAGNUM

KUWAIT
State of Kuwait

**EMIR SHAIKH JABIR
AL-AHMAD AL-JABIR AS-SABAH**

 Until 1946, when Kuwait began producing oil, the land was a place where poor Bedouins, pearl divers, and fishermen settled, eking out a living. The discovery of oil transformed Kuwait into a little nation of big money. Now schools, medical services – even telephones – are free, there is no income tax, and nearly every Kuwaiti citizen can afford servants.

Kuwait has been ruled since 1756 by the Al-Sabah family. Shaikh Jabir al-Ahmad al-Jabir as-Sabah presides as the emir. Although the realm is theoretically a constitutional monarchy, the emir began governing by decree in July 1986, when he dissolved parliament.

Kuwait invests about 10% of its oil revenue in a $100 billion financial empire that spans the globe. The London-based Kuwait Investment Office owns properties that range from skyscrapers in New York and San Francisco to rubber plantations in Malaysia.

6,880 sq. mi. (17,818 sq. km.); pop. 2,090,000, about 570,000 are Kuwaitis; the rest (prewar) were mostly Arabs, including 300,000 Palestinians. Capital: Kuwait City; pop. approx. 25% of total. People: 39% Kuwaiti; 39% other Arabs; remainder Iranians, Indians, Palestinians; 85% Muslim, most of them Sunni. Government: Autocratic but officially a constitutional monarchy. GNP: $23.1 billion (1989) Arms: 5.1% of GNP (1988). Total armed forces (1990): 20,300.
CHARLES CROWELL / BLACK STAR

ISRAEL
State of Israel

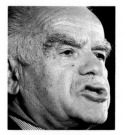

**PRIME MINISTER
YITZHAK SHAMIR**

Wars with Arab neighbors in 1967 and 1973 gained Israel additional territory. In 1979, Egypt signed a peace accord with Israel and regained the Sinai. But the conquered territories of the West Bank, the Golan Heights, and East Jerusalem remained in Israel's hands.

Prime Minister Yitzhak Shamir's hard-line Likud Party is determined to hold onto lands captured in the face of ever-increasing violence from the Palestinians, who claim rights to it. While the United States urged negotiations, Shamir backed strong measures against the estimated 1.6 million Palestinians who are living under Israeli control.

Frustrations against Israeli rule erupted in Dec. 1987, when youths started throwing stones at Israeli soldiers. This was the beginning of an uprising, the *intifada*, that thrust the Palestinian issue into the headlines and onto the evening television news. Every Arab state now had a new and potent reason to hate and threaten Israel.

8,473 sq. mi. (21,946 sq. km.); pop. 4,371,000 (plus 1,611,000 in occupied territories). Capital: Jerusalem, pop. 457,000. (Most countries, to avoid recognition of Arab-claimed Jerusalem, keep their embassies in Israel's former capital, Tel Aviv.) People: 83% Jewish, 16% Arab. Government: Parliamentary democracy. GNP: $25.9 billion (1986) Arms: 13.8% of GNP (1988). Total armed forces: 141,000.
CHRISTOPHER MORRIS / BLACK STAR

EGYPT
Arab Republic of Egypt

**PRESIDENT
HOSNI MUBARAK**

In 1978 Egyptian President Anwar Sadat dramatically broke with the past by cautiously moving toward peace with Israel. That year Sadat, Israeli Prime Minister Menachem Begin, and U.S. President Jimmy Carter signed the Camp David Accords, setting a framework for peace between Egypt and Israel. The peace agreement inflamed a group of Muslim fundamentalists, who assassinated Sadat in 1981.

Vice President Hosni Mubarak, slightly wounded in the assassination, succeeded Sadat and has been president ever since. Mubarak's close relationship with the United States, while gaining Egypt vitally needed economic and military aid, alienated him from his fundamental constituents. They supported him when, like Kuwait, Egypt aided Iraq in the Iran-Iraq War. Their support of Iraq's Saddam Hussein continued after the war, while Mubarak turned cool toward Saddam and his rabble-rousing politics.

386,662 sq. mi. (1,001,449 sq. km.); pop. 54,778,000. Capital: Cairo, pop. 5,875,000, with suburbs 10,000,000. People: 90% of ancient Egyptian descent, remainder Bedouin Arab and Nubian; 90% Sunni Muslim; some Coptic Christians. Government: Republic. GNP: $34.5 billion (1987-1988) Arms: 7.8% of GNP (1988). Total armed forces: 448,000.

ABOVE: M. PHILIPPOT / SYGMA
RIGHT: ALAIN NOGUES / SYGMA

SAUDI ARABIA
Kingdom of Saudi Arabia

**KING FAHD IBN
ABDEL AZIZ**

Abdel-Aziz Al Saud unified four Bedouin tribes and created Saudi Arabia in 1932 – just in time for the exploitation of the sheikdom's petroleum by Western oil speculators. His descendants have ruled the monarchy ever since. King Fahd, sixth of 28 sons of the founder of the kingdom, began his reign in 1982, following the death of his half-brother, King Khalid.

The Koran is the constitution of the kingdom and Saudis follow a very strict form of Islam. Alcohol and public entertainment are forbidden. The veiled women of Saudi Arabia cannot drive cars or appear with men in public places.

Other Arab countries show great deference toward Saudi Arabia because it protects within its borders the most sacred of Islamic holy places: Mecca, the birthplace of the Prophet Mohammed, where pilgrims visit the holiest of shrines, the Kaaba; and Medina, Mohammed's base for converting Arabia to Islam.

Since the beginning of the oil boom in the 1940s, the United States has provided technical aid to Saudi Arabia. More than 25,000 Americans were living in the kingdom in 1988. The Saudis have been consistent customers for high-tech U.S. weaponry.

830,000 sq. mi. (2,149,690 sq. km.); pop. 12,678,000, including 4,000,000 non-Saudis. Capital: Riyadh, pop. 1,200,000. People: 99% Muslim; 90% Arabs. Government: Monarchy. GNP: $72 billion (est. 1989) Arms: 16.5% of GNP (1988). Total amred forces: 67,500.

JORDAN
Hashemite Kingdom of Jordan

KING HUSSEIN

The assassination of Jordan's King Abdullah in 1951 put his teenage grandson Hussein on the throne.

Hussein, the most durable leader in the Middle East, is married to Lebanese-American Lisa Halaby, Queen Noor. The queen has regularly appeared in the United States to lobby for her husband and her adopted country.

Hussein joined Egypt and Syria in the 1967 Six-Day War. Defeat cost Jordan the West Bank, where 1,000,000 Palestinians lived, and the Old City. When Palestinians in Jordan rose in civil war, they were crushed by Hussein and his army, consisting mostly of Bedouins armed with U.S. weapons.

When the Gulf War began, Hussein's Palestinian population considered Iraq's Saddam Hussein a hero. Jordan got 90% of its petroleum from Iraq. Iraq borrowed heavily from Jordan during the Iran-Iraq War. Saddam's failure to repay the loans put Jordan in a dire financial situation. Hussein's refusal to unequivocally support the U.N. boycott against Iraq cast doubt over future U.S. aid, which totaled more than $1 billion during the past decade.

35,467 sq. mi. (91,860 sq. km.); pop. 2,956,000. Capital: Amman, pop. 812,500. People: 98% Arabs, most of them Palestinians, with some Circassians. Armenians, and Kurds; 95% Muslim, nearly all of them Sunni. Government: Monarchy. GNP: $4 billion (1989). Arms: 21% of GNP (1988). Total armed forces: 82,250.

SYRIA
Syrian Arab Republic

**PRESIDENT
HAFEZ AL-ASSAD**

Syria won independence from France in 1946. But after Israel defeated Arab armies in the 1948-1949 war, military dictators took power. A civilian government returned in 1956 and established a United Arab Republic with Egypt.

The alliance faltered in 1961, and out of the crisis emerged the Arab Socialist Baath Party. Its leader, President Hafez al-Assad has been president of Syria since Feb. 1971. He is a sworn enemy of Iraq's leader, Saddam Hussein. The rivalry stems from their competition for primacy in the Arab world

The United States broke off diplomatic relations with Syria in 1967, after the Arab-Israeli Six-Day War. Although U.S.-Syrian relations resumed in June 1974, U.S. antipathy toward Syria grew as Syria rejected accords for Egypt-Israel peace, supported anti-Western terrorists, and grew closer to the Soviet Union.

71,044 sq. mi. (184,004 sq. km.); pop. 12,080,000. Capital: Damascus, pop. 1,219,400. People: 90% Arab, remainder Kurds, Armenians, Circassians, Turkoman; 70% Sunni Muslim, 20% other Muslim; 10% Christians; small Jewish community. Government: Republic, but controlled by Arab Socialist Baath Party regimes since 1963. GNP: $5.83 billion (1988). Arms: 10.9% of GNP (1988). Total armed forces: 404,000.

ABOVE: DANIEL SIMON / GAMMA-LIAISON
LEFT: C. SPENCER / GAMMA-LIAISON

MIDDLE EAST LEADERS

TURKEY
Republic of Turkey

**PRESIDENT
TURGUT OZAL**

 Mustafa Kemal-Ataturk, Father of the Turks – founded the republic of Turkey in 1923, changing the Islamic land of the Ottoman Turks into a secular, Western nation. Still, beneath the modern Turkey seethed ancient rivalries and a tradition of harsh restraints on individual rights. A military coup in 1980 interrupted Turkey's republican history for three years, then restored power to an elected parliament.

Turkey joined the North Atlantic Treaty Organization (NATO) in 1952 and has been a steady – although sometimes wary – friend of the United States. Arab nations tend to treat Turkey as a European state, but in 1989 the European Community rejected Turkey's membership, citing economic problems and a poor record on human rights.

Turkey, like Iraq, has a large, unassimilated Kurdish population. Mindful of Western sensibilities, Turkey tries to subdue the Kurds through geography, not brutality, by keeping them in the southeastern mountains.

Turkey pleases Arab nations by maintaining only limited relations with Israel.

300,948 sq. mi. (779,452 sq. km.); pop. 55,356,000. Capital: Ankara, pop. 2,235,000. People: 85% Turkish, 12% Kurdish; 98% Muslim. Government: Republic. GNP: $68.4 billion (1988). Arms: 3.9% (1988). Total armed forces: 651,000.

ABOVE: AP / WIDE WORLD PHOTOS;
ABOVE RIGHT: ABBAS / MAGNUM
OPPOSITE:PETER TURNLEY / BLACK STAR

UNITED ARAB EMIRATES

**SHEIK ZAID IBN
SULTAN AN-NAHAYAN**

 The UAE, a federation of seven sheikdoms, was created after the British withdrawal from the Gulf in 1971. The biggest and richest sheikdom – Abu Dhabi – leads the other six.

Sheik Zaid, president of the UAE, is also emir of Abu Dhabi.

Oil revenues have given the citizens of the UAE one of the highest per-capita incomes in the world. In recent years, the UAE encouraged foreign investment.

32,278 sq. mi. (83,600 sq. km.); pop. 1,698,000. Capital: Abu Dhabi, pop. 243,000. People: Arabs, Iranians, Pakistanis, Indians, 95% Muslim, Sunni and Shiite; 20% of the residents are UAE citizens. Government: Federation of emirates under an emir as president. GNP: $20 billion. Arms: 6.8% of GNP (1988). Total armed forces: 44,000.

OMAN
Sultanate of Oman

 Oman, long a friend of the United States, supported the Egypt-Israel peace accord negotiated by U.S. President Jimmy Carter in 1979.

82,030 sq. mi. (212,457 sq. km.); pop. 1,420,000. Capital: Muscat, pop. 50,000. People: Arab, Baluchi, Zanzabari, Indian; 75% Muslim. Government: Sultanate. GNP: $7.3 billion (1986) Arms: 38.4% of GNP (1988). Total armed forces: 29,500.

YEMEN
Republic of Yemen

 North Yemen President Ali Abdullah Saleh of the powerful Hashed tribe became the leader of Yemen when north and south united in 1970. Pro-Western and conservative, he shrewdly played a game of non-alignment until the Persian Gulf crisis, when he put Yemen on Iraq's side.

Most of Yemen's income comes from remittances, money sent home by Yemeni working in other countries. For Yemen's siding with Iraq, host governments expelled Yemeni workers, exacerbating Yemen's economic problems.

203,850 sq. mi. (527,968 sq. km.); pop. 12,000,000 to 13,000,000. Capital: Sanaa, pop. 1,200,000. People: 99% Muslim. Government: Republic. GNP: Unknown; its underground economy, based on smuggling, may rival its official economy. Arms: 61,000-man army, largest on the Arabian Peninsula. Total armed forces:

QATAR
Kingdom of Qatar

 Qatar's people, outnumbered by foreign workers, are among the richest people on earth. Oil revenues are widely distributed for social projects, but the arid, barren land resists development. About half the population lives in Doha.

4,247 sq. mi.(11,000 sq. km.); pop. 437,000. Capital: Doha, pop. 217,300. People: 45% Arab, 15% Pakistani, 21% Indian, 6% Iranian; 95% Muslim, mostly Sunni. Government: Sheikdom. GNP: $3.8 billion (1985 est.) Arms: 25% of budget (1983 est.) Total armed forces: 7,500.

BAHRAIN
Kingdom of Bahrain

 Bahrain is an archipelago of about 35 islands off the coast of Saudi Arabia and Qatar. Oil was discovered in the 1930s; reserves could run out by 1994. To find a new source of income, the emir fosters offshore banking and accommodations for multinational companies.

267 sq. mi. (691 sq. km.); pop. 500,000. Capital: Manama, pop. 108,700. People: 73% Arab, 9% Iranian, also Pakistani, Indian; over 60% of the indigenous population is Shiite Muslim, 30% Sunni Muslim. Government: Monarchy. GNP: $3.6 billion (1988 est.) Arms: 9% of published budget (1986). Armed forces: 3,350.

LEBANON
Republic of Lebanon

By the end of 1990, Lebanon was emerging from a 15-year civil war caused by a struggle for power within Lebanon's delicately balanced government. The structure was set up when France granted independence in 1943: the president a Christian, the premier a Sunni Muslim, legislative leader a Shiite Muslim.

In the 1970s, the arrangement broke down as Beirut became divided between Christian and Muslim forces.

Syria, aligned with local Muslims , unleashed its military in Lebanon in October 1990 and defeated Christian forces. But in south Lebanon, Palestine Liberation Organization groups still fight Israeli-backed Lebanese.

4,015 sq. mi.(10,400 sq. km.); pop. 3,301,000. Capital: Beirut, pop. 1,100,000. People: 57% Muslim, 42% Christian; language officially Arabic. Government: Republic, but greatly weakened by civil war and outside pressures. GNP: $1.8 billion. Arms: 8.2% of GNP (1983). Armed forces: 21,300.

closer. The meetings produced an unprecedented peace agreement, the Camp David Accords, named after the presidential hideaway where the three leaders hammered out an agreement. Israel said it would leave the occupied Sinai Peninsula. The agreement also called for new efforts to determine the Palestinians' future in the Israeli-occupied West Bank and the Gaza Strip.

During the dismantling of the Ottoman Empire, Great Britain wanted control over territory east of the Jordan River. So, in 1921, it created Transjordan, under King Abdullah, as an entity separate from the rest of British-administered Palestine and French-controlled Syria.

Transjordan became independent in 1946. During the 1948 Arab-Israeli War, King Abdullah occupied the West Bank of the Jordan River, earning the resentment of local Arabs, who saw themselves as culturally superior to Jordan's Arabs. Abdullah also occupied Jerusalem's Old City, and renamed his kingdom Jordan. In 1951, the king was assassinated by a Palestinian. Abdullah's grandson, the current King Hussein, ascended to the throne a year later.

In the disastrous 1967 Six-Day War against Israel, Hussein – allied with Egypt and Syria – lost Jordan's portion of Jerusalem as well as the West Bank. More than 400,000 Palestinian refugees poured into Jordan. From there, Palestinian guerrillas struck at Israel, which in retaliation attacked Jordan.

The Palestinians soon became so powerful that they threatened Hussein's rule. In September 1970, the king sent his air force and Bedouin army against them, strafing refugee camps and inflicting some 20,000 casualties.

Egypt, meanwhile, was becoming a regional power. In 1952, a military coup had installed Major General Mohammed Naguib as the country's first president and premier. In 1954, Lieutenant Colonel Gamal Abdel Nasser, a reform-minded army officer, removed Naguib, established himself as premier, and in 1956 was elected Egypt's second president.

Nasser forced Great Britain out of Egypt and nationalized the Suez Canal in 1956. Earlier, Egypt had closed the canal to shipping bound for Israel. A British-French-Israeli strike against Egypt failed after the U.S.-imposed withdrawal.

Nasser died in 1970 and was succeeded by Vice President Anwar Sadat, who continued Nasser's policies: encourage private investment, seek foreign investment, remain aggressive toward Israel. But Sadat changed policy. His courageous decision to make peace with Israel cost him his life. He was assassinated in 1981 and was succeeded by his vice president, Hosni Mubarak.

Like Egypt, Iraq emerged from colonial control in the 1950s. The British-supported monarchy tottered, and leftists killed the king in 1958. The regicide set off an era of coup and counter-coup until Baath Arab Socialists took over in 1968, purged the Army, and wiped out all political opposition.

The Soviet Union helped build up the Baath war machine, which fought against Israel in the 1973 Yom Kippur War and against Iraq's Kurdish minority when it rose in rebellion. Large populations of Kurds live in northern Iraq, in southeastern Turkey, and in northwestern Iran. In 1975 the Kurds rebelled, with aid from Iran, and demanded independence and their own autonomous nation. Iran, after settling a long-simmering border dispute with Iraq, withdrew support from the Kurds. Their revolt faded but did not die.

Behind the scenes during the Baath consolidation of power was the deputy chairman of the ruling Revolutionary Command Council, the brutal chief of internal security, Saddam Hussein.

Iran, a pro-German monarchy under a shah early in World War II, was occupied during the war by British, U.S., and Soviet troops. The Soviets balked at leaving when the war ended. Soviet-aided Tudeh rebels battled the shah's troops. The Soviets, acceding to demands from President Harry S Truman, finally left. But the incident left the shah, Mohammad Reza Pahlavi, with a dread of a Communist takeover and a reliance on force against dissent.

In 1951, Iranian nationalist groups forced the appointment of Mohammed Mossadegh as prime minister. When he *Continued on page 24*

PALESTINE: SEARCHING FOR A HOMELAND. . .

PLO LEADER YASIR ARAFAT

Palestinians – Arabs and their descendants who now live or formerly lived in what was Palestine – have become a stateless political power in the Middle East. They are scattered through the region in volatile refugee camps, in closely watched communities in Israel-held territory, and in Arab countries.

The Palestine Liberation Organization (PLO) represents several factions that agree on one issue: the establishment of a permanent Palestinian homeland. Although the PLO has a history of terrorist tactics, it was recognized by the United Nations in November 1974 as the legitimate representative of the Palestinian people. The PLO has been given similar status by Arab nations. These designations form the basis for the PLO demand that it be a participant in negotiations concerning the future of the Israeli-occupied West Bank and Gaza Strip.

The PLO advocates Israeli withdrawal from the territories captured in the 1967 Six-Day

...FIGHTING FOR A HOMELAND

War, and the establishment of an independent Palestinian state, perhaps in those areas. About 655,000 Palestinians and some 2,000 Jewish settlers live in the territories.

On November 15, 1988, PLO Chairman Yasir Arafat declared Palestine to be an independent nation. He also agreed to U.N. Resolutions 242, which recognizes Israel's right to exist as an independent nation, and 338, which establishes peace in the Middle East with a vow to curb PLO-sponsored terrorism. Arafat's acceptance of the resolutions lost him the support of several PLO factions.

Arafat won some guarded U.S. support with his

Stones their weapons, masked Palestinians fight Israeli rule in the occupied territories.
CHRISTOPHER MORRIS / BLACK STAR

conciliatory actions. But that support was lost by his response to Saddam Hussein's invasion of Kuwait: Arafat fully endorsed the invasion – and the PLO launched a rocket attack on Israeli targets from southern Lebanon in support of the Iraqis. None of the missiles reached their targets.

Outlawed in Israeli-controlled territory, the PLO went underground and in December 1987 kindled the *intifada* (Arabic for uprising) in the occupied territories to draw international attention to the Palestinians and to bring Israel to the negotiating table. By the time of the Iraqi invasion, about 600 Palestinians had been killed in conflicts with Israeli soldiers and police in the occupied territories. Israeli fatalities numbered about 40.

Palestinian women mourn at the Bethlehem home of an Arab man killed in the intifada.
JAMES NACHTWEY / MAGNUM

Muslims pray at one of the many mosques in Jerusalem (right) under the watchful eyes of Israeli riot police after a confrontation between Palestinian youths and Israeli authorities. In another clash, police arrest a demonstrator (above). The blood-red handprints of Palestinians stain the wall of the Al-Agsa Mosque in Jerusalem (left).

RIGHT AND ABOVE: PATRICK BAZ / AFP; LEFT: JACQUELINE ARZT / BLACK STAR

nationalized Iran's oil, Britain retaliated with an economic boycott. The United States, after getting assurances that the British oil monopoly would be ended, intervened. The Central Intelligence Agency aided Iranian military officers in overthrowing the nationalists and in restoring the shah to his throne.

Trying to stop future rebellions, the shah pushed new laws through the Iranian parliament. Women got the right to vote. Farmers received royal land. Iran built schools and, with U.S. aid, hydroelectric dams. Although the shah put his nation on the road to modernization, he still ruled like a Persian king of old. And his subjects still plotted rebellion. Whatever his worries, the shah was treated as a friend of the West, for Iran was the strongest nation in the Persian Gulf, and from it came more than 40 percent of the imported oil used by the world's major industrial nations.

By the early 1970s, the British, who had created the mosaic of the modern Middle East, were pulling out of the region. Cutting back on defense funds, Great Britain closed bases, withdrew military forces, and ended treaty obligations with Gulf states. The decision had been made in 1968, when Arab nationalism, often borne on waves of Islamic fervor, transfixed the Middle East

with an Arab East. The future belonged to the people who lived there. But even
as the Union Jack was being hauled down, the demand for Persian Gulf oil was
increasing in Britain, as it was in industrial nations worldwide.

No longer were the oil sheiks willing to listen to advisors. Since 1960, they
had been united with other oil producing states in the Organization of
Petroleum Exporting Countries (OPEC), setting prices by controlling oil
production. In 1973, as the United States sought to halt the Yom Kippur War,
Saudi Arabia unleashed "the oil weapon": an immense price increase for nations
supporting Israel. An Arab oil embargo followed.

The Saudi Royal Family, oil-selling friends of Great Britain and the United
States since the 1930s, took the lead in wielding the oil weapon. Prices rose by
70 percent. The Arab members of OPEC said they would cut their production
by five percent and would continue to cut it by an additional five percent a
month until Israel withdrew from all occupied Arab territories.

The oil weapon found its primary target in U.S. gas tanks. Americans waited
in lines that coiled for blocks around gas stations. President Richard M. Nixon
set priorities for fuel allocations. Secretary of State Henry Kissinger juggled

Ancient religions and modern politics clash in Jerusalem, a city sacred to Jews, Christians, and Muslims. The gleaming Dome of the Rock atop Temple Mount enshrines tradition revered by the three faiths.

negotiations to end the embargo and to get a cease-fire. Both materialized, as did the realization that the Middle East was playing by new rules.

Saudi Arabia, which had been paid 22 cents a barrel for crude oil in 1948, received $11.15 in 1976. "The colonial era is gone forever," an official in Saudi Arabia said. "We are masters of our own affairs, and we will decide what to do with our oil."

During the 1973 embargo, the United States imported about 35 percent of its oil. When Jimmy Carter became president four years later, the U.S. dependence on foreign oil had increased to almost 50 percent. OPEC, which had quadrupled oil prices in 1973, doubled prices again in 1977. But Carter's struggle with the realities of the Middle East would not entirely concern oil.

The shah of Iran had met seven U.S. presidents by the time he arrived at the White House in November 1977 and shook hands with an eighth, President

Carter. The shah liked America, although democracy was a foreign abstraction to him. He ruled as an absolute monarch, and if there was dissent, his secret police – the *Savak* – put it down, sometimes murderously. "Nobody can overthrow me," the shah once said. "I have the support of 700,000 troops, all the workers, and most of the people. . . ."

In January 1979, with Iran torn by strikes and riots, the shah announced, "I am going on vacation," and fled his country, beginning a tragi-comic wandering in search of another that would accept him.

The shah's exit set the stage for the entrance of an exiled religious leader, Ayatollah Ruhollah Khomeini. A Shiite Muslim, he brought with him a dogma that would change Iran and its relations with the United States. Most Muslims are Sunni. Shiites, who make up the majority of Muslims in Iran, Iraq, and Bahrain, represent only about ten percent of the world's Muslim population.

The split traces back to the early history of Islam, when followers of Mohammed were deciding the role of Islam in civil affairs. Shiites like Khomeini preach – and, when they get the chance, practice – theocracy. Under the fiercely religious reign of Khomeini, Iranians were shoved out of the modern age. Women lost their right to education. Only religious laws were promulgated, and violators of Khomeini dogma were put to death.

Mobs marched on the U.S. Embassy in Tehran, cursing "the Great Satan" that had supported the shah. In February 1979, an armed mob burst into the embassy and briefly held everyone inside captive. That crisis passed, but anti-American marches continued, and nearly 45,000 Americans were evacuated.

Then, a little after 3 A.M. on Sunday, November 4, 1979, the U.S. Embassy placed an urgent telephone call to the operations center on the seventh floor of the U.S. State Department in Washington, D.C. Another mob, bigger than the first, had stormed the embassy and surrounded the chancery buildings.

In the days that followed, conservative Muslims attacked the Grand Mosque in Mecca, burned the U.S. embassies in Pakistan and Libya, and were repelled in an attack on the U.S. Embassy in Kuwait. Ordinary diplomacy seemed to be going up in flames as fiery Shiite action in Tehran ignited the Arab world.

On November 18 and 19, Iran released 13 hostages – including women and blacks – and threatened to try and execute the remaining 52 as spies. Israel, reportedly, offered to stage a rescue similar to its successful raid that saved Jewish hostages captured on board a commercial airliner forced down in Entebbe, Uganda, in July 1976. But President Carter decided to go it alone, trying first negotiations and then, reluctantly, turning to a military rescue.

The final plan was a compromise, involving less force than Carter's military advisors wanted and more force than *Continued on page 30*

DISPUTED TERRITORY

■ Land captured during 1967 war and still occupied by Israel.

Golan Heights
Syrian border zone annexed by Israel.

West Bank
Annexed by Jordan in 1949, held by Israel since 1967. Population primarily Palestinian.

Gaza Strip
Egyptian territory captured by Israel.

LEBANON
Damascus
SYRIA
Mediterranean Sea
Haifa
Sea of Galilee
JORDAN
Tel Aviv
Amman
Jerusalem
Gaza
Dead Sea
ISRAEL
EGYPT
Elat

0 MILES 30
0 KM 25

SYRIA
IRAQ
IRAN
Map area
SAUDI ARABIA

SOURCE: NATIONAL GEOGRAPHIC

WORLD OIL RESERVES

Estimated proven reserves at the end of 1990, in billions of barrels.

Saudi Arabia 255

Other 164

Iraq 100

Kuwait 95

Iran 93

27

56

59

59

92

United Arab Emirates
Venezuela
Soviet Union
Mexico
United States

SOURCE: AMERICAN PETROLEUM INSTITUTE

Oil commands the skyline of Saudi Arabia, under whose sands is the world's largest known petroleum reserve. Ra's Tannurah oil refinery, one of the most productive on earth, delivers its products directly to ships plying the Persian Gulf, where tankers take on oil for nations throughout the world.
BILL STRODE / WOODFIN CAMP

A little car carries a big energy message during the 1973-1974 gas crisis. Arab countries reduced oil exports in an attempt to curb U.S. aid to Israel. In the next Middle East crisis, Iranians lampoon President Carter (opposite) as they protest U.S. support of Iran's shah.
ABOVE: DENNIS BRACK / BLACK STAR
OPPOSITE: AP / WIDE WORLD PHOTOS

FOLLOWING PAGE
The shah overthrown, Iranians wildly cheer his successor, religious leader Ayatollah Khomeini.
JEAN GAUMY / MAGNUM

Carter wanted. The incredibly complex, multi-service operation involved helicopters, transport planes and an aircraft carrier. Because of a series of misfortunes, the mission was aborted. And, in one last disaster, a helicopter collided with another aircraft, which exploded into flames, killing eight and injuring five. The next day, April 25, 1980, Carter announced the failure.

The hostages were not released until January 20, 1981, hours after Carter – defeated for reelection, at least partially because of the hostage crisis – left the White House and hard-liner Ronald Reagan was inaugurated. A U.S. agreement to release frozen Iranian assets ensured the hostages' release after 444 days of captivity.

President Reagan would find his bitter Middle East experience in Lebanon. The bloody saga began in August 1982, when Reagan deployed 800 U.S. Marines to Beirut at the request of the Lebanese government. In June, Israel had invaded southern Lebanon to drive out Palestine Liberation Organization (PLO) guerrillas, who had been attacking Israeli border communities. The Marines aided in the evacuation of the PLO.

The evacuation was seemingly complete in September, when the Marines began pulling out. Then a new crisis erupted. Lebanese President-elect Bashir Gemayel was assassinated, and two days later a Lebanese Christian military force with ties to Israel massacred some 800 Palestinians in refugee camps.

In the autumn of 1983, the United States shifted its policy from maintaining a military presence to actively supporting the Lebanese armed forces. U.S. warships in the Mediterranean Sea shelled rebel positions. More Marines were sent into Lebanon. Then, on October 23, with a suicidal driver at the wheel, a truck loaded with 12,000 pounds (5,443 kg.) of explosives sped into the U.S. Marine compound at Beirut International Airport. The truck exploded, shattering a barracks and killing 241 Americans, nearly all of them Marines. Another suicide attack killed 58 French paratroopers. U.S. intelligence officials blamed the attacks on Iranians supported by the Syrian government.

U.S. Marines withdrew in February 1984, leaving behind the rubble of Beirut and a Lebanon in the midst of a seemingly endless civil war.

While two successive U.S. administrations grappled with the disasters of the Middle East, Iran fought a war with Iraq. And while the world focused on the wild-eyed image of Iran's Khomeini, another Arab leader moved to the center of the Middle East stage. He was Saddam Hussein.

In 1979, Saddam assumed control of the Baath Party, which had ruled Iraq since 1968. Soon after taking power, he purged potential rivals from his power structure. Saddam, a politically appointed lieutenant general with no military experience, gave himself the title field marshal and then began planning a war against Iran. The Iranians vastly outnumbered the Iraqis – 53 million Iranians, fired by religious zeal, opposed by 16 million Iraqis. But the Iraqis' well-trained army would be fighting an inferior army, a revolutionary force driven more by fervor than by military discipline.

What had been the shah's army had become a target of the Ayatollah's revolutionary forces. They had executed 500 general officers and had purged at least 10,000 others. "The antipathy of the Iranian clerics toward the Imperial Army was profound," says a U.S. Army War College study. "They viewed it – with some justification – as the principal agency whereby secular ideas were disseminated throughout Iranian society. . . . Certainly the clerics would have destroyed the army had not the Iran-Iraq War forced them to relent."

In September 1980, after months of skirmishing, Saddam Hussein, predicting a two-week war, invaded Iran. His immediate objective was the Shatt al-Arab waterway – a border but also a commercial artery that both nations wanted to control. Saddam ran into fanatic resistance and accepted a U.N. cease-fire. Khomeini rejected the cease-fire, and the long war began.

Soon after, U.S. policy makers tilted their support toward Iraq. Although the reasons for the tilt were never spelled *Continued on page 34*

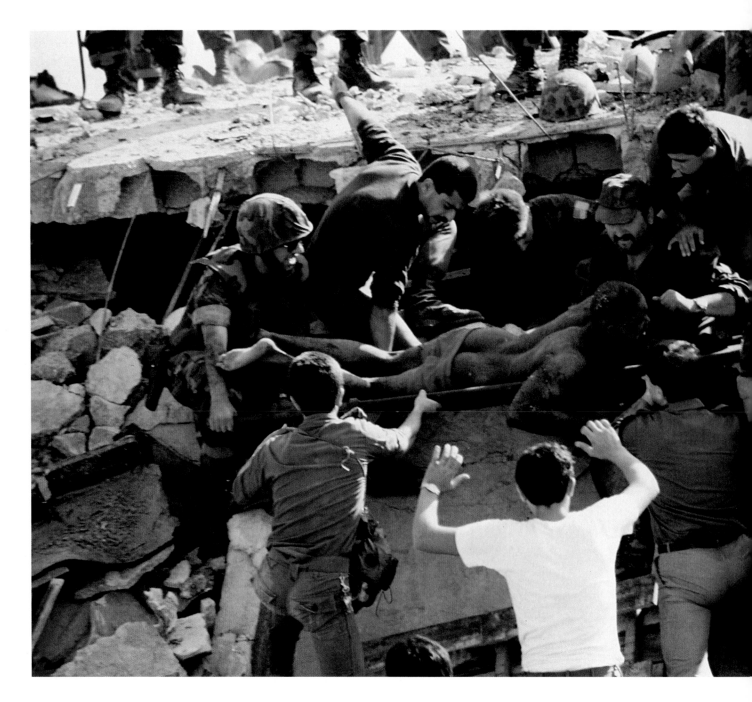

Painful memories of U.S. disasters in the Middle East: In 1979, Iranians parade a blindfolded hostage (opposite) from the U.S. Embassy in Tehran. In 1983, rescuers (above) pull a U.S. Marine from the rubble of a Beirut barracks blown up by a bomb that killed 241 Americans.

OPPOSITE:PHILIPPE LEDRU / SYGMA
ABOVE: ELI REED / MAGNUM

out, the U.S. State Department likely feared that an Iranian victory would fan the spread of Iran's fundamental Shiite branch of Islam and contribute to Middle East turmoil. Moreover, in Cold War logic, U.S. support of Iraq would drive a wedge between Saddam and the Soviet Union.

The little, oil-rich sheikdom of Kuwait also sided with Iraq, even though Kuwait had good reason to be hostile toward its powerful neighbor. In 1961, when Kuwait gained independence, Iraq, claiming the sheikdom as Iraqi territory, had threatened to invade. The Arab League set up an all-Arab force to defend Kuwait, and the crisis ended with Iraq recognizing Kuwait.

Border disputes simmered over rights to the Shatt al-Arab waterway, over possession of the Bubiyan and Warba islands, and over Iraq's supplying of fresh water to Kuwait. (To become self-sufficient, Kuwait built desalination plants, which provided drinking water.) In 1973, Iraq occupied part of Kuwait and withdrew only after being paid substantial sums.

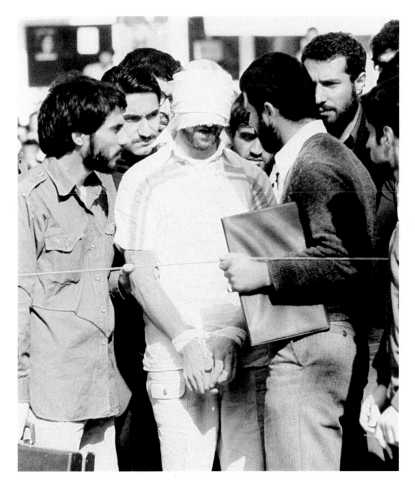

But when the Iran-Iraq War began, Kuwait loaned billions to Iraq. Kuwait, a worldly monarchy ruled by Sunni Muslims, chose to support Iraq, which kept its Shiites under control, unlike Iran and Khomeini's anti-secular Shiite cleric brethren. When Iran attacked Kuwaiti oil tankers in the Persian Gulf in July 1987, U.S. Navy warships began escorting them.

After suffering heavy losses in a major tank battle in the spring of 1981, Iranian leaders turned away from the regular army in favor of two other forces: lightly armed infantry units called the Pasdaran and a paramilitary organization called the Basij. The Pasdaran elected their own officers and favored fanaticism over training. Basij troops, recruited from Iran's underclasses, were sent to the front, given scant training, and put under the command of the Pasdaran.

In November 1981, at the town of Bostan, the Iranians shocked even the battle-hardened Iraqis with an incredibly brutal human-wave attack. First came hundreds of youths, some of them children only 12 years old. They ran

through a mine field, blowing themselves to pieces to clear a path for the Basij, who hurled themselves against the barbed-wire of the next line of defense. Most of the Basij were mowed down by Iraqi fire, but wounded and dying Basij crawled to the entanglements and cut through them. Over the corpses of the Basij came thousands of Pasdaran in waves. The Iraqis retreated at the sight of such fanaticism.

Saddam assigned his best officers to the defense of the southern Iraqi city of Basra, a Shiite stronghold and a target of Iranian religious propaganda. Around the city, the Iraqis built what they called "the Iron Ring," a defense complex of dug-in tanks, concrete bunkers, and an artificial lake.

In July 1982, the Iranians invaded. Again they used the meat-grinder tactic that had worked at Bostan and elsewhere. Now, though, the Iraqis employed a counter-tactic. The attacked Iraqi unit fell back just far enough to pull the Iranians into a killing zone, where Iraqi artillery and armored units chopped away at the Iranian flanks. The Iranians, suffering great losses, withdrew.

For the next three years, fighting in the northern mountains or in the southern swamps, Iraq repelled Iranian invasion attempts. Iraq smashed Iranian thrusts along the 730-mile (1,175 km.) frontier. Several times, according to U.S. intelligence reports, the Iraqis used mustard gas – a persistent blister agent that can blind and kill – and possibly Tabun, a lethal nerve gas.

In the first reported use of chemical weapons, Iraqis fired artillery shells containing mustard gas against an Iranian unit on a mountaintop. As the Iraqi attackers climbed the mountain, the low-settling gas drenched them, inflicting casualties and forcing a wild retreat. It was a classic example of how treacherous gas can be in battle. After this start, the Iraqis quickly improved, using gas primarily as a psychological weapon to panic massed troops.

Iraq's hit-and-run strategy attempted to wear down the Iranians and force them to bid for peace in defeat. Early in 1986, however, Iran seized Al Faw, a meagerly defended town at the end of a peninsula jutting into the Persian Gulf. Saddam sent his Republican Guard units to retake Al Faw. But, bogged down on flooded roads, Guard forces were bombarded by Iranian artillery across the Shatt al-Arab. The best the Guards could do was to isolate about 30,000 Iranian troops at the tip of the peninsula.

Saddam then took the Iranian town of Mehran, and said he would trade it for Al Faw. Instead of acquiescing, Iranian forces recaptured Mehran and drove off the Iraqis, humiliating Saddam and raising doubts about his ability to prosecute the war. Gulf states that had been supporting Saddam began flirting with Iran. Saudi Arabia, for example, agreed to oil pricing favorable to Iran.

An Iranian soldier (left) lies dead in the devastation wrought by Iraq's Saddam Hussein after he invaded Iran in 1980, launching an eight-year war. Artillery fire (lower left) evolved into missile exchanges, foreshadowing the Iraqi attacks on Israel and Saudi Arabia in 1991.

TOP LEFT: J. PAVLOVSKY / SYGMA
BOTTOM LEFT: SIPA PRESS

A few days after the debacle at Mehran, the leaders of the Baath Party held an "Extraordinary Congress" in Baghdad and decided on a mobilization. The party enlisted men as old as 42 for the Popular Army militia. Colleges were to be closed and students put into summer training camps. To sweeten the call-up for these students, the Baathists announced that volunteers would be accepted into the Republican Guard. The chance to enter the Republican Guard was attractive to ambitious students. Before the announcement, only young men from Tikrit, Saddam's hometown, were allowed into the "elite" Guard. The Republican Guard began changing from a praetorian bodyguard for Saddam to a tough, well-equipped force for special missions. Later in the war, the expanding Republican Guard would enter its final phase, becoming the Iraqi Army's major offensive element.

While the Iraqis were building their army, the Iranians were proclaiming the mobilization of 200,000 more men for an offensive that would end the war by January 21, 1987 – the Iranian New Year. "The last campaign," as it was billed, began on December 24, 1986, when a large Iranian force tried to take the small island of Umm Rassas in the Shatt al- Arab. The Iranians planned to use the island as a staging area for an assault on Basra. The loss of Basra would mean the loss of southern Iraq and, almost inevitably, the loss of the war.

The Iraqis defended Basra in a series of battles that demonstrated a new flair for maneuvering large forces. It was as if the Iraqis were fighting a World War II-style battle of armor and movement, while the Iranians were fighting a World War I-style engagement of frontal assaults and slaughter. The Iraqis, methodically trapping and annihilating isolated units, killed as many as 70,000 Iranians while suffering about 10,000 killed or wounded.

The Iraqis now began preparing for Operation *Tawakalna Ala Allah* (In God We Trust), an offensive to recapture Iraqi territory. At the same time, the Iraqis drastically changed their strategic use of air power and missiles.

In wars between Muslim nations, industries usually are not targeted. Industrialization gives former colonial states self-reliance and lessens dependency upon outside capital. So, in this Islamic view, an attack on industrial targets plays into the hands of imperial powers. In the fall of 1986, Iraq broke the taboo with a massive air raid on Iran's major oil refinery at Tabriz. Iraqi aircraft also bombed oil terminals at the mouth of the Gulf.

By the end of 1987, Iran's oil exports had dropped from 1.3 million barrels per day to 800,000 per day. Other bombings knocked out electric-power grids, disrupted commerce, and produced food shortages. The air raids built up resentment against the war and inspired widespread draft-dodging by Iranian young men who were rapidly losing their fanaticism.

. The escalating air war was probably ordered by Saddam because he believed the Iraqis no longer had an incentive to cooperate with the United States in limiting the war. Saddam apparently was reacting to disclosures about the futile U.S. deal to trade arms for hostages. The deal mushroomed into the Iran-Contra scandal. Saddam may have viewed the attempts to sell arms to Iran as proof of a U.S. shift away from Iraq. In February 1988, the Iraqis stepped up the war again, firing land-launched, Scud-B missiles into Tehran. These strikes were not the first. Since March 1985, missiles had been exploding in cities on both sides, with little impact on the real war.

But when Saddam's Scuds rained down on Tehran in 1988, the rocketing had a conclusive effect on the war. The clerics ruling Iran could not protect their people and did not have enough Scuds for a formidable response. Between February and April, Iraq fired more than 120 missiles into Tehran and other cities. Iranian front-line troops, after learning of the missile attacks on their homes, began deserting. Iranians lost confidence in their leaders.

Meanwhile, Iraq launched its ground offensive, striking Al Faw, which Iran had captured in 1986. The helicopters were flown by Iraqis in a rare combined arms operation. The Iraqis drove the Iranians from the peninsula, allowing one bridge spanning the Shatt al-Arab waterway to stand so that the shattered, fleeing Iranians had an exit from the battlefield.

By July 1988, when Khomeini suddenly accepted a cease-fire, Iran no longer was a military power; its army was all but annihilated. Iran did not admit defeat, but since the overthrow of Saddam had been a war aim, the popular judgment was that Iraq had won. Saddam, flush with the power of victory, savagely turned on the rebellious Kurds, killing thousands in northern Iraq. The Iraqi forces razed villages and snuffed out the lives of at least 5,000 Kurds with poison gas.

By U.S. intelligence estimates, the war cost $500 billion, leaving Iraq with a burden of debt that was more than 1.5 times its gross national product. Bankrupt but now in possession of a victorious war machine, Saddam conceived a brutally simple strategy: Use his army as a club to threaten – or to smash – Kuwait, seize its oil fields, and then march on to Saudi Arabia.

Burning Iraqi oil wells at Abadan blot the horizon during the Iran-Iraq War. These 1984 flames eerily portend the fires that Iraqis would set in Kuwaiti oil fields during their 1991 withdrawal.
HENRI BUREAU / SYGMA

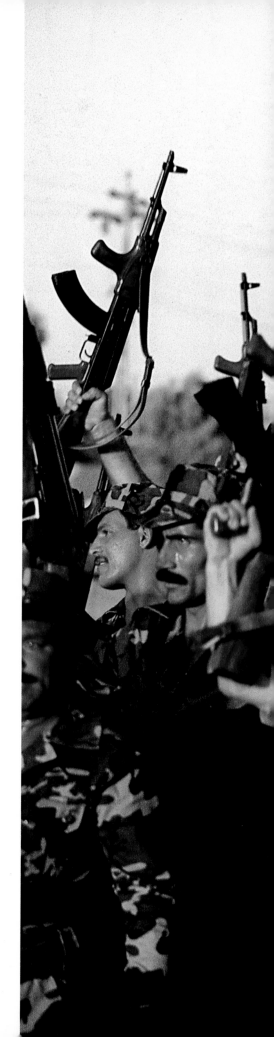

CHAPTER TWO

AN ARMED MIDDLE EAST

The Middle East in 1990 was an armed camp, the product of an international "arms bazaar." For some three decades, Middle East countries had their pick of the world's weaponry – short of nuclear weapons. Two countries, Israel and Saddam Hussein's Iraq, had decided to develop a nuclear capability and pursued their own atomic bombs.

The Middle East arms race began in the mid-1950s. In the decade after World War II, many Middle East nations were colonies or United Nations mandates, dependent upon major European nations for their defense. When they did achieve independence, they continued to procure their arms from the same nations. That changed when, shortly after the death of Josef Stalin in 1953, the Soviet government led by Nikita Khrushchev recognized the political and economic advantages of dealing with the so-called "non-aligned" nations. The first major Soviet weapons transfer was announced in 1955. The deal sent arms to Egypt, with Czechoslovakia as the intermediary. Previously, the Egyptians were dependent on Great Britain for arms. This Soviet arms agreement – valued as much as $200 million by some sources – proved significant for breaking a Western monopoly as well as for its size. The agreement, in essence a barter deal, required the Egyptian government to pay for the arms with cotton and rice over a 12-year period.

That arms deal ignited an East-West competition to arm the Arab states. The competition became all the more Continued on page 44

Guns are part of the culture of the Middle East. These Iraqi militia troops are holding aloft Soviet-supplied AK-47s.
CHRISTOPHER MORRIS / BLACK STAR

40

*More sophisticated arms
in the region include American-built
F-15 Eagle fighters of the Israeli Air
Force, shown here flying over the
fortress of Masada.*

MCDONNELL DOUGLAS AIRCRAFT

ARMS TRADE

The five permanent members of the U.N. Security Council were the top five arms exporters to the Middle East from 1984 to 1988. Their sales accounted for 75% of all arms sales to the region. The Middle East accounted for 35.8% of all world arms imports during this period.

TOP FIVE ARMS EXPORTERS TO THE MIDDLE EAST, 1984-88

$26.5 billion — Soviet Union
$16.3 billion — United States
$12.7 billion — France
$8.4 billion — China
$3.1 billion — Britain

TOP FIVE ARMS IMPORTERS IN THE MIDDLE EAST, 1984-88

$29.7 billion — Iraq
$19.5 billion — Saudi Arabia
$10.5 billion — Iran
$8.3 billion — Syria
$6.4 billion — Egypt

SOURCE: U.S. ARMS CONTROL AND DISARMAMENT AGENCY, WORLD MILITARY EXPENDITURES AND ARMS TRANSFERS, ANNUAL, 1989.

attractive with the increasing Western dependence on Middle East petroleum and natural gas. Many Arab states could use their huge oil incomes to pay for the weapons, and the wealthier states were soon subsidizing arms purchases of the poorer ones. Those have-not states, such as Jordan and Egypt, could easily buy arms on credit in return for support – real or only promised – of their arms sponsors.

Israel seemed immune to the East-West competition, being totally supported by the West – first France and then the United States, with semi-clandestine military assistance from a few other Western countries, such as West Germany. Israel, the one Westernized country in the Middle East, also became the first arms producer in the region.

Armed with mostly French and later U.S. weapons as well as indigenous weapons, the highly capable Israeli armed forces repeatedly demonstrated their military superiority over Arab states during the wars of 1956, 1967, 1973, and 1982. Israeli successes, however, solved none of the political problems of the region and exacerbated the hatred of many Arab states – especially Iraq.

The United States armed not only Israel but also Saudi Arabia and Iran under the Shah, Mohammad Reza Pahlavi. Both Arab countries were conservative, anti-Communist states, and both could afford to buy weapons in the marketplace from Britain, France, and other countries. The United States provided both countries with some of the most advanced weapons in the West's arsenal. After the 1978 Camp David Accords established diplomatic relations between Israel and Egypt, the United States added Egypt to its list of Middle East countries receiving U.S. weapons.

Iraq remained the enigma of the region. Vehemently anti-Israel, Iraq became a beneficiary of Soviet largesse in the early 1960s while still procuring arms from Great Britain. Subsequently, under Saddam Hussein, Iraq initiated major programs to develop nuclear, chemical, and biological weapons.

While such a massive arms effort concerned the United States and other countries, after the fall of the Shah of Iran in 1979, many countries, including several of the Gulf-area states, welcomed a militant Iraq as a buffer against Muslim fundamentalism. Indeed, when Iraq attacked Iran in 1980, the West and the more conservative Arab states generally hailed the move as a godsend. While Saddam's oppressive, dictatorial policies against his own population were widely criticized, the Arab saying "the enemy of my enemy is my friend," gained new currency. Even Saddam's use of poison gas against Kurdish rebels in his own country in 1987-1988 brought little censure from Western nations, with the significant exception of Israel.

The Israeli government viewed with anxiety the growth of Iraqi military power, especially the "unconventional" nuclear, chemical, and biological weapons. Although Israel had developed its own nuclear arsenal, it had sought to avoid attention to that development while working behind the political scenes – and sometimes using clandestine operations – to prevent Arab nations from developing such weapons.

However, in September 1976 a French consortium began constructing a nuclear research center at the ancient Iraqi city of Osirak, on the banks of the Tigris River some ten miles (16 km.) from Baghdad. West German technicians were also involved in the project. While Iraqi officials publicly said the project was for peaceful purposes, the governments of the United States, Israel, and Syria expressed concern.

Reportedly, Israeli covert actions failed to slow, appreciably, the Iraqi atomic program. Subsequently, on June 7, 1981, Israeli fighter- bombers attacked the Osirak reactor. During the raid, code-named Babylon, eight F-16 strike aircraft escorted by six F-15 fighters – all U.S.-built aircraft – flew about 600 miles (966 km.) through Jordanian, Saudi, and Iraqi air space to drop sixteen 2,000-pound (907-kg.) bombs on the unfinished nuclear facility. Reportedly, all bombs struck the target as each F-16 made a single pass.

The raid, intentionally conducted on a Sunday to limit casualties, wrecked

Iraqi armored vehicles parade in Baghdad in 1990. Inset: the Al-Hussein missile, modified from the Soviet Scud-B, played a major role in the Gulf War.
BOTH: KOL AL ARAB / SIPA PRESS

the facility. All of the attacking planes returned safely to their bases in Israel.

Although the Arab world expressed shock, many of Iraq's neighbors seemed genuinely pleased with the Israeli action. (A short time after the raid, a group of French engineers who had worked at the Osirak reactor announced that it had been secretly modified to produce weapons-grade plutonium outside of international inspections.)

The raid was but a brief setback for Iraqi military expansion. Engaged in a war with Iran since 1980, Iraq spent most of its own treasury and then borrowed from neighboring Saudi Arabia and Kuwait to maintain and to add to its arsenal.

Chemical and biological weapons – and a restart of the nuclear program – received priority, as did the continued buildup of conventional weapons. In 1990, Western analysts estimated that Iraq could possess nuclear weapons within five years, assisted by smuggled western technology, some from West Germany. A "sting" operation at London's Heathrow Airport in early 1990

publicized Iraq's effort to obtain "krytron" trigger devices for atomic weapons. In March, Iraq also attempted to smuggle krytron trigger devices out of the United States; a short time later the Bush administration lifted the export controls on them.

Iraq first used chemical weapons in 1983 against Iranian troops. Iran reported some 45,000 men were killed or injured by chemical weapons. The Iraqis had introduced chemical weapons to counter the Iranian "human wave" attacks, in which thousands of troops – many of them young boys with virtually no military training – would attempt to overrun Iraqi positions by sheer mass of numbers. Chemical weapons offered a nearly perfect solution to these attacks by massed, lightly armed troops. When employed in conjunction with concentrated artillery fire, the "chemical weapons were singularly effective," according to a report of the U.S. Army War College.

Use of these weapons against Iranians continued. Subsequently, in 1987-1988, Iraqi aircraft dropped chemical-filled bombs on several Kurdish villages, inflicting heavy casualties. According to some reports, about 5,000 men, women, and children died at Halabjah, along the mountainous border between Iraq and Iran, from exposure to mustard gas and a nerve agent known as Tabun. While experts believe that chemical weapons have very limited effectiveness against well-trained and protected troops, they can be very effective against poorly trained and ill-protected troops or civilians, as demonstrated by the Iraqi experiences. U.S. Senator John S. McCain, III (R-Ariz.) identified Salam Pak, located about 35 miles (59 km.) southeast of Baghdad, as the principal research center for chemical weapons. "This center includes underground sheltered facilities and is known to work on nerve gas research," he said in a paper. "It is unclear whether it is to be the center of Iraq's biotoxin effort," he added. Another research site was identified at Samarra, about 65 miles (105 km.) north of Baghdad. Technicians from several European countries, including West Germany, helped Iraq with chemical weapons development, with most of the shell and bomb casings being purchased from Spain. In the 1980s, U.S. firms attempted to help Iran develop its own chemical weapons.

William Webster, the director of Central Intelligence, told Congress in 1989 that "after several years of experience in producing chemical weapons, Iraq's well-established effort now is far less dependent on foreign assistance. . . .It is now expanding its chemical weapons capability and is taking further steps to make its program entirely independent of foreign officials." By 1990 there were said to be five chemical weapon research laboratories, six chemical production sites, and five factories for filling chemical warheads.

When the Gulf War began, public sources credited Iraq with 2,000 to 4,000

High-technology weapons have become increasingly important to the Arab nations for confronting Israel as well as their Arab neighbors. Iraqi pilots (opposite) train on French-built Mirage F1 fighters and Saudi radar operators (above) train in U.S.-built E-3A AWACS aircraft.

OPPOSITE: FRANCOIS GUENET / GAMMA-LIAISON
ABOVE: U.S. DEPARTMENT OF DEFENSE

tons of chemical agents (compared to a U.S. inventory estimated at 30,000 tons and a Soviet inventory of 40,000 to 50,000 tons). Later the Iraqi government would admit to having a weapons stockpile at the end of the Gulf War that included 280 tons of mustard gas, 75 tons of Sarin, and 500 tons of Tabun, plus 1,481 artillery shells and bombs containing chemical warheads and another 30 chemical warheads for the modified Scud missiles. (Other chemical weapons were undoubtedly destroyed during the war.)

It is not known publicly if Iraq had biological weapons at the start of the Gulf War. An Israeli official in Jerusalem told the Reuter news agency in 1989 that Israel believed Iraq had developed "a military biological capability" but had not started "to manufacture actual biological weapons nor, more importantly, have they yet acquired any airborne weapons [bombs], such as sophisticated missiles, to deliver the bacteria they worked on."

In September 1990, the Chairman of the House Armed Services Committee, Les Aspin (D-Wis.), told reporters, "Saddam Hussein . . . is expected to have a militarily significant biological program by the end of this year or early next year. This will be a new dimension to the problem. It is a more important and more serious element than the chemical threat. It is harder to deal with." The biological agents anthrax, botulism, cholera, equine encephalitis, tularemia, and typhoid have been cited in both U.S. government and media reports. Although Saddam Hussein did boast that Iraq was developing a "super weapon," an Iraqi government spokesmen stated that Iraq was not producing biological weapons.

Saddam's military efforts also have emphasized reinforced structural defenses. Saddam constructed an intricate underground bunker complex in which to hide his military equipment, communications facilities, and, if necessary, himself.

Saddam's defensive mentality could also be seen in the vast air defense complex he had built around Baghdad and several other cities. The Iraqis had Surface-to-Air Missiles (SAMs), Anti-Aircraft Artillery (AAA), early warning and fire-direction radars, and area control centers linked into an integrated network. This system, described by the Director of U.S. Naval Intelligence, Rear Admiral Thomas A. Brooks, as "square mile for square mile, the most sophisticated air defense system in the world," comprised British, Chinese, French, Italian, Soviet, and Swedish equipment, all integrated by Thomson-CSF of France.

Iraq purchased its offensive weapons from virtually every major arms supplier in the world. During 1984-1988 (the last five-year period for which full data are available), Iraq was the world's largest arms importer – $29.7 billion worth of weapons. By comparison, the Saudis, holding second place in the Middle East, bought $19.5 billion in arms, while Israel purchased $6.1 billion.

The Iraqis seemed to buy arms everywhere. From the Soviet Union, Saddam purchased tanks and armored vehicles, artillery, battlefield missiles, anti-tank missiles, SAMs, landing ships, missile craft, helicopters, and most of Iraq's combat aircraft, including about 20 MiG-29 Fulcrums, one of the most advanced Soviet-built fighters.

France provided a number of first-line aircraft, principally 64 Mirage F1 fighter-attack aircraft and 30 fighter-interceptor variants, as well as Exocet anti-ship missiles. In May 1987, an Iraqi Mirage F1 fired two Exocet missiles into the U.S. frigate *Stark* (FFG-37), apparently mistaking the ship for an Iranian target. The attack inflicted heavy damage on the warship and killed 37 Americans.

From Italy, Iraq purchased U.S.-designed helicopters, anti-tank and anti-ship missiles, and frigates and corvettes, although most of the ships were not delivered when the war began.

China had also provided aircraft to Iraq, about 40 of the J-6 versions of the Soviet MiG-19 fighter.

MILITARY BUILDUP

Iraq's military forces at the beginning of the Gulf War and those of its neighbors:

	TROOPS	TANKS	ARTILLERY	COMBAT AIRCRAFT
Bahrain	2,300	54	20	12
Egypt	320,000	2,425	1,260	485
Iran	305,000	500	800	190
Iraq	**955,000**	**5,500**	**3,500**	**665**
Israel	104,000	4,290	1,400	565
Jordan	74,000	1,130	195	100
Kuwait	16,000	245	70	23
Lebanon	21,000	100	95	6
Qatar	6,000	24	14	18
Saudi Arabia	40,000	550	475	154
Syria	300,000	4,050	2,150	460
Turkey	528,500	3,725	2,2190	485
United Arab Emirates	40,000	130	175	45

WORLD'S LARGEST ARMIES

World's 4 largest armed forces by manpower:

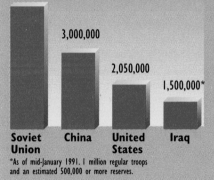

Soviet Union	China	United States	Iraq
4,400,000	3,000,000	2,050,000	1,500,000*

*As of mid-January 1991. 1 million regular troops and an estimated 500,000 or more reserves.

SOURCE: USNI MILITARY DATABASE

The United States has been a major arms provider to the Middle East. These U.S. Hawk anti-aircraft missiles (opposite) have been sold to Egypt, Iran, Israel, Jordan, and Saudi Arabia.
JOHN FICARA / WOODFIN CAMP

The only U.S.-made military equipment procured by the Iraqi armed forces in the 1980s were 45 Bell 214ST helicopters. However, close ties between Baghdad and Washington had existed since 1983, as the United States supported Iraq's war against Iran.

By that year, representatives of the United States and Iraq were meeting regularly in Europe and in the United States. In addition to trying to shut off all Western arms sales to Iran, from 1985 to 1990 the Reagan and Bush administrations allowed Iraq to purchase $1.5 billion in advanced U.S. technology. This equipment included computers, radios, graphic terminals, machine tools, and computer mapping systems. The day before Iraq invaded Kuwait, the Bush administration gave final approval for the sale to Iraq of data transmission equipment valued at $695,000. All of these sales had some relation to Iraqi military projects.

While Iraq possessed a number of aircraft capable of carrying conventional bombs and "weapons of mass destruction," including several Soviet-built Tu-16 Badger and Tu-22 Blinder turbojet bombers, conflicts with Israel had demonstrated the difficulty of penetrating the Israeli air defense system with manned aircraft.

In previous wars with Israel, both Egypt and Syria had fired missiles into Israel, with some success, although they caused no casualties and inflicted little damage. Consequently, Iraq initiated a major missile program to bombard Israeli cities.

By the late 1970s, Iraq had the land-launched SS-1c Scud-B missile, which had become operational in the Soviet Union in 1965. As many as 2,000 Scuds were transferred to Iraq. With a range of about 175 miles (282 km.), however, the Scud-B could not strike Israel from western Iraq.

Saddam Hussein built up an arsenal of unconventional weapons: chemical (gas), nuclear, and possibly biological. He used chemical weapons against the Kurds in his own country; this mother and child (opposite) were gassed in an attack on Halabjah in March 1988. After an Israeli air attack destroyed the nuclear weapons facility (above) at Osirak in 1981, Saddam ordered its rebuilding.

ABOVE; OZTURK / SIPA PRESS
RIGHT: MARC RIBOUD / MAGNUM

The Iraqis modified the Scud-B, reducing the warhead size from 2,200 pounds (1,000 kg.) to about 500 pounds (227 kg.) to accommodate additional fuel. This modified version, called the *Al-Hussein*, attained a range of approximately 400 miles (644 km.). The missile could reach far enough to strike Riyadh as well as Tel Aviv, although the accuracy of such weapons was extremely poor, measured in thousands of yards.

Iraq launched a still longer-range variant, the *Al-Abbas*, for the first time in 1989. That weapon carried a warhead of only 250 pounds (113 kg.), but could strike targets more than 500 miles (805 km.) away. And, just before war erupted, Iraq joined the Egyptian-Argentine Condor 2 venture to develop a modern, long-range, and accurate ballistic missile.

By 1990, the Iraqi Army had an estimated 400 *Al-Hussein* missiles, still referred to as "Scuds" in the West. The *Al-Husseins* could be fired from fixed or truck-mounted launchers. In addition to high explosive warheads, the Iraqi government later reported that they had chemical warheads available for use on the missiles.

Other advanced weapons that the Iraqis were apparently developing when the Gulf War began were a series of "super guns," intended, reportedly, to launch nuclear, biological, and chemical projectiles at targets up to 425 miles (684 km.) away.

These guns were designed by Dr. Gerald V. Bull, who had already produced long-range shells for Saddam's artillery. Born in Canada, Bull became a world authority on long-range artillery. Although Bull did work on some artillery projects for the U.S. Army, when the Army rejected some of his later designs he sold his products instead to other countries, including Iraq and South Africa. (Sales to the latter led to Bull spending nearly five months in a U.S. federal prison in 1980 for violating the U.S. arms embargo of South Africa.) The guns he sold to Iraq had a major role in inflicting heavy casualties on Iranian troops during the 1980s.

By early 1990, Bull was believed to be in the process of shipping super gun components to Iraq. These were part of a series of long-range artillery weapons that Bull was developing for Saddam's arsenal. On March 22, Bull was shot twice in the back of the neck with a 7.65-mm. pistol while entering his apartment in Brussels, Belgium. The motive was not robbery, as $20,000 was found on his body when police arrived.

A month later, British customs officials seized eight tubes believed to have been intended for a smooth-bore gun barrel 130 feet (40 m.) long with an interior diameter of 39.4 inches (100 cm.). If those estimates were correct, it would have been the largest gun ever built.

Iraq's massive investment in arms had, by 1990, given Iraq the world's fourth largest force, after the Soviet Union, China, and the United States. Much of its equipment was modern, and many of its commanders and troops, veterans of the Iran-Iraq War, had combat experience. This formidable military machine owed its allegiance to one man, and by early 1990 Saddam Hussein was preparing to send it on the march again.

CHAPTER THREE

THE WORLD OF SADDAM

He said he acted "in the name of God, the merciful, the compassionate." Yet, by his own accounts, he began killing people when he was a child of ten. He was born an Iraqi peasant, and he claimed the allegiance of the masses. Yet he ordered the slaughter of tens of thousands of Iraqi peasants. He proclaimed himself a champion of Islam. Yet through terror and oppression, he created a secular state. He called all Arabs his brothers. Yet he attacked an Arab neighbor.

This man of contradictions is Saddam Hussein. As Iraq's president, Saddam is the most charismatic figure to appear in the Middle East since Egyptian President Gamal Abdel Nasser confronted the West and called for pan-Arab nationalism in the 1950s and 1960s.

Saddam admired Josef Stalin and imitated the Soviet tyrant by building a dictatorship and a cult of personality. Giant portraits of Saddam smile down on Iraqis throughout the country. His birthday is a national holiday, and his followers, in the flowery rhetoric of Arabic, hail him as "the minaret of all mankind." He mystically associated himself with Saladin, the great 12th-Century Islamic warrior who fought the Crusaders; and Nebuchadnezzar, the Babylonian conqueror of the Jews. Saddam launched a project to rebuild ancient Babylon. The bricks are inscribed, "The Babylon of Nebuchadnezzar was reconstructed in the era of Saddam Hussein."

The story of his rise to power is so embellished by official propaganda that

Saddam Hussein smiles at his subjects in one of numerous portraits of him in Iraq. For his invasions of Iran and Kuwait he changed from a double-breasted suit to a field marshal's uniform.
CHRISTOPHER MORRIS / BLACK STAR

even basic details about his life are difficult to confirm. But it seems certain that Saddam Hussein was born on April 28, 1937, in a village of mud-and-reed huts near Takrit, a Tigris River town. The people of Saddam's village, al-Auja, were poor, landless Sunni Muslims in a country dominated by a Shiite majority. Life was hard in al-Auja. The village had no electricity, no running water. Baghdad, 100 miles (161 km.) to the south, was the royal city of a king, placed on his throne by the British.

Official biographies of Saddam begin like fairy tales: He was a sensitive lad cruelly treated by a stepfather. In the reverent pages that tell the saga of Saddam, his stepfather called him "a son of a dog," beat him, and refused to let him go to school. So Saddam, at the age of ten, went off to Baghdad on his own to get an education.

Then the fairy-tale biographies turn dark. One of them says Saddam was given a revolver when he was seven years old and killed his first enemy when he was ten. By then he was living in Baghdad with his mother's brother, Khairallah Talfah, a schoolteacher who taught Saddam the child much of what Saddam the leader later proclaimed. Uncle Khairallah, for example, wrote a leaflet entitled *Three Things that God Should Not Have Created: Persians, Jews, and Flies.* When Saddam came to power, he had his uncle's leaflet reprinted and widely distributed. A U.S. government psychiatrist who developed a profile of Saddam said his uncle "became not only his political mentor but also his larger-than-life father figure."

Khairallah Talfah is believed to have been a neo-Nazi Iraqi Army officer. In the mid-1930s, Germany had seen Iraq as a potential ally in the Middle East. German agents, aided by sympathetic Iraqis, spread anti-British, anti-Semitic propaganda and plotted to keep Iraq from aiding the British when World War II began. In May 1941, pro-Nazi Iraqi troops attacked British air bases in southern Iraq. British troops easily defeated the Iraqis, took control of Iraq, and jailed many pro-Nazis. Saddam's uncle was reportedly among them.

After World War II, Shiite Muslims fought with minority Sunni Muslims for the limited power dispensed by the King, Faisal II, puppet of Great Britain. His shaky throne was propped up in 1955 when, at British urging, he assembled an alliance known as the Baghdad Pact. It united Iraq, Turkey, Pakistan, and Iran against Soviet encroachments in the Middle East.

Egypt, then led by Lieutenant Colonel Gamal Abdel Nasser, opposed the pact, denouncing it as a backward step toward colonialism. Branded as pro-Communist by the West, he became a hero of nationalistic Arabs. One of them was young Saddam Hussein, who was politically adrift in Baghdad.

As the pupil of his Uncle Khairallah, Saddam espoused fascism. But young men like him were caught up in the socialist revolution. An underground plot to overthrow the monarchy attracted Saddam, who may have played a minor role in an attempted coup. Authorized accounts are not clear about whether Saddam had been inspired by a fervor for socialism or by a hatred of the monarchy. The Saddam of those turbulent days seemed to be developing not an ideology but a fascination with power.

In 1957, Saddam joined the small Iraqi Baath Party, a splinter of a large, radical movement for spreading the doctrines of Marxism and nationalism in Arab countries. Baath ideology – "Marxism in an Islamic cup," as some called it – appealed to revolutionary Muslims. In Arabic "Baath" meant "renaissance," and the party promised Arab nations a democratic, socialist rebirth.

Most military officers, including the Society of Free Officers in Egypt and the nationalists in the Iraqi Army, had no interest in democracy or socialism. They wanted to get rid of kings and install military governments.

By joining the Baath Party, Saddam put himself on the left at a time when power was destined to be taken by the right. For it was not socialists who got rid of Iraq's King Faisal II. In 1958, a clique of nationalist army officers led by General Abdul Karim Kassem murdered King Faisal in his palace and set up a military regime.

Saddam Hussein's own museum displays this photograph to portray a youthful man of the desert. But from the age of ten he lived in Baghdad and worked not as a shepherd but as a gunman for the radical Baath Party he would later control.
GAMMA-LIAISON

Saddam Hussein, in a pilgrim's religious garb, makes a pilgrimage to Mecca in 1988. Kin surround Saddam (left) in a family portrait that includes his wife Sajida, children, son-in-law, and grandchildren. Saddam, whose favorite movie is "The Godfather," gave power to his clansmen.
BOTH: SYGMA

The killing of the king sent tremors through the Middle East. Faisal's cousin, King Hussein of Jordan, feared he was next. Riots broke out in Tripoli, Libya. Muslims and Christians clashed in Beirut, Lebanon. Western intelligence agencies believed Syria was about to invade Lebanon. At the request of the Lebanese government, President Dwight D. Eisenhower sent in U.S. Marines. British paratroops landed in Jordan to protect Hussein.

That was the explosive Middle East that Saddam saw as a Baath revolutionary: the West intervening with force against the spread of nationalism throughout the Arab world. Yet, as Saddam looked at his own country, he saw the absolute rule of a king merely replaced by the absolute rule of a military dictator.

Saddam wanted to become a hero to his nation – the Nasser of Iraq. Baath leaders, playing to Saddam's enthusiasm for weapons and violence, used him as an expendable triggerman. They sent him to kill his brother-in-law, a Communist supporter of Kassem. This may have been a kind of test for his next assignment: Kill Kassem in a Baath plot to seize power.

The attempted assassination of Kassem in 1959 was dramatized some 20 years later in an Iraqi film about Saddam's life. As the film portrays him, Saddam leaps in front of Kassem's car, sprays it with machine-gun fire, and is shot by Kassem's bodyguards. Limping and bleeding, he slips away and eludes his pursuers. A comrade uses a razor blade to remove a bullet from Saddam's leg. Then, masquerading as a Bedouin, Saddam swims the Tigris River and escapes.

In reality, Saddam fled to Cairo after the botched ambush. In exile, he married his cousin Sajida Talfah, daughter of his uncle Khairallah, and enrolled in a university. During his years of study, he mixed with other revolutionaries and became known as the Egyptian representative of the Iraqi Baath Party. Saddam boasted that he was under Nasser's personal protection.

In February 1963, the Baathists, allied with military officers, finally succeeded in killing Kassem. Iraqi peasants, who adored Kassem, did not believe he had been killed. To prove it, the Baathists showed his bullet-pocked body on television for several nights.

Nine months after the murder, the army overthrew the Baathists and jailed many Baath Party members, including Saddam, who had hurried home from Cairo. In prison, Saddam read books about Adolf Hitler and Stalin, seeking the secrets of power. He had already learned one that had eluded the Baath leadership: Don't ally with the army. From the history of the early Nazi movement he learned a lasting lesson: Build a trusted armed force inside the party itself. Hitler had his storm troopers; Saddam would have his militia and later his Republican Guard.

In July 1968, the Baathists seized power again, and Saddam's cousin, General Ahmed Hassan al-Bakr, secretary-general of the Baath Party, became president and commander-in-chief. He was also chairman of the party's Revolutionary Command Council, the ruling elite of the country. Saddam was a member of the council, which was dominated by high-ranking army officers. Saddam, who

BAGHDAD BUNKER

Shelters designed by Swiss or German companies reportedly were built under several official buildings in Baghdad. Here is a typical bunker design:

Concrete stairwell leading from basement

2-foot-thick steel-reinforced concrete slab provides bomb protection

Multi-level underground complex includes barracks, communications, offices, sentry posts

Generators, food and water rations, ventilation and sewage system

One of many air shafts

80 feet (24.4 meters)

Walls: 6-9 feet (1.8-2.7 meters) thick

Hard rubber foundation with coiled springs absorbs shock waves from bombs

SOURCE: KNIGHT-RIDDER TRIBUNE NEWS

had no military experience, later gave himself a promotion to lieutenant general, then to field marshal. He also gave himself a title that translates into English as "The Awesome."

Family ties bound Iraq's leaders. Reportedly, al-Bakr's son was married to Saddam's sister-in-law, and two of al-Bakr's daughters were married to relaitves of Saddam. His uncle Khairallah became the mayor of Baghdad and grew wealthy by gaining a virtual monopoly on Iraq's citrus crops. Saddam's eldest son, Udai, had a similar monopoly on chickens, beef, eggs, and cheese. (Hotheaded Udai reminds relatives of his father as a young man, for Udai is reputed to have killed two men who insulted him. He also is said to have fatally clubbed another man, identified as his father's valet or bodyguard. The assault reportedly took place before shocked guests at a party.)

Al-Bakr made Saddam deputy secretary-general, and in 1968, at the age of 31, Saddam began his climb to power. His primary job was running the state security apparatus, which he modeled after both Nazi and Soviet organizations. Security agents ferreted out subversion, conducted espionage, and performed assassinations. Agents of the most dreaded branch, the Makhabarat, watched over other security operatives and regular policemen. Makhabarat agents prowled every neighborhood, listening for dissent and turning in traitors.

Al-Bakr gave Saddam a free hand in disposing of "enemies of the party," many of whom died in mass public hangings. Saddam's victims included the minister of defense, generals and other army officers, and 500 members of the outlawed Communist Party. He methodically eradicated al-Bakr's closest associates until few remained at al-Bakr's side, except Saddam. Al-Bakr, perhaps anticipating his own removal, resigned in July 1979 for what he said were health reasons, and Saddam became president of the police state that he had created.

To consolidate his power, the new president called a special meeting of Baath Party leaders. The men gathered uneasily. No one ever knew what Saddam would do next. He trusted no one—and he claimed to have a mysterious sixth sense that enabled him to look into the eyes of a man and decide whether he was a conspirator.

"We used to be able to sense a conspiracy with our hearts before we even gathered the evidence," he told the meeting, which was being videotaped. "Nevertheless, we were patient, and some of our comrades blamed us for knowing this and doing nothing about it."

In the video, a man stands and says that a major plot already has begun. People begin shouting for a purge. Suddenly, several burly men appear, grab an alleged conspirator, and hustle him from the room. The video lens then turns to Saddam, who is lighting a cigar. He removes the cigar, glares at the camera, and says, "The witness has just given us information about the group leaders in that organization. Similar confessions were made by the ring leaders. Get out! Get out!"

More conspirators are led away. A frenzy of shouting erupts: "Long Live the party! God save Saddam from conspirators!"

For about seven years before he became president, Saddam ran both Iraq's terror apparatus and foreign policy. Whatever Saddam's crudity in dealing with dissidents, he was remarkably effective in foreign relations. He played off the United States against the Soviet Union; managed to keep Soviet friendship, while executing Iraqi Communists; and posed as a champion of pan-Arabism, while shipping arms to warring factions of the Arab world.

Soviet technicians built an oil refinery at Iraq's Rumaila oil field. In April 1972, Saddam and Soviet Prime Minister Aleksey Kosygin celebrated the opening of the refinery by cutting a ribbon and signing a friendship agreement. Next came a deluge of Soviet weapons, including the delivery of the first Soviet-built, land-launched Scud-B missiles.

As the Soviets helped modernize Iraq's arsenal, the United States increased its

Saddam Hussein's Sajood Palace towers over the Tigris River (opposite), a marble edifice adorned with turquoise and gold. It was near completion when the bombing of Baghdad began. Bombs hit it on the second night of the war, but an underground bunker probably was not touched. A massive door (above) led to the bunker, which had its own electrical and water purifying systems. An artist's portrayal (opposite) shows the elements of a typical bunker.

BOTH PHOTOS: IAN LEGUEN / SIPA PRESS

To justify his invasion of Kuwait, Saddam Hussein pointed to the opulence of his neighbors, the stacks of money, the luxury cars, and the ways of the haughty rich. "The colonialists," he told fellow Arabs, set up "disfigured petroleum states" that "kept the wealth away from the masses of this nation. . . .Oh, Arabs, oh, Muslims and believers everywhere, this is your day to rise and defend Mecca."

CLOCKWISE FROM TOP LEFT: DIRCK HALSTEAD / GAMMA-LIAISON; GERARD RANCINAN / SYGMA (2); G. CHARPY, T. MINOSA / SYGMA

trade with Iraq, even though the two nations had had no diplomatic relations since Iraq sent forces against Israel during the 1967 Six-Day War.

Saddam opened another avenue to the West in November 1975 by signing a nuclear cooperation agreement with France and negotiating the purchase of French Mirage F1 fighter-attack aircraft. He also made a $1 billion agreement with Japan, trading oil for Japanese-financed economic development projects. In addition, he awarded Japan's Mitsubishi Group a $400 million contract for an electric power station.

Although al-Bakr was the titular head of Iraq's government, Saddam was essentially running the country, especially its foreign policy. U.S. intelligence reports on Iraq during the 1970s mention him frequently. He is cited for deciding to ally Iraq with the Soviet Union and then, in May 1978, for cooling Iraqi-Soviet relations. He made his point by executing 21 allegedly pro-Soviet Communists for "trying to organize political activity in the armed forces."

When Saddam formally took power, the United States no longer considered Iraq a Soviet client state, and when he invaded Iran in 1980, the United States secretly sided with him. The war was not quite four years old in November 1984, when President Ronald Reagan publicly signaled U.S. support by announcing the resumption of relations between the United States and Iraq.

The United States knew that Iraqi had used poison gas in the war and that Saddam ruled by terror. Amnesty International, for example, reported that in September and October 1985, Iraqi secret police held about 300 Kurdish children and youths hostage to get their guerrilla relatives to surrender; many hostages were tortured and as many as 30 were killed, Amnesty said. U.S.-Iraqi relations were only twice strained—by the abortive U.S. weapons-for-hostages deal with Iran and by the presumably accidental Iraqi attack on the U.S. frigate *Stark* (FFG-37) in May 1987.

Iraq ranked with Libya as a human-rights offender and supporter of terrorism. Iraq sheltered Mohammed Abu Abbas, who led the October 1985 hijacking of the cruise ship *Achille Lauro,* in which an American passenger was killed. But the United States removed Iraq from the U.S. list of countries sponsoring terrorism. U.S. officials explained that the relationship between the United States and Iraq was based on realpolitik: Iraq had oil reserves second only to Saudi Arabia; Iraq would be an essential player in any U.S. attempt to bring stability to the Middle East.

Saddam harangued about the "criminal Zionist spiders" of Israel, blustered about territorial claims to Kuwait, and complained about U.S. "imperialialism." But the United States continued to follow its conciliatory policy toward Iraq.

The United States did not condone Saddam's gassing of Kurds in 1988, but the U.S. State Department did regard the repression of Kurds and Shiite Muslims as internal matters. The United States tried to expand its trade with Iraq, and when U.S. firms participated in a trade fair in 1989, their Iraqi hosts saw to it that the U.S. pavilion won the best-of-fair gold medal. Early in 1990, Iraq began allowing three previously prohibited imports into the country: typewriters, computers, and blank video tapes. And, U.S. trade with Iraq was on the upswing, especially for American farmers.

U.S. Ambassador April C. Glaspie, the first woman to be a U.S. ambassador to an Arab country, saw the increase in trade as a good sign. She believed that Saddam was beginning to trust the United States and wished to improve relations. Iraq, for example, agreed to pay a total of $27 million in what Ambassador Glaspie later called "reasonable compensation" to the 37 families "who had lost their breadwinners" in the attack on the *Stark.*

Shortly after John Kelly, Assistant Secretary of State for near Eastern and South Asian Affairs, visited Baghdad on February 12, 1990, the Voice of America criticized Iraq for human-rights violations. The broadcast shocked Kelly and Ambassador Glaspie, who called on the Iraqi Foreign Ministry and expressed U.S. "regret" for the broadcast.

Iraq had emerged from its eight-year war with Iran $80 billion in debt and beset by creditors, the most insistent being Kuwait. In February, at a secret meeting with representatives of the Arab Cooperation Council nations (Iraq, Yemen, Jordan, and Egypt), Saddam indicated that he would never pay back his war debts. He pressed for even more money. Told that he could get no more money for his bankrupt nation, he reportedly said, "Go tell them in Saudi Arabia and in the Gulf that if they don't give it to me, I will know how to take it." Egyptian President Hosni Mubarak angrily walked out of the meeting.

A crisis was building, but only Saddam seemed to know where it would lead. Western experts on the Middle East insisted months later that the failure to recognize the coming crisis was not a result of cultural blindness. "The Islamic states also made mistakes about his intentions," a U.S. State Department official said. "So it was not a cultural mistake. We just didn't understand Saddam Hussein."

On March 15, rejecting the pleas of Western politicians and journalists, Saddam ordered the execution of Farzad Bazoft, an Iranian-born, British-based journalist accused of espionage. A few days later, U.S. and British authorities arrested several Iraqis in a "sting" operation against an Iraqi-run ring that was trying to smuggle missile components out of the United States and Great Britain. Then on March 22, Gerald Bull, an artillery expert who had been developing a super-cannon for Iraq, was found shot to death in Brussels—

apparently because of his Iraqi connection.

Saddam, who continually suspected U.S. plots against him, interpreted these events as part of a conspiracy leading to an imminent Israeli attack on Iraq, and issued a warning on April 2: "We will make the fire eat up half of Israel." Iraq, he admitted to the world, had chemical weapons.

Outraged U.S. Congressmen demanded economic sanctions against Iraq. Assistant Secretary Kelly tried to calm down Congress by telling a Senate committee that the Bush administration opposed sanctions because they would impair the U.S. "ability to exercise a restraining influence on Iraqi actions."

Meanwhile, U.S. Senators Howard M. Metzenbaum (D-Ohio), Robert J. Dole (R-Kan.), and Alan K. Simpson (R-Wyo.) met with Saddam in Baghdad. According to a transcript provided by Iraq and telecast on NBC, Metzenbaum told Saddam, "I am now aware that you are a strong and intelligent man," and Simpson told Saddam, "I believe that your problems lie with the Western media and not with the U.S. government."

The senators later said that the transcript had been edited—Saddam's censors removed the senators' remarks about the gassing of Kurds and the making of nuclear weapons. But the transcript's words were those of the senators; they obviously had not seen Saddam as a man planning an invasion.

In mid-July, in a nationwide broadcast, Saddam threatened to use force against any Arab oil-exporting nation that continued to pump excess oil. The threat was clearly aimed at Kuwait, which had angered Saddam by producing more oil than had been allotted under Organization of Petroleum Exporting Countries (OPEC) agreements, causing oil prices to plummet. In early 1990, oil was selling for $20.50 a barrel. By summer, the price had dropped to $13.60,

Man with a golden gun: Saddam examines his kind of work of art, a gold-plated AK-47. The trophy could be an emblem for his lifelong love of guns – and gold. Investigations into his wealth turned up fortunes hidden in foreign banks. A tableau of Saddam's justice (opposite): an Iraqi accused of spying is hanged on a public gibbet.

OPPOSITE: GAMMA / LIAISON
ABOVE: CNN

61

with each dollar drop equating to a $1 billion loss for Iraq, worsening Iraq's already difficult financial problems. Iraq also accused Kuwait of allegedly slant-drilling along the Iraq-Kuwait border, stealing an estimated $2.5 billion in oil from the Iraqi side of the Rumaila oil field.

"The oil quota violators have stabbed Iraq with a poison dagger," Saddam charged. "Iraqis will not forget the saying that cutting necks is better than cutting means of living. Oh God Almighty, be witness that we have warned them!"

Iraq began moving troops toward the border with Kuwait. The emirates and Kuwait tried to placate Saddam one more time by accepting a proposed oil price increase and by agreeing to limit their oil output, thus aiding a financially strapped Iraq. But again, Saddam warned Kuwait and the other Arab states that his "country will not kneel."

Saddam Hussein and U.S. Ambassador April Glaspie shake hands after their meeting on July 25, 1990. Exchanging smiles, she believes he will not attack Kuwait and he knows that more than 100,000 Iraqi troops are poised to invade Kuwait.

Like the leader in heroic scale behind her, this girl (opposite) with her AK-47 marches in a nation perpetually mobilized for war. Unlike other Arab states, Iraq allows women to bear arms; they also can appear in public unveiled.

ABOVE: CNN
RIGHT: CHRISTOPHER MORRIS / BLACK STAR

On July 18, in a letter from Iraq's foreign minister to the Arab League, Iraq charged Kuwait with "systematically, deliberately, and continuously" harming Iraq by encroaching on its territory, stealing its oil, and destroying its economy. "Such behavior," the minister said, "amounts to military aggression." Two days later, Israel offered the United States evidence that Iraq had deployed offensive missile batteries along the Kuwaiti and Jordanian borders.

By July 23, U.S. intelligence satellites confirmed that at least 30,000 Iraqi troops had massed on the Kuwaiti border. The next day, however, the U.S. State Department declined an opportunity during a press briefing to stand up, publicly, for Kuwait. Spokesperson Margaret D. Tutwiler sidestepped questions about the imminent invasion, saying that the United States had "no defense treaties with Kuwait; no special defense or security commitment to Kuwait."

After days of meetings with Iraqi officials, on July 25, Ambassador Glaspie was summoned to Iraq's Foreign Ministry. To her surprise, she was ushered into the presence of Saddam Hussein, who appeared in a well-tailored suit instead of his usual crisp military uniform. What was said at the meeting is less clear than what Saddam wore.

The Iraqi government issued a transcript that quoted the ambassador as telling Saddam, "We have no opinion on the Arab-Arab conflicts, like your border disagreement with Kuwait." Ambassador Glaspie herself later told the Senate Foreign Relations Committee that the Iraqis had edited out her warning that "we would support our friends in the Gulf, we would defend their sovereignty and integrity." Also omitted, she said, was a warning that "we would insist on settlements being made in a nonviolent manner, not by threats, not by intimidation, and certainly not by aggression."

When the Iraqis issued the transcript, the assumption was that it accurately reflected conciliatory U.S. policy. The State Department did not repudiate the transcript. Another version of the meeting, Glaspie's "memcom" (a memorandum of the conversation cabled to the U.S. State Department in Washington), was not made public. This memorandum could undoubtedly clarify the dispute over exactly how conciliatory the United States had been toward Saddam.

Whatever was said when the ambassador and Saddam met, the meeting was soon eclipsed by events along the Kuwait border. The next day, high-ranking Iraqi and Kuwaiti officials met in Jiddah, Saudi Arabia. As Iraq made its demands – that Kuwait forgive Iraq's war debts and hand over to Iraq the Kuwaiti island of Bubiyan – the Iraqi troop buildup continued. And while the world still wondered about Iraq's intentions, Saddam followed through with what he had threatened: "If they don't give it to me, I will. . . .take it."

At 2 A.M. on August 2, Saddam Hussein's troops began to take Kuwait.

CHAPTER FOUR

ASSAULT ON AN ARAB NEIGHBOR

In the predawn darkness of Thursday, August 2, 1990, some 100,000 Iraqi troops began crossing the border into Kuwait. For the two previous weeks, officials of the Iraqi and Kuwaiti governments had held talks in Jiddah, Saudi Arabia, to discuss their differences. No agreement was reached, and the Iraqi delegates had walked out on August 1, complaining that Kuwait was not taking the negotiations seriously.

During the abortive negotiations the U.S. Central Intelligence Agency (CIA) reported the massing of about 100,000 Iraqi troops with at least 300 tanks on the border with Kuwait. The source for this intelligence was primarily the KH-11 spy satellite, developed originally to photograph Soviet weapons and forces. Not only were Iraqi troops being built up on the border, but the satellite photos revealed a "logistics train" of fuel and ammunition trucks and other equipment moving into position to keep those troops supplied.

Most U.S. intelligence analysts interpreted the Iraqi buildup as either a move to intimidate the Kuwaitis negotiating at Jiddah, or the prelude for an attack to seize the Rumaila oil fields in western Kuwait from which, the Iraqis claimed, Kuwait was siphoning off Iraqi oil by way of slant drilling. Alternatively, some analysts suggested, the Iraqis could be preparing to seize the islands of Bubiyan and Warba, essentially mud flats that blocked Iraq's access to the Gulf. Few Washington observers of the Middle East scene believed that the buildup was for an all-out assault on an Arab neighbor. But among those who did predict that Iraq was on the verge of war was Israeli Defense Minister Moshe Arens.

Smoke engulfs minaret-shaped water towers as Iraqi troops assault Kuwait City. Saddam's plan to unify the Arab world had begun.
SAUDI ARABIA TELEVISION

Meeting in Washington with Secretary of Defense Dick Cheney in late July, he is said to have shown evidence that Iraq was positioning offensive missiles along the Kuwaiti and Jordanian border, the latter for a possible strike on Israel.

By July 26, intelligence reports confirmed a buildup of Iraqi forces along the Kuwaiti border after Saddam Hussein had assured U.S. Ambassador April Glaspie that Iraq would not invade. A senior White House official privately admitted that the administration was confused. The U.S. Defense Intelligence Agency reported that the situation was serious, but did not believe that Iraq would invade Kuwait. The estimates of the Central Intelligence Agency were more ominous: the CIA believed that an invasion is planned and perhaps imminent.

On August 1, the Iraqi ambassador in Washington, Mohammed Sadiq Al-Mashat, met with U.S. officials at the State Department's sprawling headquarters a few blocks west of the White House. Al-Mashat down-played the reports of Iraqi troop movements and blamed American rhetoric for raising anxieties among Washington officials.

U.S. Assistant Secretary of State for Near Eastern and South Asian Affairs John Kelly said that U.S. concern over the 100,000 troops massing on Kuwait's border was real. Mashat responded that Iraq had the right to move troops wherever it wished within its own borders and declared, "We are not going to move against anybody."

Consultations were held over secure telephones among officials at the State and Defense Departments and with top staff members on the National Security Council. Then it was time for face-to-face meetings to decide a coordinated U.S. position and begin fashioning responses.

Two hours after the State Department meeting with Al-Mashat, at 5 P.M., officials from State, the White House, the Joint Chiefs of Staff, and CIA met in the seventh-floor conference room at State. Deputy Director of Central Intelligence Richard Kerr brought the latest synthesis of intelligence from all sources. He predicted Iraq would invade Kuwait within 24 hours. The burning question, and the one with no answer as yet, was how far the Iraqi troops would go.

At 2 A.M. (Kuwait time) on August 2, the Middle East was again plunged into war, as Iraqi troops crossed the border into Kuwait. It was 7 P.M. (Eastern Daylight Saving Time) in Washington, D.C.– less than two hours after Kerr had made his prediction. The Iraqi columns sped unimpeded along the six-lane super highway toward Kuwait City, 80 miles (129 km.) from the border. As dawn broke, Iraqi jet fighter and attack aircraft and armed helicopters arrived over the advancing troops. Kuwait's Continued on page 70

An Iraqi 152-mm. self-propelled gun (opposite) is photographed clandestinely through a car window as Iraqi troops roll through Kuwait City. Insets: Home video captures the first scenes of the invasion.
STEPHANIE MCGEHEE / AP / WIDEWORLD PHOTOS
INSETS: CNN

FOLLOWING PAGE
An Iraqi firing squad executes soldiers who had looted in Kuwait; inset: an officer gives the coup de grace with his pistol. Kuwaitis were assembled to watch the executions. Unpunished pillage of the country soon followed.
BOTH: AHMED A / SIPA PRESS

Building support: U.S. Secretary of State Baker speaks to a British diplomat (below), while Kuwait's Emir Shaikh Jabir al-Ahmad al-Jabir as-Sabah (opposite) addresses the United Nations, asking for help.

BOTH: CHRISTOPHER MORRIS / BLACK STAR

UNITED STATES

12 KEY UNITED NATIONS RESOLUTIONS ADOPTED AGAINST IRAQ

660 AUG 2 Condemned Iraq's invasion of Kuwait. Demanded Baghdad withdraw.

661 AUG 6 Imposed sanctions on all trade to and from Iraq except for medicine and, in humanitarian circumstances, foodstuffs.

662 AUG 9 Declared null and void Iraq's annexation of Kuwait.

664 AUG 18 Demanded Iraq allow foreign nationals to leave Iraq and Kuwait and rescind its order to close diplomatic missions in Kuwait.

665 AUG 25 Permitted use of limited naval force to ensure compliance with economic sanctions, including the right to inspect cargos.

666 SEPT 13 Approved food shipments to Iraq and Kuwait for humanitarian purposes, if distributed by international groups.

667 SEPT 16 Condemned raids by Iraqi troops on French and other diplomatic missions in occupied Kuwait.

669 SEPT 24 Entrusted sanctions committee to evaluate requests for assistance from countries suffering due to embargo.

670 SEPT 25 Prohibited non-humanitarian air traffic into Iraq and occupied Kuwait.

674 OCT 29 Asked states to document financial losses and human rights violations resulting from the invasion.

677 NOV 28 Asked the U.N. secretary-general to safeguard a smuggled copy of Kuwait's pre-invasion population register.

678 NOV 29 Authorized states "to use all necessary means" against Iraq unless it withdrew from Kuwait on or by Jan. 15.

armed forces totaled 20,300 men, plus some foreign specialists hired under contract.

Indeed, the country's entire native population was smaller than the active Iraqi armed forces. Kuwait did not mobilize its army against Iraq because its leaders envisioned another diplomatic solution to the confrontation. Their inaction made the job of the attacking forces easier, but it would have been a walkthrough in any case: Iraq's best divisions, equippped with first-line equipment, were rolling and flying into Kuwait in overwhelming numbers. The outcome was preordained.The defending Kuwaiti forces were quickly overrun, and the Iraqis smashed into Kuwait City.

The first targets of the Iraqi forces entering Kuwait City were the palace of Shaikh Jabir al-Ahmad al-Jabir as-Sabah, the Emir of Kuwait; the central bank, where Kuwaiti's gold reserves were stored; and the Ministry of Information building, which housed Kuwait's radio and television studios. The few attempts by Kuwaiti troops to engage the attackers were simply brushed aside, with Iraqis making use of overwhelming firepower. With no time to lose, the emir and most members of his family escaped south, to Ad Dammam in Saudi Arabia, by naval small craft. Many Kuwaiti troops and more than 20 Kuwaiti-piloted, U.S.-built A-4KU Skyhawk attack planes were also able to cross into Saudi Arabia before the Iraqi attackers completely sealed off the border and seized control of the airfields.

On August 8, over Baghdad radio, Saddam Hussein defended his invasion of Kuwait as "necessary" to redress what he called the "flawed regional borders" drawn up by colonial powers that left a "corrupt minority" in control of some of the Arab world's richest territory. He announced the permanent annexation of Kuwait as Iraq's 19th province and ordered foreign embassies in Kuwait to close down. Most nations complied, but U.S., British, French, and Soviet diplomats defied the edict and kept their embassies in operation. In the American Embassy, Ambassador Nathaniel Howell and his staff had made preparations to survive a siege. Among their survival rations were countless cans of tuna fish.

Meanwhile, the rape of Kuwait had begun. Torture, killings, and mass arrests had started on the day of the invasion. Men and women were pulled off the streets for interrogations. The wrong responses brought pain, mutilation, and in many cases death. Iraqi soldiers also raped women. After the war, Iraqi "torture centers" in Kuwait were found to contain bloodstained saws, axes, pick handles, meat hooks, a power drill, hand vise, and electric cattle prods: pliers to extract fingernails; carpenter planes to shave off skin; and a pair of industrial dryers, also stained inside with blood. Liberators also discovered a bed frame and a hot plate that had been wired to give electric shocks.

The number of Kuwaitis tortured and murdered during the six months of Iraqi occupation is estimated to be in the thousands. Twenty-one university professors who refused to take down a picture of the emir and replace it with one of Saddam were said to have been executed. Other accounts claim that Iraqis disconnected and removed several incubators from hospitals – even those supporting premature babies.

It was a "planned rape plus 'free enterprise' by the troops," said a senior U.S. intelligence official. The Iraqis stripped everything of value from Kuwait. "The stripping was orderly, organized, premeditated," said the official. Museums were looted as well as the nearly century-old Sief palace, home of the royal family that had ruled Kuwait since 1756. Some losses were irreplaceable, such as those from the world's most comprehensive collection of Islamic art. Also stolen was a display of Islamic art on loan to Kuwait from the Hermitage Museum in Leningrad. The buildings housing these collections, like other structures, were ravaged by Iraqi troops.

The embargo imposed by the United Nations was implemented almost immediately. A U.S. Navy SH-2F helicopter (above) flying from a nearby frigate looks over a liquid natural gas carrier in the Persian Gulf. Armed U.S. Coast Guardsmen climb aboard a container ship (opposite).
ABOVE: SCOTT M. ALLEN / U.S. NAVY
OPPOSITE: DENNIS BRACK / BLACK STAR

A Kuwaiti later explained, "They tried to wipe out the identity of Kuwait, as if Kuwait did not exist." This practice of eradicating an enemy's society was based on tribal mores that went back thousands of years, predating the Koran's call to obey the "the All-merciful, the All-compassionate" God.

"The violence against Kuwaitis reflected traditional Arab secret police tactics," in the words of the U.S. intelligence official. Beatings and rapes were common. Kuwaitis were required to become Iraqi citizens in order to obtain medical care, procure automobile license plates, and purchase gasoline and other goods. They were often hounded and harassed.

The Iraqi's also attacked the elaborate Kuwaiti national zoo. Soldiers – and even a general officer – used caged animals for target practice and carted off elephants, giraffes, and monkeys to the Baghdad zoo. Later, when food for Iraqi troops became scarce, soldiers ate the zoo's sheep, deer, and gazelles. Surviving animals starved, although Kuwaitis rescued some of the smaller ones by taking them in as house pets.

As the Kuwaiti society disintegrated, shortages of fresh foods, especially fruits and vegetables developed. Ample stocks of canned goods and staples, coupled with the exodus of Kuwaitis to the south helped to stave off widespread hunger for those who remained in Kuwait. But the situation worsened as the Republican Guard and other first-line Iraqi troops were withdrawn and less disciplined units, comprised mostly of poorly trained volunteers, arrived. Reportedly, Kuwaitis who offended soldiers were shot on the street. Soldiers seeking food entered houses at random and confiscated stereo and television sets, jewelry, and other personal possessions that had not been hidden.

In the early days of the occupation, Iraqi troops were ordered to rig Kuwaiti government buildings, utilities, and oil fields with explosives for demolition. There are indications that within four or five days of the invasion, Iraqi soldiers had affixed plastic explosives to most of Kuwait's 1,080 working wellheads. The rigging of explosives had been carefully planned before the invasion. Six of the oil wells were detonated in December 1990 to determine the effectiveness of the scheme. It was, a U.S. official later explained, "as if Saddam knew from the outset that someday he would eventually have to give up his 19th province." That might be, but at the time Saddam and his forces held Kuwait in an iron grip that tightened with every passing day.

A small Kuwaiti resistance movement fought back throughout the occupation. At first, Kuwaiti citizens openly opposed the takeover. At night, some climbed to the tops of buildings to unfurl large banners in Arabic and English calling for the Iraqis to leave and for the return of the emir. But the arrival of the Iraqi second-line troops led to more brutality and repression. The last few international telephone lines were cut, although some Kuwaitis with direct satellite phones were able to maintain communication links throughout occupation. Reportedly, some Kuwaitis periodically crossed the border into Saudi Arabia to carry information on Iraqi troop locations and movements to the coalition forces. This "human intelligence" was a welcome addition to the information being collected by U.S. aircraft and surveillance satellites, and being correlated with data provided by other countries.

Kuwait formed an anti-Iraqi guerrilla movement, which had some successes. It killed some Iraqis; and it gave some others – disarmed and detained after straying into the wrong Kuwaiti home – the choice of deserting and going back to Iraq or being killed. Using guns, grenades, explosives, and even shoulder-fired missiles, the guerrillas launched both carefully planned attacks and struck impulsively, even firing a rifle grenade at the Iraqi Embassy in mid-August. There is also a claim that Kuwaiti guerrillas had shot down an Iraqi helicopter. These valiant efforts had little impact on the Iraqi occupation, except to accelerate the retaliation underway against Kuwaiti citizens.

Under the clamp-down, the Iraqis began rounding up the hundreds of thousands of foreigners working in Kuwait. These men and women served in virtually every possible role, from engineer and physician to housekeeper and garbage collector. Similarly, foreigners working in Iraq were rounded up. Those from most Arab countries were expelled into Jordan. Others, principally Americans and Europeans, were detained as "guests." A few thousand foreigners, mostly Palestinians, were permitted to continue at their jobs.

On August 2, immediately after learning of the assault against Kuwait, President George Bush publicly condemned the invasion and asked the United Nations Security Council to demand an Iraqi withdrawal. That same day, the Council passed Resolution 660, calling for Iraq's immediate and unconditional withdrawal. The vote was 14 to 0, with Yemen not voting.

President Bush then flew to Aspen, Colorado, where he was scheduled to give a speech on East-West relations to commemorate the 40th anniversary of the Aspen Institute. The speech included President Bush's articulation of his new national strategy, now about to be tested before the speech could be reported in the media. While in Aspen, Bush met with British Prime Minister Margaret Thatcher, who was also attending the celebration. According to some reports, she encouraged Bush to undertake a military response. In his speech, the President deplored Iraq's invasion of Kuwait, terming it "naked aggression." As Mrs. Thatcher stood beside the President during the subsequent news conference, Bush affirmed that Great Britain was "standing shoulder to shoulder with the United States," to counter Saddam's aggression. Thatcher's

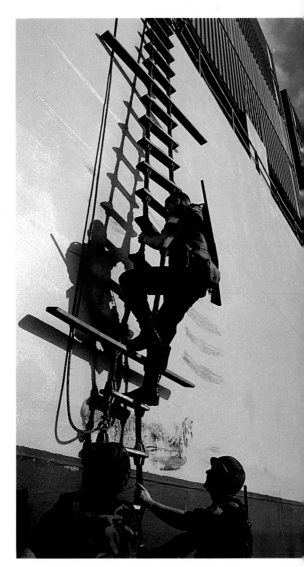

support would serve as the foundation upon which Bush would build an international coalition against Iraq.

News of the Iraqi invasion brought immediate and generally negative reaction from the world economic community. Iraq and Kuwait together controlled almost 20 percent of the world's proven oil reserves. Removal of that oil from the world market, coupled with the threat of further Iraqi aggression and the impact on the availability of oil from Saudi Arabia and other Gulf states, brought about a crisis in oil trading. The Japanese Nikkei stock market fell 593 points on announcement of the news of the Iraqi action; oil futures on all markets skyrocketed.

In the United States, President Bush immediately felt pressure to release oil from the national petroleum stockpile to ensure that gasoline prices would not rise. But because of the futures situation, prices at gasoline pumps rose throughout the world. Consumers fumed and blamed the oil companies, who in turn pontificated about the uncertainties of supplies in the future.

Meanwhile, the Bush administration advanced a three-prong approach, using political, economic, and military strategies to force Iraqi troops out of Kuwait. World leaders were urged to give their support, with President Bush himself "working the phones." Some of the results were surprising: The day after the invasion, Secretary Baker and Soviet Foreign Minister Eduard Shevardnadze issued an unprecedented joint denunciation of the Iraqi invasion. (The Soviet Union was not only Iraq's chief arms supplier but had several hundred advisors in the country at the time of the invasion.) A day later, the European Community imposed broad sanctions against Iraq, including embargoes on oil imports and arms sales. Simultaneously, to bring further economic pressure against Iraq, Bush ordered an economic embargo against the aggressor, and joined Britain and France in freezing Iraqi and Kuwaiti assets in their countries.

While Saddam prayed in his newly occupied 19th province, much of the world allied against him. The end of the Cold War enabled both of his former supporters, the United States and the Soviet Union, to reach an agreement opposing his actions.
CNN

The condemnation of Iraq, however, was not universal. Jordan's King Hussein described Saddam as a patriot for the Arab world. Geographically trapped between Iraq and Israel, the king, perhaps, feared the sentiment of Jordan's large Palestinian population, which viewed Saddam as a hero.

With regard to military strategy, the U.S. Joint Chiefs of Staff met with General H. Norman Schwarzkopf, Commander-in-Chief of the U.S. Central Command, the multi-service headquarters charged with planning Middle East operations. Secretary of Defense Dick Cheney and Schwarzkopf then flew to Saudi Arabia, arriving on August 6 to confer with King Fahd Ibn Abdel-Aziz about the threat of an Iraqi assault on Saudi Arabia. Schwarzkopf later recalled that he and Cheney told the King, "If asked to defend Saudi Arabia, we would; we would also leave when asked to leave, and we wouldn't establish any permanent bases."

The two Americans expected that the king would confer with his ministers and advisors before making the momentous decision to ask a Western army into Saudi Arabia. The king is known as the "keeper of the faith," with his country containing two of Islam's most holy shrines, at Mecca and at Medina. Inviting in foreign troops—most Christians, with many women and Jews— would be interpreted by some in the Muslim world as desecrating their holy land. "We want you to come," was King Fahd's immediate response, recalled General Schwarzkopf.

The next day, August 7, President Bush ordered U.S. military aircraft and troops to Saudi Arabia. U.S. warships were already in the Arabian Sea and Persian Gulf, with more en route. The massive buildup was given the code name "Desert Shield" (see Chapter 5). Troops from other nations were being readied to go to the Gulf. Egypt, embarrassed by the Iraqi invasion and in debt to the United States for economic aid, was the first country to commit to sending troops to join the U.S. and Saudi forces. Other nations soon followed, a credit to Bush's persuasiveness as well as to the threat from Saddam. Additional U.S. warships arrived in the Gulf, as Bush ordered the Navy to enforce the U.N. embargo against Iraq. Immediately, numerous U.S. Coast Guard detachments were dispatched to the warships to lend their considerable experience in maritime interdiction, boardings, and searches.

Within days, warships flying the flags of Australia, Britain, Canada, France, Italy, and the Netherlands began sailing into the Gulf, further reducing Iraq's chances of receiving goods and war supplies through Gulf shipping and of exporting oil. At the same time, Turkey, which provided a pipeline to the Mediterranean for Iraqi oil, added its support to the coalition, halting the oil flow. Earlier, Saudi Arabia had closed the pipelines from Iraq to ports across the Saudi peninsula.

With the Gulf blockaded by coalition warships and the pipeline through Turkey closed, the only means of getting oil out of Iraq was by truck into Jordan. Only Jordan, which shares a long, common land border with Iraq, continued to engage in commerce. Soon Jordanians and Palestinians were demonstrating in support of Saddam and denouncing the United States and its allies. (In late August, brief demonstrations erupted in several Syrian towns in support of Saddam and against Syria's decision to dispatch forces to Saudi Arabia; Syrian troops suppressed the demonstrations, and several demonstrators were killed.

Bush and Gorbachev, meeting in Helsinki, Finland, on September 9, 1990, called for Saddam to leave Kuwait.
J.L. ATLAN / SYGMA

Jordan, however, was in the minority among the Arab states. Most Arab nations sought to find an "Arab solution" to the crisis. But the annexation and Saddam's vocal assaults against the leaders of oil-producing nations only hardened Arab resolve against Iraq. When the Arab League met in Cairo, Egypt, on August 9-10, thirteen of 21 League members agreed to send military forces to Saudi Arabia and to other Gulf states to protect them from possible Iraqi attack. Twelve of the member countries endorsed a resolution that condemned Iraq's annexation of Kuwait, denounced the Iraqi military buildup on the border with Saudi Arabia, and demanded the return to power of Kuwait's legitimate ruler.

In response, on August 12, Saddam offered to resolve the crisis if Israel agreed to withdraw from the occupied West Bank, Golan Heights, and Gaza Strip. This attempt to link the invasion of Kuwait to the Palestinian issue, like his efforts to incite the Arab masses to rise up against their leaders, would fail. But while Saddam attempted his own diplomatic solution to the crisis, he continued to secure his military footing. On August 15, Saddam surprised most observers by offering to withdraw his troops from the Shatt al-Arab waterway, his trophy from the 1980-1988 war with Iran. The Iranians accepted, and Iraqi troops began dismantling the fortifications. This move freed several Iraqi divisions for potential operations to the south.

Within weeks of the invasion, Iraq had entrenched nearly a quarter of a million troops in or near Kuwait. It was not clear whether or not Saddam planned to send these forces south, to invade Saudi Arabia or to take control of the so-called "neutral zone" between the countries. The buildup was greater than required either to occupy Kuwait or to defend it against possible Saudi military efforts. Indeed, the Iraqi "logistics train" was building up stockpiles of munitions and supplies in the area far in excess of what would conceivably be needed to defend Kuwait.

As the Iraqi buildup went on, Saddam moved many of the several thousand detained foreigners, including U.S. and British citizens, to military installations in Iraq to serve as "human shields." However, when Western public opinion began to denounce Saddam, he quickly appeared on Iraqi television visiting with British hostages to demonstrate that they were safe and well treated. Iraq

Kuwaitis in London (opposite) protest Saddam's ravaging of their country. Anti-war protests erupt in many countries, including the United States (above), where Americans opposed going to war for oil.
ABOVE: DAVID BUTOW / BLACK STAR
RIGHT: AP / WIDE WORLD PHOTOS

released some French nationals as a sign of the special relationship between the two countries; the French government responded by demanding the immediate and unconditional release of all hostages. Americans reacted spontaneously, showing support for the hostages by displaying yellow ribbons, as had been done during the 1980 hostage crisis in Tehran. (The yellow ribbon demonstrations were based on then-popular song "Tie A Yellow Ribbon" sung by the group Tony Orlando and Dawn.)

The yellow ribbons soon appeared across the United States for the American troops who were rapidly deploying to Saudi Arabia, and for the sailors and Marines sailing for the Red Sea and Persian Gulf. Some 200,000 U.S. troops had been ordered to the Gulf in early August, followed on August 22 by the first activation of military reserve units – about 12,000 members of the Army National Guard. President Bush's decision to mobilize the reserves was a move that had been largely avoided by Presidents John F. Kennedy and Lyndon B. Johnson during the Vietnam War because of their fear of political repercussions.

On November 8, President Bush ordered another 200,000 troops sent

for duty in the Middle East. By year's end, more than a half million coalition troops and airmen would be positioned in Saudi Arabia and on board amphibious ships offshore. The message to Saddam was clear: Leave Kuwait or face military action.

In response, the Iraqi government announced on November 19 that it was sending another 250,000 troops into the Kuwaiti area. Western analysts estimated this would raise the Iraqi strength to about 550,000 men. The troops began erecting fortifications along the border with Saudi Arabia and along the coast of Kuwait. Those facing Saudi Arabia consisted of two "belts" of fighting positions and obstacles, protected by minefields, pools of oil that could be ignited, and barbed wire. Heavy artillery and rockets were carefully sighted on the approaches to these fortifications. In the latter stages of the Iraq-Iran War, such fortifications had withstood the mass attacks by Iranian troops and exacted a heavy toll of casualties. Saddam's generals appear to have planned a similar slaughter should the United States and its allies attempt to oust their troops. "In effect, these generals were displaying a purely defensive mentality. They were betting their troops' lives on the dubious proposition that the allies would behave as the Iranians did," was the way that U.S. Army Chief of Staff General Carl Vuono later assessed the Iraqi strategy.

In the Uinted States, facing criticism from members of Congress as well as public groups, President Bush sought to mitigate the attacks by calling on members of his newly forged coalition and other allies to help support the war with financial as well as military contributions. The contributions would go not only to the United States, but to Egypt and Turkey, which were being financially hurt by the situation in the Middle East. Bush solicited hardest from the Kuwaiti government in exile, Saudi Arabia, West Germany, and Japan. All responded rapidly with pledges of financial support. Although both Germany and Japan were prohibited by law from sending combat troops to the Gulf, Germany, did send specially equipped vehicles fitted to detect chemical contamination to U.S. troops in the Gulf.

Meanwhile, a parade of diplomats engaged in rounds of "shuttle diplomacy." Jordan's King Hussein flew to Baghdad for talks with Saddam and then on to Washington. Austrian President Kurt Waldheim followed the king to Baghdad, as did former British Prime Minister Edward Heath, former West German Chancellor Willy Brandt, and former Japanese Prime Minister Yasuhiro Nakasone. Yassar Arafat, nominal leader of the Palestine Liberation Organization, who publicly sided with Saddam, also engaged in shuttle diplomacy without effect.

U.N. Secretary General Javier Perez de Cuellar met with Iraqi Foreign Minister Tariq Aziz in Jordan. Aziz told de Cuellar, who had played a major role in the 1988 cease-fire between Iraq and Iran, that Iraq would release the hostages if the United Nations provided guarantees that Iraq would not be attacked by coalition military forces. No agreement was reached, and a short time later Aziz flew to Moscow to meet with Soviet President Mikhail Gorbachev. While Aziz said the meeting was "constructive, cordial, and frank," the Soviets reaffirmed their support of the U.N. resolutions. Thereafter, the Soviets continue to search for a Middle East settlement that would benefit their position in the region. Aziz also flew to Iran to meet with his now-former enemies.

Similarly, U.S. Secretary of State Baker and Secretary of Defense Cheney, the latter often accompanied by General Colin Powell, Chairman of the Joint Chiefs of Staff, flew throughout Europe and the Middle East to cement the coalition and to gain pledges of financial support. Former U.S. presidential candidate Jesse Jackson also tried his hand at negotiations. Jackson interviewed Saddam for a television program and sought the release of hostages. Saddam had previously announced he would release women and children, and Jackson obtained the release of some ailing male hostages.

During these months, only a trickle of Americans and Europeans found their way out of Kuwait and Iraq. But

Saddam (top) attempted to portray compassion by asking 5-year-old British hostage Stuart Lockwood, "Are you getting your milk, Stuart, and corn flakes, too?" The Reverand Jesse Jackson with U.S. Ambassador Nathaniel Howell in Kuwait (above).

BOTH: CNN

hundreds of thousands of Third World workers fled both countries. The exodus caused severe economic and humanitarian problems. For years, those workers had sent home most of their pay, contributing greatly to their nations' economies. (For instance, about one million Egyptians worked in the two countries.) The loss of income, coupled with the increase in oil prices, hurt several Third World countries. More troubling, millions of refugees camped on Jordan's doorstep, because they lacked proper documents or had no funds to travel to their own countries. Once inside Jordan, the refugees created a massive economic burden, creating food and water shortages. Tensions in the country increased.

This situation contributed to the periodic rioting by Arabs in the West Bank and East Jerusalem. On October 8, Palestinians attacked Jews celebrating the holiday of Sukkoth at the Wailing Wall in Jerusalem. When Israeli police responded, as many as 24 Arabs were killed and more than 100 injured. It was the worst clash of Israelis and Arabs since the older portion of the city was captured in 1967. Fighting continued in the West Bank and Gaza areas, fueling Saddam's demands that all occupied areas be given to the Palestinians as a part of any Middle East settlement.

In late November, as the crises escalated and hopes for a peaceful solution diminished, Senator Sam Nunn (D-Ga.), chairman of the Senate Armed Services Committee, held hearings on the issue of sanctions versus war. Most witnesses, including former Secretary of Defense Robert McNamara, former Chairmen of the Joint Chiefs of Staff Admiral William J. Crowe, and Air Force General David C. Jones, recommended against offensive action. They advocated giving economic sanctions more time to work, perhaps 12 to 18 months. They also foresaw the possibility of massive U.S. casualties if there was war.

On November 29, the U.N. Security Council adopted Resolution 678, which established a six-week deadline for Saddam to withdraw from Kuwait. The Council authorized the coalition "to use Continued on page 82

Saddam curried favor with certain countries by releasing their hostages, including 263 from France.
PATRICK DURAND / SYGMA

FOLLOWING PAGE

Saddam's assault on Kuwait displaced millions of workers in Iraq and Kuwait. Refugees clamor for water at the Jordanian border; thousands of Kuwaitis (inset) were able to flee across the border to Saudi Arabia.
PETER TURNLEY / BLACK STAR
INSET: WILLIAM FOLEY / TIME MAGAZINE

all necessary means to . . . restore international peace and security in the area." It also gave Saddam a deadline for complying with this and previous U.N. resolutions: Midnight, Eastern Standard Time, January 15, 1991.

A week later, on December 6, Saddam asked Iraq's parliament to release the last of the foreigners he had held in Iraq and Kuwait. Within two days, about 565 hostages, including 175 Americans, returned home in time for the year-end holidays. With the Americans freed, U.S. Ambassador Nathaniel Howell and his skeleton staff that had kept the American flag flying at the embassy in Kuwait City finally locked the doors on December 13. Bedraggled, suffering from the scarcity of water, and tired of eating canned foods, especially tuna fish, the five American diplomats left for home.

Perhaps believing that his release of hostages would defuse American resolve to go to war, Saddam announced on December 22 that he was not giving up Kuwait, and that if attacked, Iraq would use chemical weapons.

On January 9, 1991, President Bush dispatched Secretary Baker to meet Iraqi Foreign Minister Aziz in Geneva as a final gesture to show desire for a peaceful Iraqi withdrawal. Bush had insisted that the meeting was not for negotiations but solely to inform the Iraqis that they had to get out of Kuwait or face war. Baker carried a letter from the President to Saddam. Aziz refused to accept it. Their day-long meeting produced no results. International efforts to negotiate an agreement for Iraq's withdrawal from Kuwait would continue up until the war began. Perez de Cuellar would travel to Baghdad with new proposals as late as January 12.

Meanwhile, in Washington, the members of the 102nd Congress confronted a fundamental question: whether to authorize President Bush to use force to back the U.N. mandate, or to delay action and give the sanctions more time. Both the House of Representatives and the Senate offered resolutions supporting each course of action. It was decision time, and the world was watching—the debates were broadcast live on television. The leadership in both houses put the resolutions on the fast track for debate and then a vote, to settle the issue before the U.N. deadline.

House Speaker Thomas S. Foley (D-Wash.) described the resolution, sponsored by the chairman of the House Foreign Affairs Committee, Dante B. Fascell (D-Fla.), as the "practical equivalent" of a declaration of war. The final vote in both houses would be remembered as, perhaps, the most important of some members' careers. Moreover, the resolution's approval signaled a rare coming-together of the nation.

House Majority Leader Richard A. Gephardt (D-Mo.), whose own no–war resolution was defeated, framed it best on January 10, the first day of the debate: "In this vote, we are not Democrats. We are not Republicans. We are Americans. We expect and want all of the members to vote their conscience, what in their mind is the right thing for this country to do."

Those who supported President Bush from the outset included Congressman Stephen J. Solarz (D-N.Y.), who, two decades earlier, was a leader of the anti–Vietnam War movement. Solarz and other early advocates of using armed force in the Gulf, if necessary, generally argued that Saddam was dragging his feet, that he should not have invaded Kuwait to begin with, and that he could not be allowed to defy the United Nations. They argued that appeasing Saddam, like appeasing Adolf Hitler, would bring disaster.

Representatives who rejected this view tended to argue that sanctions were working, and even if they were not, the country would, once again, have to

Both President Saddam and President Bush attempt to influence their opponents with television messages. Both leaders explained their views and forecast dire consequences for the other should conflict come to the Middle East. In retrospect, both messages were ineffective.
BOTH: CNN

suffer grievous battlefield losses to restore Kuwait. Senator Edward M. Kennedy (D-Mass.) was expansive:

"Let there be no mistake about the cost of war. We have arrayed an impressive international coalition against Iraq, but when the bullets start flying, 90 percent of the casualties will be Americans. It is hardly a surprise that so many other nations are willing to fight to the last American to achieve the goals of the United Nations. . . . Most military experts tell us that a war with Iraq would not be quick and decisive, as President Bush suggests; it'll be brutal, and costly. It'll take weeks, even months, and will quickly turn from an air war to a ground war, with thousands, perhaps even tens of thousands, of American casualties. The administration refuses to release casualty estimates, but the 45,000 body bags the Pentagon has sent to the region are all the evidence we need of the high price in lives and blood we will have to spare. . . . In other words, we're talking about the likelihood of at least 3,000 American casualties a week, with 700 dead, for as long as the war goes on."

When the congressional debate over going to war began in January, a Senate debate on Iraq, which had erupted in July 1990, was already forgotten. That debate—over whether to provide Iraq with loans guaranteed by the U.S. government—had come on the eve of Iraq's invasion of Kuwait. But revelations that had surfaced in the Senate in July were pertinent to understanding the Bush administration's pre-invasion attitude toward Iraq, a major Middle East trading partner and a leading customer for U.S. agricultural products.

At the time of the invasion, critics and supporters of the Bush administration focused on U.S. oil interests in Kuwait and Saudi Arabia. But the Senate debate showed that the United States also had great current and potential financial interests in Saddam Hussein's Iraq.

Revealed in the Senate debate was the fact that Iraq owed $2 billion in loans backed by U.S. taxpayers through the Commodity Credit Corporation (CCC) of the Department of Agriculture. The government uses these loans as an incentive to get other nations to buy U.S. commodities. Iraq began getting such loan guarantees in 1983. Through the time of the invasion, Iraq borrowed $5 billion in CCC-backed loans for the purchase of U.S. agricultural goods. Iraq repaid the loans regularly as they came due, but still owed $2 billion when Iraqi troops invaded Kuwait.

"Do you think we are going to get paid?" asked Senator Alfonse M. D'Amato (R-N.Y.) on July 27. "This is not a loan. We are backing this up. We are not going to get paid. He does not have the money."

The debate had been touched off by what seemed to be a dull parliamentary maneuver. Senator Phil Gramm (R-Tex.), an ardent supporter of the Bush administration, introduced an amendment to an amendment to an agriculture trade act. The first amendment, introduced by D'Amato, barred Iraq from receiving any loans guaranteed by the CCC. This meant that Iraq could buy agricultural products from U.S. farmers, but, if Iraq wanted to get a loan from a private financial institution, the loan would not be backed by the federal government.

Gramm's amendment would give either of two Bush cabinet members, the Secretary of Commerce or the Secretary of Agriculture, the power to waive the D'Amato restriction, thus killing it. Gramm's argument was that Saddam would go elsewhere to buy farm goods if denied U.S.-backed loans.

Farm state Senator Nancy L. Kassebaum (R-Kan.) sharply disagreed, arguing, "It is not just food we are dealing with in this amendment; it is also banning the sale of weapons that are on the [banned] munitions list, as well as weapons equipment that has dual-use purposes."

Senator William Cohen (R-Me.), vice chairman of the Senate Intelligence Committee, introduced a new revelation: The Bush administration had just lifted export controls "on the very nuclear weapon devices, the so-called krytons, that Iraq tried to smuggle out of the United States in March." Also decontrolled, he said, were "skull furnaces, which Iraq has been trying to get

from a manufacturer in New Jersey. These can melt plutonium for nuclear bomb cores and titanium for missile nose cones." Cohen called the administration policy toward Iraq "appeasement," inspired by "the smell of oil and the color of money."

The Gramm amendment was defeated, 57 to 38, in what looked at the time to be an economic strike at Iraq. Six months later, as the House and Senate debated full-scale war against Iraq, the Bush administration had shifted its policy. In July, U.S.-backed loans to Iraq were encouraged and U.S. Ambassador April Glaspie had been instructed to make conciliatory moves toward Iraq. But in January, on the erratic march toward war, the Bush administration denounced Iraq and dismissed economic warfare as being

enough to force Iraq to leave Kuwait.

The January 1991 debate raged in both houses for three days. William Webster, the Director of Central Intelligence, wrote to congressional leaders, saying economic sanctions would not force an Iraqi withdrawal from Kuwait for at least a year.

Then on Saturday, January 12, President Bush marked an important victory. The resolution passed 52 to 47 in the Senate, and 250 to 183 in the House. It was only the sixth time in the nation's history that Congress had acted formally to declare war – or, in this case, to allow the president to use force, if required, to end the Gulf crises. (In the Senate, 42 Republicans and 10 Democrats voted for the resolution; two Republicans and 45 Democrats opposed the measure. In the House, 164 Republicans and 86 Democrats voted yes; three Republicans, 179 Democrats, and one Independent voted no.)

With the war resolution passed, members of Congress closed ranks. Debate ended. Both houses voted unanimously to support the President's decision to initiate armed action against Iraq. Senator Robert Dole (R- Kan.), minority leader of the Senate, placed the debate in context this way: "As soon as the vote was completed, there was a change across the country. The people realized that Congress has a role to play, and played it in this situation. The American people were waiting for Congress to make a judgment. When the Congress did, then the people swung behind the president." In the Middle East, U.S. and other coalition forces assembled and readied themselves to provide the necessary military might to enforce the U.N. resolutions. As the U.N. deadline neared, men, ships, planes, and weapons from a score of nations continued to arrive "in country," as those in Saudi Arabia began to refer to their location. Saudi Arabia already had a large number of airfields and several military bases. Overnight, tent cities sprang up to house the coalition armies, while offshore, in the Gulf, the Red Sea, and eastern Mediteranean, warships and amphibious ships maneuvered at a high state of readiness. Throughout this period people in many countries demonstrated and prayed for peace. In the United States, on January 14, anti-war demonstrators gathered at the National Cathedral in Washington, D.C., and marched in a candlelight procession to the White House. Chanting "peace now," and singing songs from the Vietnam era, these and other protestors then gathered in a candlelight prayer vigil in front of the Lincoln Memorial.

President Bush spent January 14 in meetings with foreign officials in the White House. Presidential spokesman Marlin Fitzwater warned that coalition military action could occur at any point after the U.N. deadline. "Any moment after the 15th is borrowed time," he said.

As armies, planes, and ships are moved to prepare for the opening gambit in the Middle East, millions pray that war will not come. On the eve of war, a prayer vigil is held at Washington's National Cathedral.
DAVID BURNETT / CONTACT

BUILDING A COALITION

When Iraq invaded Kuwait several U.S. warships were on station in the Persian Gulf, where the United States had maintained a continuous naval presence since 1949. The U.S. naval presence in the region had reached the size of a fleet in the late 1980s, when the Iran-Iraq War had threatened commercial tankers carrying crude oil out of the Gulf.

But when Kuwait was invaded, the nearest U.S. tactical aircraft were on board the aircraft carriers *Independence* (CV-62), steaming in the eastern Indian Ocean, and on the carrier *Dwight D. Eisenhower* (CVN-69) at Naples, Italy; each ship carried an 80-plane air wing. The nearest U.S. ground combat forces were the four "heavy" armored and mechanized divisions of the U.S. Seventh Army in Germany, supported by nine U.S. Air Force tactical fighter wings at bases in Britain, Germany, and Spain. In the Far East, a Marine battalion and aircraft squadron were embarked in amphibious ships at Subic Bay in the Philippines. Meanwhile, a major U.S. planning staff had its eyes on the Gulf and was prepared for an immediate military response, if so ordered. This was the U.S. Central Command, called CENTCOM in Pentagon jargon. Its headquarters were at MacDill Air Force Base, near Tampa, Florida, almost 8,000 miles (12,870 km.) from the Persian Gulf. CENTCOM is a "unified" command with its Commander-in-Chief, Army General H. Norman Schwarzkopf, reporting directly to the Secretary of Defense and Joint Chiefs of Staff. It has the responsibility for planning potential U.S. military operations in 19 Middle East countries. The term "unified" means that Schwarzkopf could direct forces of all services in carrying out his assignments.

Thus, General Schwarzkopf, a 56-year-old soldier who had served two combat tours in Vietnam, was called early *Continued on page 92*

Preparing to fight against the threat posed by Iraqi chemical weapons, a U.S. soldier trains under the discomfort of protective mask and smock in 100-degree Fahrenheit Saudi weather.

CHRISTOPHER MORRIS / BLACK STAR

Raising clouds of talcum-powder Saudi sand, troopers of the U.S. 1st Cavalry Division move out toward base camp.
GREG ENGLISH / AP / WIDE WORLD PHOTOS

The U.S. aircraft carrier America *(CV-66) sails through the Suez Canal in January 1991, with the aircraft and crews of Carrier Air Wing 1 on board.*
MIKE NELSON / AFP

on the morning of August 2, 1990, by General Colin Powell, Chairman of the Joint Chiefs of Staff, and told of the Iraqi invasion. A short time later he was in Washington, D.C., to confer with senior U.S. political and military leaders. Then, on August 6, Schwarzkopf accompanied Secretary of Defense Dick Cheney to Saudi Arabia. Schwarzkopf's staff had long planned for a number of possible contingencies in the Gulf; among them, as the general had explained to a congressional committee on April 20, 1989: "Iraq's persistent claims to strategic portions of northeastern Kuwait which could be a problem in the future." Even as these discussions were under way, U.S. military units were being brought to a higher state of readiness and preparing for possible deployment to the Gulf area. The carrier *Independence* battle group, which had been in the eastern Indian Ocean, arrived in the Gulf of Oman, just south of the Persian Gulf, on August 7. That same day the *Eisenhower* battle group passed through the Suez Canal, while another carrier, the *Saratoga* (CV-60), and the battleship *Wisconsin* (BB-64) departed U.S. East Coast ports en route to the

Middle East.

These preparatory moves were harbingers of a massive U.S. buildup in the Gulf area ordered on August 7 by President Bush to deter a possible Iraqi attack. The operation was given the code name Desert Shield.

In response to the presidential order, on August 8 the first F-15 Eagle fighters and E-3 Sentry AWACS (Airborne Warning And Control System) aircraft began arriving in Saudi Arabia. The F-15s were air superiority fighters, intended to defend Saudi air space from Iraqi aircraft. The fighters, from the U.S. Air Force's 1st Tactical Fighter Wing based at Langley Air Force Base, Virginia, flew nonstop to Saudi Arabia. They were in the air for 15 hours and refueled in flight seven times from U.S. tanker aircraft while in route.

The E-3 AWACS aircraft were flying radar stations, providing long-range surveillance of Saudi and Persian Gulf air space. Air controllers in the AWACS – built on a Boeing 707 airframe – could direct defensive fighters to intercept approaching Iraqi aircraft. The Saudis already operated five American-built

A warrior and his loved one (opposite) enact once more the rituals of farewell. In cities and small towns across the United States, yellow ribbons and national flags (above) blossomed everywhere in support of the men and women deployed to the Gulf.
OPPOSITE: TIM WRIGHT / GAMMA LIAISON
ABOVE: MICHAEL BAYTOFF / BLACK STAR

AWACS aircraft as well as F-15C fighters, providing some support for the arriving U.S. Air Force squadrons. For the next seven months, U.S. Air Force and Saudi AWACS aircraft and U.S. Navy carrier-based E-2C Hawkeye radar aircraft would be airborne over the Middle East continuously.

On August 9, transport aircraft began landing troops from the Army's 82nd Airborne Division from Fort Bragg, North Carolina. The 82nd, the Army's only parachute division, kept a brigade in a high state of alert, ready to be flown into trouble spots. The 2,300 troops of the division's "ready brigade" arrived at Saudi bases to provide a defense against Iraqi airborne or commando assaults.

The 82nd Airborne soldiers were lightly armed troops, without tanks or heavy artillery. As the troop-carrying transports arrived in Saudi Arabia, General Schwarzkopf made certain that they were well covered by live television to convince the world – and Saddam, who was known to be watching CNN – that a defensive force was rapidly being put in place.

General Schwarzkopf gambled that he could move in "heavy" forces and close this "window of vulnerability" before Saddam realized his opportunity and launched an offensive. Had Iraq's troops and tanks rolled across the Saudi border, the newly arrived U.S. troops could have offered only limited resistance. At the end of the first week of August 1990, the only forces that could have effectively resisted the assault were the Saudi Air Force, planes from U.S. aircraft carriers, and the U.S. fighters being flown over from the United States, after their crews had rested.

The major U.S. military problem was how to transport the large numbers of tanks, heavy artillery, helicopters, trucks, bulldozers, ammunition, and the mass of other materiel needed by a modern army for war in the desert. The task would not be easy.

An old military axiom says that amateurs think about tactics while professionals think about logistics. The logistics required carrying huge amounts of war materiel more than 8,500 nautical miles (15,740 km.) from U.S. East Coast ports to the Persian Gulf. Only ships could carry that materiel.

General Schwarzkopf had several aces up his sleeve that were called "prepositioning ships." By the time of Desert Shield, three prepositioning squadrons existed, each with four or five ships. Each squadron carried the tanks, weapons, ammunition, supplies, and equipment for a 16,000-man Marine brigade to operate for 30 days. One MPS squadron was normally anchored at Diego Garcia in the Indian Ocean; one at Guam in the western Pacific; and one in the Atlantic. In addition, 12 merchant-type prepositioning ships were anchored off Diego Garcia carrying fuel and supplies for the Army and Air Force, and a Navy field hospital.

On August 7, "sail orders" were issued to the Indian Ocean and Guam squadrons to head to the Persian Gulf to support Desert Shield. The 7th Marine Expeditionary Brigade from Twenty-Nine Palms, California, was flown into Saudi Arabia and began "marrying up" with the MPS equipment on August 15; the 1st Marine Expeditionary Brigade, flown in from Oahu, Hawaii, arrived and joined up with the equipment carried by the second MPS squadron on August 26. Although the Marines were relatively light units, they did have some M60A1 tanks and 155-mm. howitzers as well as light armored vehicles and amphibian tractors that could serve as armored personnel carriers. The other prepositioning ships began unloading their Army and Air Force cargoes on August 17. The Atlantic prepositioning squadron with supplies for another Marine brigade set course for the Persian Gulf.

The Army's heavy gear began arriving in Saudi Arabia on August 27. First came the 24th Infantry Division (Mechanized), which General Schwarzkopf had

The U.S. aircraft carrier **Dwight D. Eisenhower** *(CVN-69) passes northbound through the Suez Canal, in August 1990. The U.S. rapidly brought tactical aircraft into the Gulf area.*
FRANK A. MARQUART / U.S. NAVY

One of 24 French Air Force Jaguar attack aircraft (opposite) committed to the Gulf forces refuels over Saudi Arabia from a French KC-135 tanker aircraft. France also sent Mirage 2000 and Mirage F1 fighters plus support aircraft.
JEAN-CLAUDE COUTAUSSE / CONTACT

commanded earlier in his career. The 24th "Mech," based at Fort Stewart, Georgia, had been loaded onto trains, carried to the port of Savannah, and there embarked in seven of the world's fastest cargo ships, the Navy's fast sealift ships. The Army's 2d Armored and 1st Cavalry Divisions and the 101st Airborne Division (Air Assault) all used sealift for their heavy equipment, while troops and light equipment went by air.

On August 27 – 12 days after the first Marine ground combat forces arrived – the first two fast sealift ships began unloading M1A1 tanks of the 24th Division in Saudi Arabia. The division's 200 main battle tanks along with the M60A1 tanks of the Marine brigades gave the United States the heavy forces required for desert warfare.

General Colin L. Powell, Chairman of the U.S. Joint Chiefs of Staff (left), briefs President Bush in the Oval Office at the White House in September 1990. Secretary of Defense Dick Cheney (back to camera), National Security Advisor Brent Scowcroft (standing), and White House Chief of Staff John Sununu listen to the briefing.
SUSAN BIDDLE / THE WHITE HOUSE

FOLLOWING PAGES
Heavy armor of the U.S. 24th Infantry Division (Mechanized) lined up for loading on board ship for the long voyage to the Gulf in late August 1990. M1A1 Abrams main battle tanks, M2 Bradley fighting vehicles, and M109 self- propelled 155-mm. howitzers are shown here.
U.S. DEPARTMENT OF DEFENSE

More merchant ships went to sea carrying weapons, munitions, rations, and fuels to Saudi Arabia. Most of the fast sealift and prepositioning ships were pressed into cargo-carrying service after delivering their equipment. Additional cargo ships were chartered from merchant service and pulled out of the U.S. Maritime Administration's reserve or "mothball" fleet.

Finding crews to man the ships was a critical issue. A shrinking U.S. merchant marine had created a shortage of merchant seamen. But enough were found – the average age of these seamen was 49 compared to under 20 for the sailors manning the U.S. Navy warships in the Gulf area. Many of the merchant seamen were in their 60s and 70s, and two were in their early 80s.

On September 28, the Desert Shield sealift reached a peak with 90 ships at sea – 69 were en route to the Middle East from the United States and Europe, and 21 "empties" were returning for more cargo. Had these ships been evenly spaced on the route from the U.S. East Coast to the Persian Gulf, there would have been one ship every 100 miles (161 km.). When phase II of Desert Shield began in November 1990 to build up a U.S. offensive force in the area, a peak of 172 ships at sea on a given day was reached on January 2, 1991.

The order to activate two hospital ships – the *Mercy* (T-AH-19) and the *Comfort* (T-AH-20) was given on August 9. "These ships were a tremendous signal that no bluff was involved," recalled Vice Admiral Frank Donovan, Commander, Military Sealift Command. "It meant that we were expecting casualties. . . . it was a hell of a signal," he said.

Ships carried 95 percent (by weight) of the fuel, weapons, equipment, and food delivered to the Middle East during Desert Shield. Aircraft carried high-priority equipment, including Army helicopters and troops.

The U.S. Air Force's Military Airlift Command flew 115 of the C-5 Galaxy and 260 of the C-141 Starlifter long-range cargo/transport aircraft for the massive airlift. Within Saudi Arabia, the Air Force operated several hundred C-130 Hercules turboprop transports to distribute men and supplies to the many bases across the country.

The trans-ocean "aluminum bridge" of long-range military aircraft stabilized the situation while the sealift geared up. However, the number of military aircraft was insufficient to meet the demands, and on August 18 the Defense Department activated the Civil Reserve Air Fleet (CRAF).

Through an earlier arrangement, commercial airlines provided jumbo jets, especially Boeing 747s with reinforced cargo decks, the first time CRAF had been called into service. Eventually, 129 of these aircraft, flown by their civilian crews, carried troops and cargo to the Gulf.

The massive airlift and sealift were unprecedented in the post- World War II period. By the end of August, the airlift alone had delivered 72,000 troops as well as 100,000 tons of cargo to the Gulf. *Continued on page 103*

COMPARISON OF ARMED FORCES DEPLOYED IN THE GULF WAR

Countries that deployed military forces for Operations Desert Shield and Desert Storm.

MULTINATIONAL FORCE

	Troops	Combat aircraft	Warships
Argentina	100		2
Australia			2
Bangladesh	2,000		
Canada		CF-18 Hornets 24	2
Czechoslovakia	170 Anti-chemical warfare troops		
Egypt	40,000 Plus 5,000 in U.A.E.		
France	15,200 Including 4,000 rapid deployment and 1,200 chemical warfare troops	42 18 Mirages and 24 Jaguars	7
Great Britain	25,000 Including the 1st Armoured Division, plus 9,000 support troops	54 Tornado and Jaguar fighter-bombers	17
Gulf Cooperation Council Saudi Arabia, Oman, Qatar, U.A.E., Bahrain, Kuwait	145,000 Including rapid deployment force of up to 10,000 troops, plus 7,000 Kuwaiti troops who escaped after Iraqi invasion	330	36
Honduras	150		
Italy		Tornado fighter-bombers 10	5
Morocco	1,200 Plus 3,500 in U.A.E		
NATO members			10 Belgium 2, Denmark 1, Greece 1, Netherlands 2, Norway 1, Portugal 1, Spain 2
Niger	480		
Pakistan	7,000 Plus 2,000 in U.A.E. (up to 6,000 more arrived by G-Day)		
Senegal	500		
Sierra Leone	200		
Syria	15,000 Including in U.A.E		
Soviet Union			2
United States	425,000 Major ground units: 82nd and 101st Airborne Divs., 1st, 2nd and 3rd Armored Divs., 1st and 24th Infantry Divs. (Mech.), 1st Cavalry Div., 197th Infantry Bde. (Mech.), 11th Air Defense Arty. Bde., 2nd and 3rd Armored Cav. Regts., 1 Marine Expeditionary Force with 1st and 2nd Marine Divs., 4th and 5th Marine Expeditionary Brigades.	More than 1,200 Including: 360 carrier-based A-6E, A-7E, F/A-18, and F-14 attack and fighter aircraft; over 850 land-based F/A-18, AV-8B, F-4G, F-15, F-16, F-111F, F-117A, and A-10 attack and fighter aircraft; plus long-range B-52G bombers.	About 65 Including six aircraft carriers, two battleships and 31 amphibious ships.
Total:	**More than 695,000**	**More than 1,650**	**About 174**

IRAQ's FORCES

Troops	Combat aircraft	Warships
Deployment to Kuwait Theater of Operations (KTO): 540,000 Three corps in Kuwait and two corps (one reserve) in Iraq, plus 160,000 troops in seven Republican Guard Divs. and two Army Divs. assigned to Republican Guard Forces Command on border. Regular army: 955,000 Reserves: about 500,000	Overall: About 665 Includes MiG-29 fighters and Mirage F1 fighters among many older Soviet-built types. Iraqi air defenses include more than 330 surface-to-air missile launchers, some of them captured in Kuwait.	No significant navy One training frigate, about eight missile attack craft and six torpedo boats. Shore defenses against seaborne attack include Silkworm anti-ship missiles, some of which may have been deployed in Kuwait.

ALLIED FINANCIAL CONTRIBUTIONS TO OPERATION DESERT STORM

Other	Korea	UAE	Germany	Japan	Kuwait	Saudi Arabia
$0.003 billion	$0.4 billion	$4 billion	$6.6 billion	$10.7 billion	$16 billion	$16.8 billion

NOTE: All figures are estimates of forces deployed in or near Saudi Arabia, Kuwait and Iraq or committed to be transported there. Merchant and hospital ships, transport aircraft and countries sending exclusively medical support units are omitted. Support ships, ships in the Eastern Mediterranean that replace U.S. ships moved to the Gulf, and aircraft stationed in Turkey, Diego Garcia, and other nearby bases are included, but Egyptian, Turkish and Syrian forces in their home countries are omitted. Div=division; bde=brigade; regt=regiment; arty=artillery.

SOURCES: USNI, USAF WHITE PAPER—AIR FORCE PERFORMANCE IN DESERT STORM, FOR YOUR EYES ONLY.

PRECEDING PAGE

Cases of plastic bottles reflect the extraordinary quantities of water required to sustain troops in the Saudi desert.
CHRISTOPHER MORRIS / BLACK STAR

Inset: Troopers of the 101st Airborne Division handle boxes of ammunition off a C-5 Galaxy in Saudi Arabia.
INSET: MARTIN JEONG / UPI / BETTMAN

This was just the beginning. At the airlift's peak, more than 125 U.S. military and CRAF aircraft were landing every day in Saudi Arabia, averaging one arrival every 12 minutes around the clock.

The task of determining what materiel was needed for a war and stockpiling it fell to a small army of logisticians led by Army Major General William (Gus) Pagonis. As General Schwarzkopf's logistics chief, Pagonis had to win the war of supply before any of Schwarzkopf's tactical commanders could seek victory on the battlefield.

While airlift brought in all of the Army troops and most of the Marines from bases in the continental United States, Hawaii, Okinawa, and Germany, Marines also arrived by sea.

First came the 13th Marine Expeditionary Unit, a 2,300-man force that had departed Subic Bay in the Philippines in amphibious ships when Iraq invaded Kuwait. They were followed by the 4th and 5th Marine Expeditionary Brigades, each with more than 7,000 troops embarked in amphibious ships. As these Marines arrived, they began conducting exercise landings off the coasts of Oman and Saudi Arabia in preparation for a possible amphibious assault against the coast of Iraq or occupied Kuwait.

Shortly after Desert Shield began, General Schwarzkopf moved his headquarters to Riyadh, locating his command center in a bomb-proof facility three levels beneath the Saudi Ministry of Defense.

His principal subordinates were the Central Command's Army, Navy, Air Force, and Marine commanders, plus the senior coalition officers such as British Lieutenant General Sir Peter de la Billiere and Saudi Lieutenant General Khalid bin-Sultan.

The U.S. Army component commander, Lieutenant General John J. Yeosock, would direct most of the coalition's ground troops. Yeosock was no stranger to the Middle East; in the early 1980s he had led the U.S. military team that had helped modernize the Saudi National Guard, as the country's ground forces are called. Schwarzkopf's air commander was Lieutenant General Charles A. Horner, a former fighter pilot who had flown 111 combat missions in F-105 fighter-bombers in the Vietnam War.

The naval commander for CENTCOM was Vice Admiral Stanley R. Arthur, commander of the Seventh Fleet in the Pacific-Indian Ocean areas. Arthur, too, had Middle East experience, having commanded U.S. naval forces in the Gulf in the early 1980s. Arthur was also in direct command of the 17,000 Marines embarked in amphibious ships in the Persian Gulf, as Marines afloat invariably come under naval command.

The Marines ashore came under the command of Lieutenant General Walter E. Boomer, whose I Marine Expeditionary Force would embody the largest Marine deployment since World War II. Boomer worked closely with

A Saudi tank crewman preparing for action is draped with automatic cannon ammunition.
ABBAS / MAGNUM

French Foreign Legionnaires (opposite above) debark in Saudi Arabia to join the coalition forces.
GILLES BASSIGNAC / GAMMA-LIAISON

Saudi soldiers (opposite) pray to Mecca five times each day.
BARRY IVERSON / TIME MAGAZINE

103

General Norman Schwarzkopf (above right) speaks with troops in training as the weather turned from searing heat to clammy cold. A U.S. Marine (above) personalizes his camouflage cover. A column of ubiquitous "Hummers" (opposite) winds across the sands; bedrolls and tents are tied down. More than 20,000 of these vehicles served in the Gulf War.

ABOVE RIGHT: DAVID TURNLEY /
DETROIT FREE PRESS / BLACK STAR
ABOVE: CHRISTOPHER MORRIS / BLACK STAR
OPPOSITE:PETER TURNLEY / BLACK STAR

General Yeosock, but was not subordinate to him in the CENTCOM structure; thus in practice Schwarzkopf had two U.S. ground force commanders.

Admiral Arthur's principal mission was enforcing the embargo of Iraq. U.N. Resolutions 661 and 665 called on members "to halt all inward and outward maritime shipping in order to inspect and verify their cargoes and destinations." U.S. warships, soon joined by destroyers and frigates from Australia, Britain, France, Italy, and the Netherlands, and smaller warships from Gulf states, began stopping and, on a regular basis, searching merchant ships in the Gulf that could be steaming to or from the Iraqi port of Basra.

On August 31, the U.S. missile cruiser *Biddle* (CG-34) intercepted and a Navy-Coast Guard team boarded the Iraqi tanker *Al Karamah*. This was the first Iraqi ship to be boarded since the intercept operation began. The tanker was empty and was allowed to continue southward, to Jordan's port of Aqaba. The coalition ships were averaging 40 intercepts and four boardings per day. Only one merchant ship actively resisted. On December 26, several U.S. and coalition ships stopped the Iraqi-flag freighter *Ibn Haldoon* ("Peace Ship"). The freighter's crew refused requests to stop and then attempted to stave off a boarding team. After firing warning shots into the air, exploding smoke and noise grenades, the U.S. search team examined the ship's papers and cargo, found cargo prohibited by the U.N. embargo.

By the start of Desert Storm in mid-January, coalition ships had recorded 6,960 intercepts with 832 boardings. Thirty-six ships were diverted from their intended destinations, because they carried prohibited cargo.

The carrier *Independence* entered the Persian Gulf on October 1, the first time a "flattop" had entered that waterway since 1974. This operation demonstrated the feasibility of large carrier operations in the Gulf's relatively restricted waters. The "Indy" was relieved in the Gulf on November 1 by the USS *Midway* (CV-41). Thereafter, aircraft carriers and battleships sailed continuously in the Gulf, demonstrating the ability of the U.S. *Continued on page 108*

PRECEDING PAGE

Coalition troops take a break from training as a column of camels passes by, they are a welcome diversion during the routine of preparing for war.
DENNIS BRACK / BLACK STAR

"blue water" ships to operate anywhere that the water was deep enough.

By early November 1990, the United States had assembled a military force of some 230,000 men and women in the Gulf. The force was about half the size of that the United States had put into Vietnam in the mid-1960s, a buildup that took several years. In contrast, the Desert Shield force was deployed in only three months.

Other countries were also sending troops, aircraft, and ships to the Gulf, making the forces arrayed against Saddam truly an international coalition. Of particular significance was the arrival of troops from Syria and Egypt, Arab states that did not border on the Gulf. From France came troops of the Rapid Action Force and the famed Foreign Legion, and from Britain the 7th Armoured Brigade, which traced its lineage to the "Desert Rats," who had gained renown in desert battles against German Field Marshal Erwin Rommel in North Africa

during World War II.

As these troops waited, they had to adjust to a harsh environment of hot days and cold nights; a rainy season in winter; and, everywhere, sand— a fine sand, almost like talcum powder, that seemed to permeate every piece of clothing and equipment. They also had to adjust to an unfamiliar Islamic culture and regional customs. Inadvertent slights could blossom into larger problems unless the troops were briefed and understood the conduct required. No alcoholic beverages were permitted. No erotic magazines could be brought into the region. Female soldiers and airmen were told they could not bare their arms or legs in public, and men and women could not be seen holding hands. Women in a Massachusetts reserve military police battalion were told that they could appear in Saudi towns out of uniform only if they wore long, black dresses, and walked 12 paces behind any man they accompanied. *Continued on page 112*

True "sandlot football" (opposite) breaks the routine of training and waiting. In the weeks just before Christmas (top), video cameras enable troops to make video recordings for the folks at home. A soldier of the 197th Infantry Brigade (above) places a telephone call to his familty at Fort Benning, Georgia.

OPPOSITE: DAVID TURNLEY / DETROIT FREE PRESS / BLACK STAR
TOP: DENNIS BRACK / BLACK STAR
ABOVE: DENNIS BRACK / TIME MAGAZINE

But on many occasions U.S. women in uniform were stopped in the streets by Saudi men, who would engage them in conversation – something they would never do with Saudi women. To the credit of troops and officers alike, the number of incidents with Saudis was small. U.S. forces concentrated on training, training, and more training.

The American public seemed surprised by the number of instances in which active duty and reserve spouses were both deployed to the Gulf, often with no option but to leave their children in the care of others. Operation Desert Shield separated families in ways not frequently experienced in past conflicts. The American news media devoted considerable coverage to the large number of women in uniform going to the Gulf.

While congressional legislation prevents women from serving in combat units or on board warships, women, in fact, served in front-line units as aircraft mechanics, nurses, physicians, and helicopter pilots. A few flew as flight crew in E-3 AWACS aircraft that, although they remained mainly over Saudi territory, could have been high-priority targets for Iraqi fighters.

The typical soldier, airman, and Marine – in active duty as well as reserve units – under General Schwarzkopf was 27 years old, six years older than the average in the Vietnam War. And, he or she was much more likely to be married and have children than were previous Americans in uniform.

One of the oldest Americans serving in the Gulf was Lorain Kuryla, from Chicago, an Air Force reservist who was a personnel officer with the 928th Tactical Airlift Group – and the 63-year-old grandmother of five. Twenty years of an all-volunteer military force had created this older, more stable force, the oldest U.S. military force to be sent into the field since the Civil War.

PRECEDING PAGE
President and Mrs. Bush visited the troops for Thanksgiving, touching hands with thousands. They, like all the men and women serving in the Gulf, had protective gas masks handy.
DENNIS BRACK / TIME MAGAZINE

The number of blacks in the Gulf (25.4 percent), which reflected the large number of blacks in the U.S. armed forces, drew criticism from some black leaders. A few condemned the use of black troops "to fight the white man's war," but their arguments were effectively countered by the articulate voice of General Colin Powell, the first black to serve as Chairman of the Joint Chiefs of Staff. Without question, the U.S. forces deployed to the Middle East were diverse, well trained, and highly motivated.

When General Schwarzkopf came to Washington on Thursday, August 2, he briefed President Bush at the White House. When he again met with Bush on Saturday, at Camp David, the presidential retreat in Maryland, he addressed the forces needed to defend Saudi Arabia. But his last briefing chart, Schwarzkopf later recalled, stated, "in the event that we changed our objective from one of defending Saudi Arabia to one of taking him [Saddam] on offensively, here is his offensive capability, and it will take many, many more troops [to take him on] than we plan to deploy."

During the first week of November 1990, President Bush and his principal cabinet secretaries and advisors decided to take the offensive against Iraq – carrying out the actions necessary to force Saddam to comply with the U.N. resolutions. On November 8, Secretary Cheney announced that more men, ships, aircraft, and tanks would be sent to the Gulf. The troop increase would be about 200,000, and a few days later Cheney authorized an additional 72,500 reservists to be called to active duty and extended the active duty for reservists from 90 to 180 days. Among the newcomers would be the U.S. Army VII Corps – nearly 100,000 troops – based in Germany. The troops in the heavy armored and mechanized formations of VII Corps had spent years practicing to fight the Warsaw Pact. Now they would fight in a very different environment.

While the terrain and weather would be different, the VII Corps would find familiar targets: Soviet-made T-72 tanks and BMP infantry fighting vehicles.

The attitude of the troops in Saudi Arabia appeared to change with the shift to an obviously offensive force. Men and women, already working and training hard, seemed to try harder. Relationship between coalition forces grew closer.

Without question, that battle for the liberation of Kuwait was near. On January 16, 1991, at the CENTCOM press briefing in Riyadh, U.S. troop strength in the Gulf area was listed at 425,000.

The U.S. forces were aligned with the combat and support units of 28 other countries in the Gulf, raising the allied force to almost 700,000 men and women.

At midnight Eastern Standard Time on January 15, Iraqi forces remained entrenched in Kuwait. U.S. intelligence agencies estimated that the Iraqis had 545,000 troops in the Kuwaiti Theater of Operations. The following evening, radio and television newscasts were reporting a very high number of takeoffs of military aircraft from airfields in Saudi Arabia.

In Lafayette Square across from the White House (opposite) protesters march, hold up placards, and beat drums(above). President Bush said the loud drums kept him awake. When the drumbeats exceeded the allowable sound level of 60 decibels, police made them pound more softly.

OPPOSITE: DENNIS BRACK / BLACK STAR
JONATHAN ELDERFIE / BLACK STAR

113

CHAPTER SIX

DESERT STORM

THE AIR CAMPAIGN

During the night of January 16-17, 1991, U.S. Navy weapon specialists inside cramped compartments in several warships huddled over computer consoles as their ships steamed in the Persian Gulf and Red Sea. They were entering targeting codes into computers that fed complex geographic data into Tomahawk cruise missiles. The missiles' powerful microcomputers stored intricate digital maps of terrain and images of targets several hundred miles away, in Baghdad. Throughout the ships – battleships, cruisers, and destroyers – other crewmen worked at their battle stations and waited.

High above Saudi Arabia, well out of range of Iraqi radar, large KC-135 aerial tankers flew oval-shaped "racetrack" patterns while pumping thousands of gallons of jet fuel through refueling booms and drogue hoses into trailing combat aircraft. When their fuel tanks were topped off, those aircraft entered into their own holding patterns at prearranged altitudes and locations. Other fighters and heavily laden attack planes then moved into position to repeat the delicate refueling maneuver.

Closer to the Saudi-Iraq border, E-3 AWACS or Airborne Warning And Control System aircraft, each with a large, rotating radar dome mounted atop its fuselage, flew on stations, retracing the same orbiting patterns they had flown for months. Their radars swept the skies over southern Iraq, tracking aircraft movements. Below, to the north, Iraqi radar operators and commanders tracked the AWACS aircraft. The Iraqis had grown accustomed to the flight paths and maneuvers of the U.S. and Saudi E-3s and their protective F-15 Eagle fighters, and nothing unusual appeared on their screens. *Continued on page 118*

Sailors and Marines of the battleship Wisconsin *(BB-64) watch a Tomahawk land-attack cruise missile begin its flight to Baghdad. The 290 Tomahawks were fired at high-value targets that were strongly defended.*
JOHN MC CUTCHEN / SAN DIEGO UNION

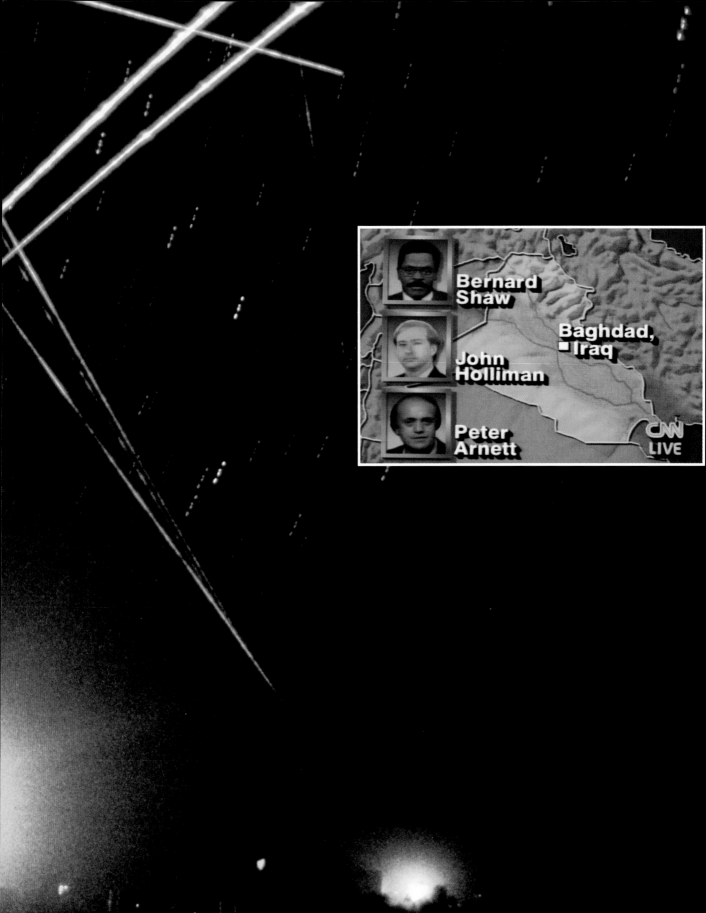

On the flight line of a Saudi Arabian air base, pilots of the U.S. 37th Tactical Fighter Wing finished pre-flight checks of their F-117A Stealth attack planes and, with the help of their crew chiefs, strapped themselves into their cockpits. After rolling into takeoff position on the long runway, the aircraft roared into the soft blackness and headed north, toward Iraq. With the new moon showing its dark side toward the Earth, only the stars and the plumes of jet exhaust breached the darkness.

Between 2 and 2:30 A.M. (Gulf time) on January 17, nearly 700 aircraft of the coalition forces assembled in airspace beyond Iraqi radar range – each pilot prepared to execute his or her assigned mission. They were all part of a meticulously planned, carefully executed strike. The initial attacks were aimed at destroying Iraqi air defenses and command, control, and communications centers.

The first allied weapon to strike Baghdad was a Tomahawk Land-Attack Missile (TLAM), launched from the U.S. cruiser *San Jacinto* (CG-56) in the Red Sea. The Tomahawk is a cruise missile that flies at high subsonic speeds (about 550 m.p.h./885 km.p.h.) and carries either a single 1,000-pound (454-kg.) high-explosive warhead or multiple smaller warheads against targets several hundred miles from the launching ship or submarine.

The nine warships, including the battleships *Missouri* (BB-63) and *Wisconsin* (BB-64), fired 52 Tomahawks in the opening salvo of the air war. Because of their speed and ability to fly at altitudes of only 100 feet (30.5 m.), these missiles were able to strike targets that were heavily defended by anti-aircraft weapons. All but one Tomahawk in the attack— the first use of the missile in combat—are believed to have struck their targets.

Slipping past Iraqi air defenses at almost the same moment as the Tomahawks were the F-117 Stealth attack aircraft. The futuristic-looking F-117's angular shape and construction using composite materials reduces the possibility of radar detection. Each plane carried a single, 2,000-pound (909-kg.), laser-guided "smart" bomb to attack "point" targets, such as the Baghdad telecommunications building.

Capitalizing on the confusion and damage to air defenses and communications facilities caused by the first waves of the attack, hundreds of coalition aircraft then struck Baghdad and other targets throughout southern Iraq and occupied Kuwait. During the first 24 hours of the air war, more than 1,000 sorties (one sortie equates to one flight by one aircraft) were flown by U.S. Air Force, Navy, and Marine Corps fixed-wing aircraft, plus Army AH-64 Apache attack helicopters, Saudi and British Tornado strike aircraft, French Jaguar strike aircraft, and Kuwaiti A-4 Skyhawks. The RAF Tornados executed the especially hazardous low-level strikes against Iraqi air bases to blow craters in their runways to prevent takeoffs. Aircraft from the six U.S. carriers in the area flew 228 of those initial sorties.

One of the most critical assignments of the opening attack was flown by eight AH-64 Apaches from the U.S. Army's 101st Airborne Division. Before the main air strikes began, the AH-64s darted undetected across the far western border of Saudi Arabia and Iraq, flying without lights, at high speed, and close to the ground. The Apaches had a vital mission: to destroy two in a line of Iraqi radar stations that provided early warning of air intrusions into Iraq and controlled intercept aircraft.

At 2:38 A.M., the Apaches fired laser-guided Hellfire missiles at the radar sites and adjacent buildings, followed by clusters of 2.75-inch (70-mm.) Hydra rockets and streams of 30-mm. cannon fire. One of the aviators yelled into his radio, "This one's for you, Saddam," playing on a popular beer commercial. Destruction of the radar sites created a "radar-black" corridor, through which the coalition strike aircraft flew into Iraq undetected by radar.

BAGHDAD AIR STRIKES

Major targets attacked by Coalition Forces during the air war.

SOURCE: KNIGHT-RIDDER TRIBUNE NEWS

PRECEDING PAGE

Time: near 3 A.M. Date: January 17, 1991. Tracer rounds from anti-aircraft guns lace the night sky over Baghdad, competing with the flashes from bursting bombs and missiles to break the darkness. Iraqi radars and fire-control systems were early coalition targets, resulting in AAA gunners firing mostly by sight.

NOEL QUIDU / GAMMA - LIAISON
INSET: CNN/ TERRASCAPE™ MAP
© HAMMOND, INC.

Beyond the hundreds of strike aircraft, the coalition air sorties included fighters flying Combat Air Patrol (CAP) missions to intercept any Iraqi fighters that sought to interfere with the attacks; electronic intercept and jamming aircraft; aerial tankers to refuel planes; and rescue helicopters to recover downed fliers. At higher altitudes, the all-seeing U.S. and Saudi E-3 AWACS aircraft and Navy E-2C Hawkeye radar planes provided overall control of air operations and issued warnings of hostile aircraft. In total, more than 1,000 coalition aircraft flew combat and support missions on the first night of Desert Storm – a night that initiated a spectacular, violent air war.

Throughout the day following the U.N. deadline for Iraq's withdrawal from Kuwait – midnight, Eastern Standard Time (EST), January 15 – the world watched and waited for the coalition's next move. In Washington, D.C., at 6:35 P.M., CNN's David French was interviewing former Secretary of Defense Caspar Weinberger on the television program "The World Today," when French paused suddenly and then told his audience, "We're going to Bernard Shaw in Baghdad."

Viewers heard Shaw's voice and saw his picture superimposed over a map of Iraq displayed on their screen. Then CNN producers added photos of Shaw's colleagues in Baghdad, John Holliman and Peter Arnett, as they made their reports from the ninth floor of the Al-Rashid Hotel. Shaw: "This is – something is happening outside. Peter Arnett, join me here. Let's describe to your viewers what we're seeing. The skies over Baghdad have been illuminated. We're seeing bright flashes going off all over the sky. Peter?"

Peter Arnett came on the air. In his distinctive New Zealand accent he gave the first of countless reports that would be heard during the next 43 days.

Arnett: "Well, there's anti-aircraft gunfire going into the sky. We hear the sound of planes. They're coming over our hotel. However, we have not yet heard the sound of bombs landing. But there's tremendous lightning in the sky, lightning-like effects. Bernie?"

Shaw: "I have a sense, Peter, that people are shooting toward the sky, and they are not aware or cannot see what they're shooting at. This is extraordinary. The lights are still on. All the street lights in downtown Baghdad are still on. But as you look, you see trails of flashes of light going up into the air, obviously anti-aircraft fire. We're getting starbursts, seeming starbursts, in the black sky. We have not heard any jet planes yet, Peter."

Arnett agreed that they had not yet heard any jet planes. Then, over his voice, sirens began to wail.

Arnett: "Now the sirens are sounding for the first time. The Iraqis have informed us. . . ."

At that moment, CNN's satellite communications link to Baghdad was broken. Viewers next saw the young, bearded face of CNN's Wolf Blitzer at the Pentagon in Washington.

Blitzer: "David, there are strong indications here at the Pentagon that this war may, may be beginning right now and that the President may be going on television later this evening to explain exactly what is going on."

French interrupted Blitzer to switch back to Baghdad. Holliman was calling, trying to reestablish contact with CNN headquarters in Atlanta. That contact was lost, and French returned to Blitzer at the Pentagon.

Blitzer: "Only moments ago, Before I came into the studio here at the Pentagon, I had a chance to see two very senior Pentagon officials almost running through the halls, going up to Secretary (Dick) Cheney's office."

The program switched back and forth from Baghdad to Atlanta to the Pentagon and to the White House. In Baghdad, Shaw, Arnett, and Holliman continued to report the sights and sounds of war. It was the first time in history that a war's opening engagement was broadcast live.

Holliman: "I can see much of the city blacked out. There are no lights on the major telecommunications center in Baghdad, but it is still intact. It is still standing. As I look off more to the southwest, I can see a large section of the city that has not been blacked out. There is one broadcasting tower, radio or

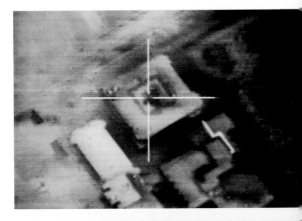

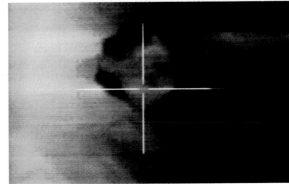

Pilot of a strike aircraft holds the crosshairs squarely on the air shaft on the roof of Baghdad's air ministry. A precision guided bomb homes on the spot, descends into the airshaft, and explodes inside the building.
BOTH: U.S. DEPARTMENT OF DEFENSE

television. It still has the red lights up its 250-foot [76-m.] tower."

Arnett: The sky is lighting up, I guess to the south, with anti-aircraft fire. Some are bright red. Others are splashes of yellow liquid."

Holliman: "Oh-oh! Oops! Now there's a huge fire that we've just seen that is due west of our position. And we just heard – whoa! Holy cow! That was a large air burst that we saw. It was filling the sky." (Sounds of gunfire.)

Arnett: "And I think, John, that air burst took out the telecommunications (building)." (Sounds of explosions.)

The first night's attacks were an immense success, according to Secretary of Defense Cheney. He told a Pentagon press conference on the night of January 16. "It would appear, based upon the comments that were coming in from the CNN crew in the hotel in Baghdad, that the operation was successful in striking targets with a high degree of precision, at least that's the reporting according to CNN."

Military officials in Washington and Riyadh claimed that the Tomahawk missiles and strike aircraft were 80 percent effective (80 percent of the bombs and missiles struck their targets).

The first day of the air war was not without losses to the coalition. Iraqi anti-

aircraft guns and missiles shot down four aircraft: One U.S. Navy F/A-18 Hornet strike-fighter, two Royal Air Force Tornado GR.1 attack aircraft, and one Kuwaiti A-4KU Skyhawk. Their crews – two men in each Tornado and one in each of the others – were listed as missing in action.

The number of coalition losses among the more than 1,000 sorties flown was remarkably low, amounting to a loss rate of four-tenths of one percent. In World War II, a bomber loss rate of five percent was considered "good." In comparison, the August 1, 1943, heavy bomber raid on the Ploesti oil facilities in Rumania suffered a 25 percent loss rate. In the "Linebacker" bombing of Hanoi conducted during the final days of the Vietnam War, B-52 jet bombers suffered a loss rate of two percent. The only precedent for such low loss rates was in previous Arab-Israeli conflicts.

During the first night and day of the air campaign, the Iraqis lost eight aircraft in air-to-air combat with U.S. fighters. The first was a French-built Mirage F1 fighter shot down by a U.S. Air Force F-15C Eagle flown by Captain Steve Tate. In those first hours of the war, the pilots from the Air Force 1st and 33rd Tactical Fighter Wings downed three Mirage F1s (two by one plane) and three MiG-29s, all with radar-guided Sparrow missiles. The other kills in the first 42 hours of the war were a pair of Iraqi MiG-21s, an older Soviet fighter, by a pair of U.S. Navy F/A-18 Hornets.

The Hornet was long advertised as a dual-mission aircraft, that could perform strike and fighter missions, changing missions by the pilot pushing a single switch on the aircraft's weapon control panel. On January 17 four F/A-18s from the carrier *Saratoga* (CV-60) in the Red Sea had streaked across Saudi Arabia and were entering Iraqi air space. The Hornets each carried four 2,000-pound (909-kg.) bombs for one of the first daylight strikes of the war as well as Sparrow and Sidewinder air-to-air missiles.

The Hornets were called by an AWACS and then by an E-2C Hawkeye that warned of approaching Iraqi fighters. Hornets flown by Lieutenant Commander Mark Fox and Lieutenant Nick Mongillo of Navy Strike-Fighter Squadron 81 got a radar lock on two Iraqi fighters at a distance of about ten miles (16 km.). Fox fired a heat-seeking Sidewinder missile and then a radar-guided Sparrow; Mongillo a Sparrow. Fox's first missile hit as did Mongillo's; two MiG-21s were destroyed in the Navy's only kills of fixed-wing aircraft in the war. The Hornets then resumed their bombing mission. (The only other Navy air-to-air kill of the war was a helicopter shot down by an F-14A Tomcat with a Sidewinder missile.)

During the air campaign, coalition aircraft would destroy 40 Iraqi aircraft in air-to-air combat; 33 were fixed-wing planes, all fighter types, and seven were helicopters. All but one of the kills were made by coalition fighter-type aircraft. Two Air Force pilots flying the A-10 Thunderbolt, universally known as the "Warthog," destroyed a pair of Iraqi *Continued on page 126*

Morning coffee drinkers in Rock Falls, Illinois, on January 17 read about the air war that began during the night.
STEVE LISS / TIME MAGAZINE

FOLLOWING PAGE
Nicknamed Shaba (Ghost) by Iraqis, a U.S. Air Force F-117A Stealth attack aircraft displays its radar-evading shape. The F-117As struck at night with pinpoint accuracy. They flew only 2.6 percent of the strike sorties, but struck 31 percent of the high-priority fixed targets.
U.S. DEPARTMENT OF DEFENSE

"I LOCKED HIM UP AT 16 MILES"- THE FIRST KILL

Air Force Captain Steve "Tater" Tate
1ST TACTICAL FIGHTER WING / U.S. AIR FORCE

In the first hours of the air war against Iraq, U.S. Air Force Captain Steve "Tater" Tate scored the first aerial kill of Desert Storm. When the war began, Tate was at 30,000 feet (9,144 m.) over Iraq, leading a flight of four F-15C Eagle fighters of the 71st Tactical Fighter Squadron, 1st Tactical Fighter Wing. Tate, age 28, had flown more than 1,000 hours in the F-15C before this mission. Providing "offensive counter-air," Tate and his fighters were hunting Iraqi aircraft that could interfere with coalition planes flying strikes against targets in Iraq.

"The cities were all lit up. You could see the Euphrates and Tigris rivers," Tate recalled. The F-15s flew without navigation lights in a disciplined, strung-out formation. A layer of thin, broken clouds at 25,000 feet (7,620 m.) reduced the clarity of the country below them, but did not obscure the view. Tate's wing man was Captain Bo Merlack; Captains Damon Harp and Mark Atwell flew in the number three and four positions of the four-plane formation.

Tate's flight proceeded deeper into Iraq toward its assignment over Baghdad at an airspeed approaching 600 knots. Tate checked in with the E-3 AWACS controllers on the tactical radio frequency and ordered his pilots to arm their weapons. Each F-15 carried four Sidewinder infrared, heat-seeking missiles, four Sparrow radar-guided missiles, and 940 rounds of 20-mm. ammunition for the plane's Vulcan rotary cannon.

Fifty miles inside Iraq, Tate and his flight had lofty ringside seats for the war's opening hours. "Everywhere, the cities were lighted," he recalled. "And then you saw a twinkling begin, like Christmas lights, in all colors. It was the triple-A (anti-aircraft artillery) being shot at us and the other aircraft in the (strike) package. The solid streams of tracers from the medium triple-A (57-mm. and 85-mm. guns) looked like colored snakes streaking up. The real heavy artillery (100-mm. and 135-mm. guns) would blink on the ground, then explode like big popcorn puffs at 30,000 feet – our altitude."

Closer to Baghdad, the fighter pilots could see much of Iraq. Their eyes made out four major target areas, lit up by the flashes of exploding bombs below. One was to the east, in Kuwait; another ahead and just west of Baghdad; and a third to the far west. Their own strike target area was in Baghdad. Iraqi air defenders began launching Surface-to-Air Missiles (SAMs) against the attack force.

Tate and Merlack descended to 10,000 feet (3,048 m.) to fly the low Combat Air Patrol (CAP) mission, while Harp and Atwell flew their CAP above 30,000 feet. Tate and Merlack approached the Iraqi airfield that was their biggest concern. When Tate picked up an aircraft on his radar, he and Merlack jettisoned their external fuel tanks and prepared to fight, in case the contact was a "bandit." The blip turned out to be a friendly F-111 Aardvark. Then the AWACS controllers radioed, "Possible hit – a bogey 12 miles behind Numbers 3 and 4." Tate and Merlack added power and pulled into a 270-degree right turn to maneuver into position in front of the target, with Tate in the lead and Merlack trailing about three miles behind.

Tate recalled, "I got a radar contact that appeared to be what AWACS called out. It was a short-range setup. I 'locked him up' (in his fire control system) at 16 miles (26 km.)." It took about 20 seconds for Tate to make a positive identification of the "bandit." It was an

Iraqi Mirage F1. (French Mirage F1s also flew in the coalition air forces but, to avoid accidental engagements, were not aloft that night.)

The enemy aircraft showed up squarely inside the target box of Tate's Head-Up Display (HUD), projected on the windshield in front of him. "I called out 'Fox One' for the Sparrow missile and fired. There was a large bright flash under my right wing, as the Sparrow dropped off and its motor ignited. . . . It seemed to start slow and then pick up speed really fast. You could see the missile going toward the airplane, and about two seconds after (the missile) motor burned out, the airplane blew up.

"A huge engulfing fire billowed up. It lit up the sky. You could see pieces of the aircraft in the glare. They burned as they fell," Tate said.

It was 3:15 A.M., and Tate had scored the first aerial kill of Operation Desert Storm.

Tate and Merlack pulled away to continue the offensive counter-air mission. Iraqi forces countered with SAMs, trying to knock down the attackers. In response, F-4G Wild Weasel aircraft detected the radar transmissions from the Iraqi control sites. They homed on the sites that were active, and prepared to fire HARMs (High-Speed Anti-Radiation Missiles). When the enemy site came within range of the HARM missiles, the Wild Weasel crews launched them. The sensors in the nose of the HARM missiles homed on the enemy radar sites, blowing them up with hundreds of pounds of high explosives. The Wild Weasels were F-4 Phantom fighters modified to become flying radar-killers. The airplanes were nearly a quarter-century old, but still performed the vital mission of suppressing enemy air defenses. Other aircraft, such as the Air Force EF-111 Raven and the Navy and Marine EA-6B Prowler, engaged in electronic warfare to neutralize the threats to the strike and CAP aircraft.

The defense suppression worked. All coalition aircraft that were downed were victims of AAA fire or SAMs. But the loss rate of 41 in nearly 110,000 sorties was phenomenally low, due in a significant degree to the stellar performance of the several types of suppression aircraft committed to the battle.

For Steve Tate and almost all of the other aviators aloft that night, this was their first combat experience. However, their tactics and techniques for combat had been honed by years of realistic combat training against all possible air and ground threats. Both the Navy and Air Force operated "aggressor" squadrons that flew against front-line squadrons to simulate enemy tactics they might encounter.

Tate estimated that his Iraqi F1 adversary had been airborne for only two minutes. Other Iraqi fighters lined up on the airfield below, apparently stunned by the violent allied air attack, returned to their dispersed, hardened shelters. They believed the shelters would keep them safe. They were wrong. Of 594 Iraqi aircraft shelters identified, some 375, with at least 141 aircraft inside, were damaged or destroyed during the air campaign. Although the shelters were "hardened" – built of reinforced concrete – the heavy precision weapons available to allied forces penetrated them. Runways and taxiways at Iraq's 54 air bases were disabled by heavy bombing. The preferred coalition weapon for knocking out a runway was the JP 233 munition, carried only by Royal Air Force Tornado strike aircraft. The JP 233 blows craters in runways, and at the same time sows explosive mines over the area to impede repair work.

Captain Tate's flight continued in its CAP role, protecting additional waves of incoming strikes. The four F-15s remained aloft until the last strike aircraft had delivered its missiles and bombs. Then they pulled out and refueled once more from the orbiting tankers. The flight returned to its operating base at 5:30 A.M., where ground crews refueled and readied the aircraft for their next missions and loaded a new Sparrow missile on Tate's empty missile rack. His jubilant ground crew proudly stenciled a green star on his aircraft's fuselage to mark the victory.

During the next six weeks of Desert Storm, Captain Tate flew 34 additional missions, amassing 200 combat flying hours, almost the number of hours an F-15 pilot logs in one year during peacetime. Tate and his squadron mates averaged one sortie per day, each lasting from six to nine hours and involving three to six aerial refuelings.

Most of the F-15C pilots logged 30 or more missions, flying the primary air superiority fighter of the campaign. F-15C Eagles scored the most aerial kills during Desert Storm, 36 of the total of 41 downed from January 16 through March 22. The number includes two downed by a Saudi F-15C pilot. The unit with the highest number of victories was the 33rd Tactical Fighter Wing, based at Eglin AFB, Florida. Its pilots shot down 17 Iraqi aircraft.

The thousands of allied sorties flown were controlled by crews in the E-3 Sentry AWACS aircraft. Mission controllers in the aircraft are able to detect and track enemy aircraft operating at low altitudes over all terrain, and identify and control friendly aircraft operating in the same area.

On the days when more than 3,000 sorties were being flown, the AWACS controllers were handling more flights per day than land and take off from Chicago's O'Hare International Airport, the busiest in the United States.

FOLLOWING PAGES
*What comes down must be loaded up.
U.S. Air Force ordnance specialists
bomb-up an F-15E Strike Eagle with
cluster bombs for a Scud-busting
mission. The container on the right
houses a pod for night navigation and
target-finding. The F-15E carries four
times the load of a World War II B-17
Flying Fortress.*
MARK PETERS / DOD / SIPA PRESS

*The boom operator in a U.S. Air Force
tanker and the pilot of an approaching
F-16C maneuver to insert the refueling
boom precisely into the receptacle atop
the fighter. (Right) The weapon system
officer in the back seat of a U.S. Air
Force F-15E Strike Eagle signals
"thumbs up" during an aerial refueling.*
BOTH: U.S. DEPARTMENT OF DEFENSE

helicopters in the air with their 30-mm. anti-tank cannons. Two Mirage F1 kills
were made by a single Saudi F-15C on January 24.

One of the most unusual aerial kills occurred when an Air Force plane put the
beam from its laser designator on a helicopter just taking off and dropped a
"smart" bomb on the helicopter. That kill is not listed in the official U.S. account
of aerial kills. (In late March, after the cease fire in Iraq, two F-15C Eagles
downed two Iraqi Su-22 fighters that had violated coalition terms; heat-seeking
Sidewinder missiles killed both.) Allied guided-bombs and missiles also
destroyed an estimated 141 Iraqi aircraft on the ground, most of which were in
protective shelters. Still, considering the size of the Iraqi Air Force at the
beginning of the war, a large number of aircraft survived, many of which were
"hidden" in civilian areas where they would not be attacked by coalition planes.
After the end of January, no Iraqi aircraft flew combat missions against coalition
forces.

A minute after the explosions began in the Baghdad area on the morning of
January 17, David French told television viewers around the
world: "U.S. armed forces in Saudi Arabia have now confirmed
that war has begun in Baghdad." Presidential spokesman Marlin
Fitzwater then appeared on the screen and read a statement from
President Bush: "The liberation of Kuwait has begun. In
conjunction with the forces of our coalition partners, the United
States has moved, under the code name Operation Desert Storm,
to enforce the mandates of the United Nations Security Council.
As of 7 o'clock P.M. (EST), Operation Desert Storm forces were
engaging targets in Iraq and Kuwait."

The coalition had waited almost 24 hours beyond the U.N.
deadline before launching the air war. The suddenness with
which the air war exploded, after months of building up forces in
the Middle East and the magnitude of the attacks, stunned the
Iraqis and most everyone else in the world who watched and
listened to the events as they unfolded on television.

The air campaign against Iraq was characterized by its brilliant
orchestration. The rivalries and infighting often characteristic of
allied military coalitions failed to materialize in Desert Storm. The
credit for this success goes to Lieutenant General Charles A.
Horner, head of the Air Forces Central Command (AFCENT), and his staff.
During the Desert Shield buildup, his legion of target analysts and strike
planners, working closely with the several U.S. and coalition air force
commanders, developed one of history's most comprehensive and devastating air
campaign plans.

Not only did the various types of air operations have to be coordinated, but air
space corridors had to be kept clear for Tomahawk cruise missiles. Every day, a
single air tasking order assigned strict routes, times, and altitudes for each aircraft
of every service and country in the coalition. Air control centers on the ground
and the airborne E-3 AWACS planes kept track of each aircraft, identified
through Identification Friend or Foe (IFF) electronic codes. The massive air
campaign was flown with a minimum of mutual interference and suffered by no
aerial collisions. An officer who directed one of the tactical air control centers
attributed the amazing record to "training, planning, and an awful lot of luck."

The air war was fought in three phases. Phase one concentrated on preventing
Iraqi interference with allied air operations. Once air superiority had been
established, the coalition air forces could isolate and grind down the Iraqi field
army; destroy Saddam's strategic capabilities – his nuclear, biological, and
chemical weapons and the modified Scud-B missiles (known as the *Al- Hussein*);
and to disrupt Iraqi command and communication networks.

With the nervous system of the Iraqi forces damaged, phase two of the air
campaign would suppress Iraqi air defenses in the Kuwait Theater of Operations
(KTO). This phase was expected to last no more than two days.

During phase three, coalition air forces *Continued on page 132*

The U.S. Air Force F-15E Strike Eagle (above) is a dual-role aircraft, capable of all-weather attack as well as fighter missions. Strike Eagles were mainstays of the "Great Scud Chase" to knock out mobile missile launchers.
MCDONNELL DOUGLAS CORP.

Strike and reconnaissance versions of the Tornado were flown by the British, Saudi, and Italian air forces. An RAF Tornado streaks by (left).
YVES DEBAY

The rotating radar dome (rotodome) on the E-3 Sentry AWACS aircraft (right) provided continuous surveillance of the air space over Saudi Arabia and most of Iraq during the war. Navy E-2C Hawkeye radar planes gave coverage over the Gulf area. A formation of U.S. Marine Corps F/A-18C Hornet strike-fighters (far right).
U.S. DEPARTMENT OF DEFENSE

would pound the Iraqi field army in the KTO over a period of three to four weeks. Intense air strikes would soften enemy positions in preparation for the ground campaign, whereupon coalition air forces would shift their emphasis to air support of ground operations.

The Iraqi air forces available to deter such an air campaign were impressive. Iraq's Air Force – the world's sixth largest – flew about 950 aircraft dispersed among 54 bases throughout the country. Some 665 were combat aircraft, "shooters", 85 armed helicopters, and 200 were transports and other support aircraft. Saddam's offensive fire power included more than 90 French Mirage F1 fighter and attack aircraft as well as 20 Soviet MiG-29 Fulcrum fighters, among the most advanced in the world. For offensive strikes Iraq had a few Tu-22 Blinder and Tu-16 Badger bombers, and several hundred modified Scud-B missiles.

Iraq had numerous early-warning and fire-control radars, as many as 17,000 Surface-to-Air Missiles (SAMs), and about 10,000 Anti-Aircraft Artillery (AAA) guns, all tied into an integrated, "state of the art" air defense system. Fiber-optic cables linked the principal air-defense components, with control centers housed in buried, hardened concrete bunkers.

Generals Schwarzkopf and Horner anticipated resistance to the initial air assault, but the Iraqi Air Force was far less aggressive than expected. The ferocity of the allied air strikes across Iraq and Kuwait in the opening hours had stunned the Iraqi high command, and it never recovered. During the first and second days of the air war, only 25 Iraqi aircraft attempted to oppose coalition aircraft. Iraq lost eight planes in aerial combat on the first night and day of the air campaign. There were no allied losses in air-to-air combat. However, there were still numerous anti-aircraft guns and surface-to-air missiles in Iraq and they remained potent threats to allied aircraft.

On the third day, January 19, Iraq launched 55 aircraft. Six were shot down. In the following two weeks, the Iraqi Air Force never mounted more than 40 sorties per day, and most of those aircraft seemed more intent on fleeing to the sanctuary of neutral Iran than on fighting. The first surge to Iran, from January 22 to 24, consisted mainly of transport and support aircraft. Then, from January 26 to 29, a total of 76 fighters fled to Iran. U.S. officials soon dubbed these planes the "white-feather squadron."

Coalition AWACS aircraft and fighters belatedly took up positions to guard against further aerial escapes. No flights to Iran occurred for several days, but they resumed during February 4 to 9, with 47 Iraqi aircraft evading coalition fighters and fleeing into Iran. Only three more Iraqi aircraft fled during the next two weeks, at which time the ground war began. This brought the total to 137.

U.S. intelligence officials believe that the first Iraqi aircraft to flee to Iran were flown on the initiative of their pilots, who wished to save their lives and planes. Subsequently, it is thought the flights were condoned by Iraqi air commanders in an effort to preserve planes and pilots from the coalition air assault. Analyzing television film of the aircraft on Iranian airfields, U.S. analysts soon determined that the Iraqi aircraft were not being maintained and even if Iran were to permit them to arm and take off, they would not be a threat to allied forces.

The exuberance over the success of the first air strikes continued unabated as Desert Storm progressed. By the end of the third day of air operations, coalition aircraft had flown 4,700 combat and support sorties, and U.S. Navy ships had launched 216 Tomahawk missiles against Iraq. After that day, the coalition's aircraft sortie rate increased as more aircraft arrived in Saudi Arabia. By the end of the first week of the air war, the coalition force flying against Iraq consisted of warplanes from Bahrain, Britain, Canada, France, Italy, Kuwait, Qatar, and the United States.

Lieutenant General Horner and his airmen gained additional flexibility and air power because of aerial refueling. Through years of practice and many agreements, the NATO air forces had evolved "interoperable" air refueling systems and techniques. This paid off in the Gulf air campaign. Royal Air Force tanker aircraft, such as the VC10 and *Continued on page 136*

A Tomahawk cruise missile rides a plume of flame as it roars from an armored box launcher on the cruiser Mississippi (CGN-40). The airburst explosion (right) of a Tomahawk's 1,000-pound (454 kg.) warhead destroys aircraft target during testing.
GUILLES BASSIGNAC / GAMMA-LIAISON
RIGHT: TRIPPETT / SIPA PRESS

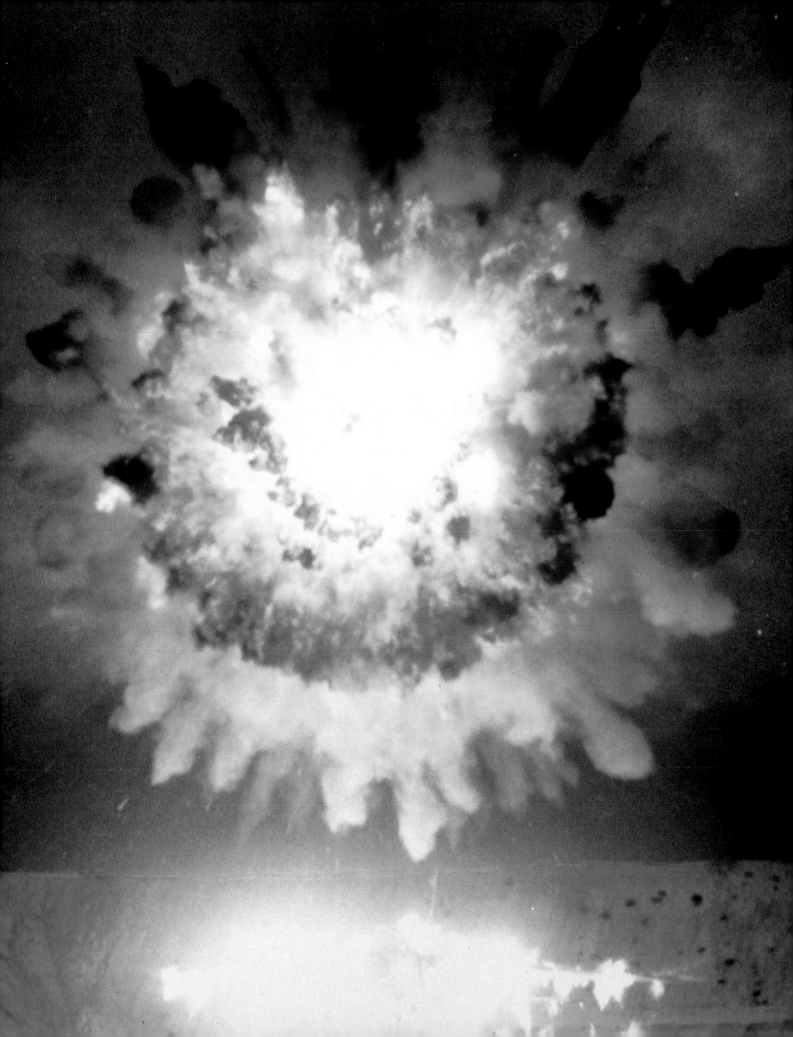

Reinforcing steel rods and concrete in this Baghdad building (right) were penetrated by an allied bomb, opening the interior to sunlight. Precision bombing gutted this office building in Baghdad (above), while surrounding structures were undamaged.
BOTH: NOEL QUIDU / GAMMA-LIAISON

GETTING CLOSER TO THE TARGET

The Gulf War showed the changing nature of air warfare. Instead of attacking a target with thousands of bombs and aircraft as in earlier conflicts, it can now be done with a single plane.

SORTIES NEEDED TO DESTROY A TARGET:

WORLD WAR II: **MORE THAN 500**

VIETNAM: **MORE THAN 5**

DESERT STORM: **1 OR 2**

ACCURACY: (CEP*)

WORLD WAR II: **THOUSANDS OF FEET**

VIETNAM: **HUNDREDS OF FEET**

DESERT STORM: **WITHIN FEET**

Bombing Accuracy Graphic

*Circular Error Probable — 50 percent of the bombs will fall on average within a circle of the specified radius.

SOURCE: U.S. AIR FORCE STAFF

Tristar, and French KC-135FR tankers could provide fuel not only to aircraft of their own air forces, but also to U.S. and coalition aircraft. On the U.S. side, Air Force KC-135 and KC-10 tankers could refuel most coalition planes, while Navy KA-6D and Marine C-130 tankers could refuel their own aircraft. The payoff was longer missions and quicker response times to calls for immediate air strikes.

The air efforts were hampered, however, by the region's worst winter weather in 14 years. Cloud cover and rain swept across the battle area during the first two weeks of the air campaign, hindering but certainly not grounding coalition fliers. The Central Command's air planners at Riyadh were usually able to vector the coalition aircraft around the storm fronts. U.S. Air Force F-111 Aardvarks, F-15E Strike Eagles, Royal Air Force and Italian Tornados, and U.S. Navy A-6E Intruders were able to press on during the bad weather and at night, executing around-the-clock strikes against Iraqi targets. Despite the logistical and maintenance problems of operating in a desert environment, ground crews were able to increase aircraft availability rates.

Often, however, the cloud cover inhibited other strike aircraft, including the F-117 Stealths, from locating their targets. These conditions forced pilots to return to base with their weapons still on board. Coalition rules of engagement restricted fliers from releasing bombs or missiles unless their targets could be positively identified to avoid injuring civilians.

In addition to the weather, the threat posed by Iraq's modified Scud-B missiles required changes to the air plan. The first Scuds fell on Israel and Saudi Arabia early on the morning of January 18. The coalition air planners immediately increased the number of search and attack sorties sent against both fixed and mobile Scud launchers in Iraq. Coalition aircraft destroyed most of the fixed Scud launchers on the first day, but they could not target Iraq's unexpectedly large number of mobile Scud launchers. Finding and destroying mobile Scud launchers required more resources than anticipated. Mobile Scuds were, apparently, hidden in civilian neighborhoods during daylight hours. At night, mobile scuds were driven to pre-marked launch positions and fired — what some called a "shoot and scoot" tactic. While U.S. officials would claim that the Scud attacks had no military affect, in fact, the strikes caused thousands of air sorties to be diverted from other targets.

The U.S. Air Force began using A-10 Warthog anti-tank aircraft to fly road reconnaissance missions in search of Scud-carrying trucks. At higher altitudes, electronic specialists in Air Force-Army E-8A J-STARS (Joint Surveillance Target Attack Radar System) aircraft scanned the likely areas for Scud launches with wide-area search radar. The operators in J-STARS aircraft had continuous electronic data-link contact with airborne F-15E Strike Eagles. When J-STARS located a moving target, it passed the information to the Strike Eagles, which then attacked with Maverick infrared-guided missiles which homed in on the heat generated by the truck's exhaust.

The anti-Scud tactics required three times the anticipated air effort. During the first ten days of the air war, Iraqi forces launched an average of five Scuds each day. Throughout the remaining 33 days of the war, the number of launches diminished to an average of one per day. But the massive air effort was never able to completely halt the Scud attacks until Saddam capitulated.

Beyond this concern, coalition forces continued to target Iraq's other strategic weapon facilities, its command and control structure, and, of course, its air defenses. This accomplished, coalition aircraft could range freely over Iraq and Kuwait. Saddam's Command, Control, and Communications (C^3) system was a "damn hard (target) . . . duplicated, sophisticated, hardened, redundant," according to one U.S. intelligence official. But using a variety of intelligence sources, including help from people who had built some of the facilities, U.S. attack aircraft destroyed dozens of hardened shelters with laser-guided "smart" bombs.

These attacks, coupled with the statements made by U.S. military spokesman at the daily press conferences in Riyadh and at the Pentagon, led Saddam to

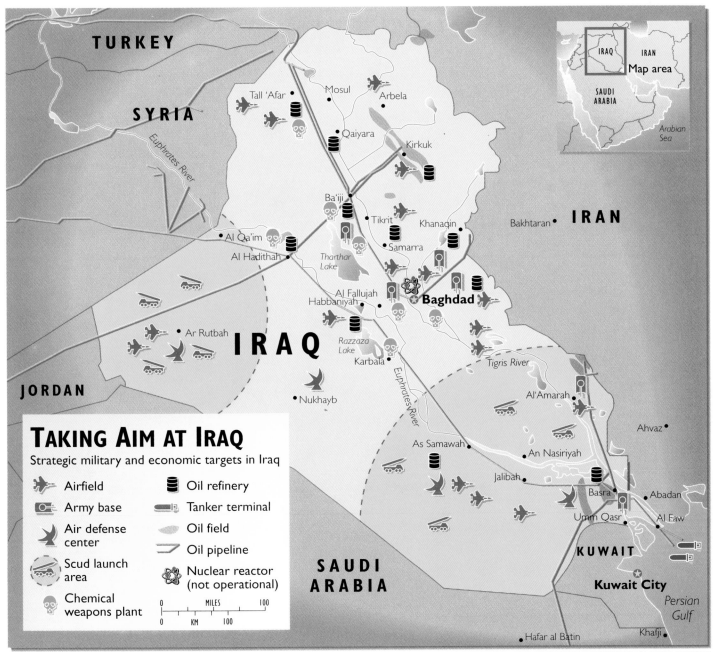

TAKING AIM AT IRAQ

Strategic military and economic targets in Iraq

- ✈ Airfield
- 🚗 Army base
- 🦅 Air defense center
- Scud launch area
- 💀 Chemical weapons plant
- 🛢 Oil refinery
- Tanker terminal
- Oil field
- Oil pipeline
- ⚛ Nuclear reactor (not operational)

```
0        MILES        100
0         KM          100
```

SOURCE: NATIONAL GEOGRAPHIC, KNIGHT-RIDDER TRIBUNE NEWS, U.S. DEFENSE DEPARTMENT

believe that the Central Command planners knew the location of every one of his command centers. "We could tell him that we knew where the bunkers were and we could strike them. . . [It] forced him to evacuate his best C^3 spaces." Rather than fighting the war from his carefully prepared command bunkers, Saddam and his generals were forced to direct their forces from a variety of secondary command shelters and private houses, and from mobile command vehicles.

One of the two most controversial strikes of the war was directed against an Iraqi bunker. At 4:30 A.M. on February 13, 1991, two laser-guided bombs destroyed the bunker in downtown Baghdad. It was bounded on two sides by residential areas; located nearby were a school, a mosque, and a recreation center. The attack did not cause any damage to nearby buildings, that is, no "collateral" damage. But the bombs killed more than 100 men, women, and children sheltered inside the bunker.

The Iraqis claimed that the building was an air raid shelter, and charged that it had been attacked deliberately by *Continued on page 140*

Aftermath of a bombing: a Baghdad citizen wails for his dead family, killed in the bombing of a controversial building. The remains of casualties (inset) are taken away for burial.
CNN VIA AFP
INSET: PARIS MATCH

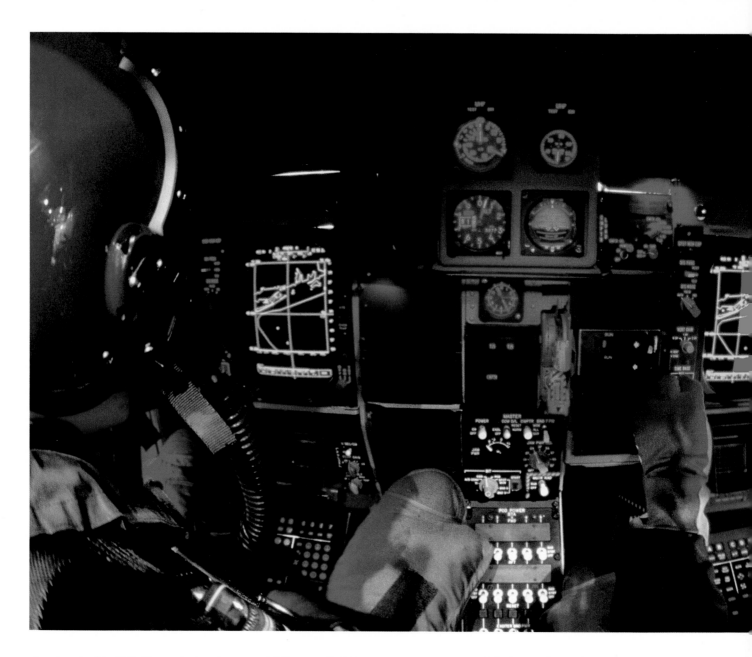

A prime tool in U.S. Navy electronic warfare is the EA-6B Prowler (above) aircraft. It is a variant of the A-6 Intruder flown by Navy and Marine squadrons. The Prowler can detect, identify, and jam hostile radio and radar transmissions.
GRUMMAN CORP.

U.S. aircraft. Western newsmen in Baghdad were brought to the scene, shown the wreckage, introduced to eyewitnesses of the attack, and presented with a sign (in English) identifying the structure as a bomb shelter.

The bunker was built in the early 1980s as a bomb shelter and upgraded to a command center in the late 1980s, according to U.S. officials. At a Pentagon press conference held on the day of the attack, U.S. Department of Defense spokesman Pete Williams commented on the changes that had been made to it in the late 1980s: "Not only was the physical building reinforced, but there was additional protection put in the building to shield communications equipment from an electromagnetic pulse. . . what you get if there is a nuclear explosion."

Officials explained that the roof had been painted with a camouflage design, a chain link and barbed wire fence was installed around the facility, and gate access was limited – features that would not be found in a civilian bomb shelter. Perhaps most telling, television and still pictures of the shattered structure showed computer cables in the wreckage. A Central Command spokesman in Riyadh summarized the official U.S. position when asked if he shared the regrets being offered by the British government on the loss of life.

Marine Brigadier General Richard (Butch) Neal snapped back: "You're damn

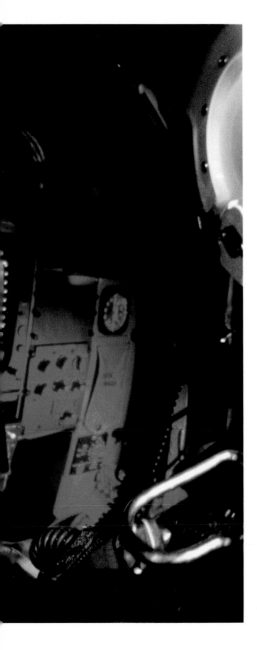

Crew stations of the EA-6B: pilot and bombardier / navigator in front; two electronic warfare specialists in back.
BOTH: GRUMMAN CORP.

right! If 400 civilians [the number originally reported by Baghdad] were killed, logic would tell you that of course the American public and the coalition forces are saddened by that fact. But I would add very quickly that this was a legitimate military target, attacked by professional officers, and it was struck as planned and as it was targeted. But yes . . . and again I have to emphasize that because I don't know all the facts as to how many people were in the bunker. . . it is a tragedy."

The bunker issue was never completely resolved. The other highly controversial strike was against a facility that the Iraqis labeled as a baby milk factory and U.S. intelligence reported as a chemical weapons plant. (See Chapter 7.) Still, the number of civilian casualties in the air campaign was small. According to Peter Arnett, "After the first few days the Iraqis were not afraid of our bombs. They knew we were only going after military targets."

After the first week of the air war, Western television viewers saw civilians in Baghdad going about their normal activities despite the blaring of air raid sirens. The Iraqis, however, did fear the Tomahawk missiles, which, said Arnett, they believed were less accurate (because they were not piloted) and liable to be skewed away from their targets by anti-aircraft fire.

As coalition aircraft quickly won total control of the air, the sortie rate climbed steadily. By mid-February, 2,800 to 2,900 sorties were being flown every day. Of those, some 100 to 200 sorties per day were flown against specific Republican Guard units in the Kuwaiti area and about the same number were flown against Scud launchers.

The strikes against Republican Guard units were part of the effort to "shape the battlefield" for the coming ground battle. The principal targets were the Iraqi artillery and tanks in the Kuwaiti area, especially guns defending the obstacle belts in southern Kuwait. These targets were hit by tactical fighters and attack planes as well as B-52 long-range bombers.

The B-52s were built in the early 1950s to deliver nuclear weapons against the Soviet Union. They later were modified for conventional bombing operations. During Desert Storm, each B-52 could carry fifty 750-pound (340-kg.) bombs – a total of almost 19 tons (19.3 metric tons) of high explosives. The B-52 poundings were devastating, to both structures and morale, although the soft sand made the bombings less effective than they had been in the Vietnam War.

These bombers initially flew strikes against Iraqi fortifications in Kuwait and Republican Guard forces. However, the failure of tactical aircraft to stop the Scud launchings led to B-52s being assigned to pound Scud launch sites away from populated areas beginning in late February.

The B-52s operated from the U.S. air base in Diego Garcia in the central Indian Ocean, a round-trip flight of about 5,000 miles (8,050 km.). Subsequently, the giant eight-engine planes also flew from bases in Britain and Spain and, on occasion, from Saudi Arabia, although Saudi airfields were already overcrowded with tactical aircraft and cargo planes. (One B-52 came down at sea while approaching Diego Garcia after a bombing mission; three of the six crewmen were lost.)

Iraqi airfields and air defense installations were bombed regularly by coalition aircraft and, during the first few days of the war, struck by large numbers of Tomahawk missiles. Whenever an Iraqi air defense or fire-control radar was activated, it would be quickly attacked by U.S. Air Force F-4G Wild Weasels or Navy EA-6B Prowlers. These aircraft were fitted with equipment to detect radar emissions. They would identify the radars as being associated with air defenses, lock onto the emitting radars, and then launch their HARMs (High-Speed Anti-Radiation Missiles).

General Colin L. Powell, Chairman of the Joint Chiefs of Staff, summarized in his mid-January briefing how the Desert Storm campaign would develop. He said: "Our strategy to go after this army is very, very simple. First we're going to cut it off and then we're going to kill it."
TERRY ASHE / TIME MAGAZINE

Iraq lost much of its radar coverage during the first few days of the air war. Soon, Iraq's SAMs and AAA were being fired by local controllers with optical sights. But these air defense crews were able to bring down only a small number of coalition aircraft. By the time hostilities ceased on March 6, 1991, the coalition air forces had flown 109,876 combat and related support sorties in the 43-day air campaign. These did not include transports and cargo planes bringing troops and materiel into the area. U.S. Air Force planes flew 59 percent and U.S. Navy and Marine planes, flying from land bases as well as aircraft carriers and amphibious ships, flew 23 percent. In flying those sorties, 41 coalition planes – 32 from the United States and nine from other countries – were shot down by ground fire; another 26 U.S. and two allied aircraft were lost in non-combat operational accidents.

The loss rates were remarkably low considering the Iraqi air defense threat. Indeed, higher loss rates had been sustained in intensive airborne training exercises. U.S. Marine aircraft suffered the heaviest loss rate, principally because they flew close-air support of ground troops; the British Tornado losses were relatively high because their targets primarily were airfields, requiring them to fly low into heavily defended areas. No aircraft of any coalition nation was shot down by Iraqi fighters.

Some pilots and air crewmen of the downed coalition aircraft were killed, but others were picked up – sometimes far behind Iraqi lines – by U.S. search-and-rescue helicopters. Several U.S. and other coalition fliers were captured by Iraqi troops. Saddam – in violation of the Geneva Convention that governs the treatment of war prisoners – displayed the downed fliers on television, forced them to make statements, and threatened to use them as human shields at military installations. But his exhibition of captured pilots backfired.

Instead of winning sympathy for his people, Saddam inspired sympathy for the pilots. The puffy, bruised, scabbed face of U.S. Navy Lieutenant Jeffrey Zaun was unforgettable. Zaun, a bombardier-navigator in an A-6E Intruder off the carrier *Saratoga*, suffered facial injuries when he ejected from his damaged aircraft over southwestern Iraq. He and his pilot, Lieutenant Robert Wetzel, parachuted safely to the ground, but Wetzel was injured. Zaun decided to stay with him rather than try to escape. Mistreated by his captors, Zaun smashed his nose himself, hoping that the injuries would prevent him from being exhibited on Iraqi television. Still, the Iraqis forced Zaun to make a videotaped statement.

He spoke slowly, haltingly:
Question: "Would you tell us your rank and name?"
Zaun: "My name is Lieutenant Jeffrey Norton Zaun, United States Navy."
Question: "Your age?"
Zaun: "I am 28."
Question: "Your unit?"
Zaun: "I am from Attack Squadron 35 on the U-S-S *Saratoga* in the Red Sea."
Question: "Your type of aircraft?"
Zaun: "I fly the A-6E Intruder attack aircraft."
Question: "Your mission?"
Zaun: "My mission was to attack H-3 airfield in southwestern Iraq."
Question: "Alone?"
Zaun: "I flew as part of a formation of four aircraft in order to commit this attack."

This sequence of a building about to be hit was seen by the pilot of an attack aircraft, transmitted by the television camera in a guided bomb.
U.S. DEPARTMENT OF DEFENSE

Continued on page 147

Was it a "Baby Milk Plant," as the sign propped against the fence proclaimed in English and Arabic, or a plant for making chemical weapons? Baghdad said the former, Washington claimed the latter. Refinery tanks and pipes at the oil city of Kirkuk (right) in northern Iraq are smashed by a coalition air strike. After suspension of the allied offensive, Kurdish rebels and Iraqi troops fought over Kirkuk.

INSET: EYUP COSKUN / SIPA PRESS
NOEL QUIDU / GAMMA-LIAISON

RAINING DESTRUCTION FROM THE AIR

The non-stop bombing of targets in Iraq and Kuwait played an integral part in operation Desert Storm. How five types of bombs work:

STANDOFF LAND ATTACK MISSILE

SLAM is a derivative of the Harpoon anti-ship missile. It provides surgical strike capability against fixed land targets or ships.

1 Target location and other mission data are loaded into the missile's computer prior to takeoff aboard an A-7E Corsair II.

2 A-7E Corsair II launches SLAM missile in excess of 50 nautical miles from target.

3 While the missile is in flight, the satelite receiver/processor updates the missile's inertial navigational system.

4 As missile nears target, the infrared seeker is activated, sending a video image to the pilot of the A-7E for guiding missile to a specific point on the target.

"DUMB BOMBS"

Three B-52 bombers flying in formation seven miles (11.27 km.) up, can release 153 bombs to carpet bomb an area 1 mile (1.6 km.) wide, 1 1/2 miles (2.4 km.) long.

Each bomb 750 lbs. (340 kg.)

1 Bombardier identifies targets; lines up plane when less than 1 mile away.

2 Bomb bay doors open.

3 Data fed into a computer for target accuracy: altitude, bomb weight, speed, and wind speed/direction.

4 Bombs released less than a quarter-mile (.4 km.) from target.

CLUSTER BOMBS

A-10 Thunderbolt can drop cluster bombs to destroy Scud missile launchers and tanks. Cluster bomb contains 202 assorted tennis ball sized bomblets:
- 1/3 anti-personnel
- 1/3 anti-armor
- 1/3 incendiary

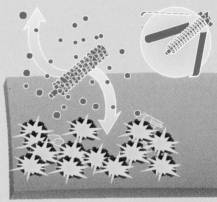

1 Dropped like a "dumb" bomb; fins spin bomb 2,500 revolutions per minute; the spinning allows bomblets to fly outward with great force.

2 Bomb's casing fans open.

3 Bomblets pour out onto targets.

"SMART BOMBS"

"Smart bombs" can be guided by lasers, TV camera or infrared signals.

1 F-111F's laser beam illuminates target.

2 Laser light reflects off target, detected by bomb.

3 Bomb's computer steers bomb by adjusting control fins.

4 F-111F continues illuminating target after bomb is released or it can leave target area.

5 Bomb's computer continues to guide bomb toward target.

F-111F fighter-bomber

Control fins

PAVEWAY
Laser-seeking guidance unit
General-purpose 2,000-lb. (907 kg.) bomb outfitted with contol fins and laser-seeking guidance unit.

AIR-TO-GROUND MISSILES

Rocket-powered Maverick missile can be guided by laser, TV or infared signals.

1 Pilot selects target with help of targeting pod, lines target up within cross hairs.

2 Locks target information into computer memory; relays information to missile, which also locks onto target.

3 Missile is launched; measures distance by sensing heat; flies itself to the target; plane breaks away after launch.

Pilot can fire missile 10-15 miles (16-24 km.) from target; less risk for aircraft and crew from being hit.

SOURCE: KNIGHT-RIDDER TRIBUNE NEWS

Question: "What do you think, lieutenant, about this aggression against Iraq?"

Zaun: "I think our leaders and our people have wrongly attacked the peaceful people of Iraq."

President Bush immediately condemned the Iraqi mistreatment of allied prisoners of war. He said of Saddam Hussein, "If he thought this brutal treatment of pilots is a way to muster world support, he is dead wrong, and I think everybody's upset about it."

Zaun and the other captured coalition airmen, several of whom were paraded on Iraqi television, were returned safely when hostilities ended.

As the air war progressed, the terms "smart bombs" and "guided weapons" entered the popular vocabulary. Smart bombs, or Guided Bomb Units (GBU), are bombs ranging up to 2,000-pound (909-kg.) size. Their guidance can be by laser, infrared, or electro-optical. Laser-guided bombs follow a light beam that is projected on a target from the attacking aircraft or another plane. Infrared-guided bombs home in on the heat given off by a target. Electro-optical guidance systems place a television camera in the nose of the weapon. (Those television sequences were recorded, and often found their way into the Riyadh or Pentagon briefings.)

Guided weapons or missiles, such as HARM and Maverick and Hellfire, are self-propelled and have internal guidance to seek out specific targets. HARM, for example, uses sensors in its antenna to home on enemy radar emissions from missile sites. The Hellfire (derived from the term "helicopter-launched, fire and forget) can use laser designation, heatseeking infrared, or radar homing guidance.

Video tapes and photos – some taken by cameras in the weapons themselves – provided the public with unprecedented views of precision bombing. Although the term "surgical bombing" had been touted since World War II, it was not achieved until Desert Storm. For example, during the Vietnam War more than 700 bombing sorties over seven years failed to destroy two critical targets near Hanoi—the Paul Doumer and Thanh Hoa (Dragon's Jaw) bridges. Both were attacked using unguided "iron bombs," and more than 30 U.S. Air Force and Navy aircraft were lost over the Thanh Hoa bridge alone. In May 1972, U.S. F-4 Phantom aircraft attacked both bridges with early model electro-optic and laser-guided bombs. Using fewer than 20 guided bombs, the attackers dropped both spans into the water. Even more efficient weapons than these were used against Iraqi targets.

In shaping the battlefield for the coming ground war, smart bombs and the massive B-52 bombardments destroyed about half of the Iraqi tanks and artillery in Kuwait. The severing of roads and bridges from the Kuwaiti theater almost stopped food and other supplies from reaching the troops in the area. The pounding was heavy and continuous, and greatly demoralized the Iraqi troops. Leaflets were dropped on these troops – by aircraft and in artillery shells – urging them to surrender. In the leaflets, General Schwarzkopf's psychological warfare specialists told the Iraqis which units would be bombed the next day. Further, the leaflets promised good treatment for prisoners. "We told them our concern was not to destroy Iraqi troops but to get their leaders to leave Kuwait," said Central Command's Brigadier General Neal.

"We told them in the leaflets," he added, "to stay away from equipment as we would bomb that. This gave them a perception that "they weren't dealing with infidels . . . we had a face of humanity."

Coalition air forces in Desert Storm dropped 88,500 tons (80,308 metric tons) of bombs on targets in Iraq and occupied Kuwait. About 6,520 tons (5,917 metric tons), over seven percent, were smart or guided bombs; they hit their targets some 90 percent of the time. In contrast, the majority of the bombs, 81,980 tons (74,392 metric tons), 93 percent, were iron bombs.

General Merrill A. McPeak, U.S. Air Force Chief of Staff, in briefing the effects of the air campaign, noted that "all the services made a very important contribution" to the war, but added: "My private conviction is that this is the first time in history that a field army has been defeated by air power."

Saddam did not withdraw from Kuwait nor did he asked for "terms" during the air campaign. Rather, he awaited the "Mother of all battles," in which he foresaw that he would defeat the coalition forces, and strike back at his antagonists.

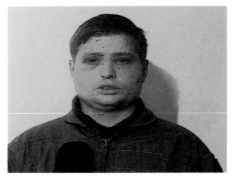

Violating the Geneva Conventions on the treatment of prisoners of war, Saddam Hussein paraded downed airmen in public, had them beaten, and forced them to make statements on television. RAF Flight Lieutenant John Peters (top) was captured when his Tornado was downed by Iraqi air defenses; U.S. Navy Lieutenant Jeffrey N. Zaun's face was bloody and puffy from ejecting from his stricken A-6E Intruder. Iraqi violations of the Geneva Conventions stirred worldwide outrage.
CNN

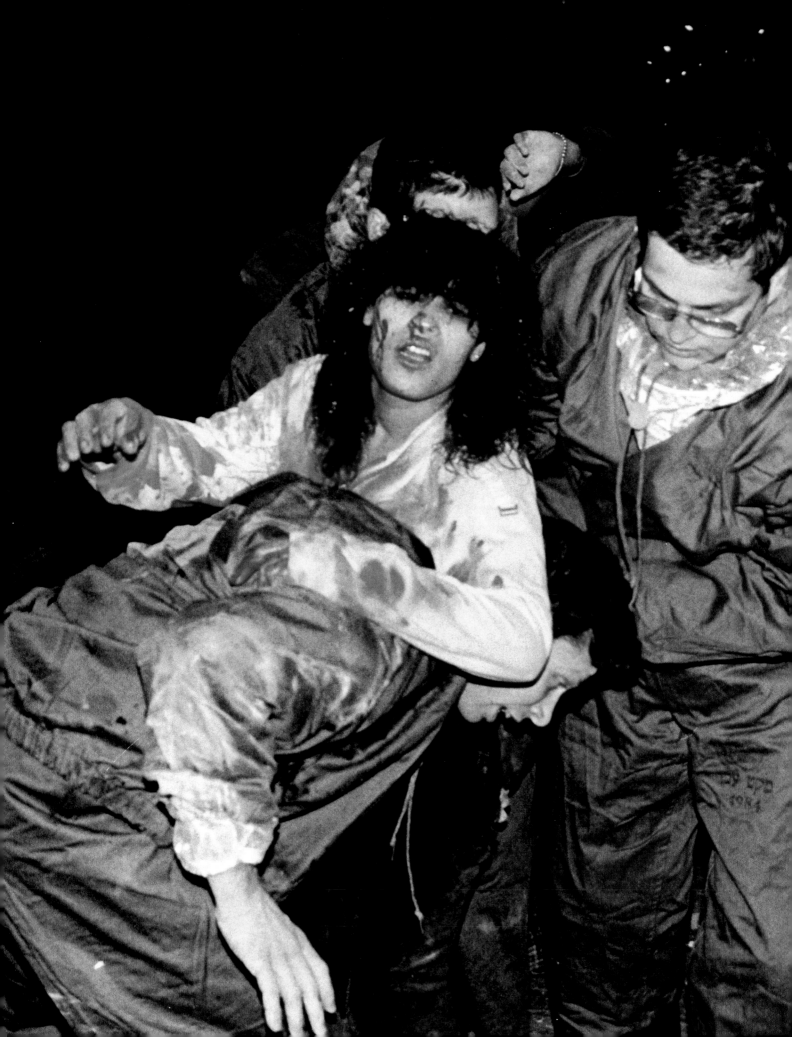

CHAPTER SEVEN

SADDAM STRIKES BACK

Huddled with his generals in a command bunker on January 17, 1991, Saddam Hussein plotted a response to the air attack on his capital. In this strategy session, Saddam, as usual, listened to no advice. "He was neither a military leader nor a strategist," as U.S. General Norman Schwarzkopf later remarked. But Saddam's strategic response would not be military. He was a man of power and guile, and those attributes drove his decision: He would not attack the coalition forces that were bombing him around the clock. He would attack Israel.

The world learned of his decision when the first modified Scud-B missile – called *Al-Hussein* by the Iraqis – slammed into Tel Aviv shortly after 2 A.M. on January 17, just in time for the start of prime time television on the East Coast of the United States. News reports showed confusing scenes of frantic correspondents donning gas masks, of terrified Israeli families in masks, of rescuers pulling people from rubble. For hours, viewers throughout the world watched and waited for the answer to the dreaded question: Did the missiles carry poison gas or lethal bacteria?

When Saddam launched the first Scuds of the war, he was gambling for the third time since August. He believed then that he could invade Kuwait with impunity. He was wrong. He next speculated that the coalition would not use force against him. The coalition's thunderous night attack on Baghdad had shown him to be wrong, again. (No one at Saddam's headquarters would dare to mention his woeful lack of prophecy. Reportedly, he had already ordered the execution of two air commanders, the latest in a long line of officers to fall victim to what a U.S. general called Saddam's "fairly dynamic zero-defects program.")

The third gamble involved more favorable probabilities, although it was far more complex than the first two. Saddam hoped the Scud attacks would pull Israel into the war. This would add a *Continued on page 152*

Rescue workers rush a wounded woman from a Tel Aviv apartment building hit by a Scud missile. At least 100 Israelis were injured in the night attack.
SVEN NACKSTRAND / AFP

149

PRECEDING PAGE
The smoldering wreckage of a Scud,
brought down by a Patriot missile, lies
on a street in Riyadh. Another Scud
aimed at Saudi Arabia explodes
(inset) when a Patriot intercepts it.

JACQUES WITT / SIPA PRESS
INSET: CNN VIA ITN

potent new enemy to the foes arrayed against him. But an Israeli retaliation could actually improve the odds on his side of the equation, by his reasoning and by the power-and-hate algebra of the Middle East.

For Saddam knew that Israel's entry would almost certainly drive many, perhaps all, of the Arab nations out of the coalition. An Israeli counter-strike would force Arab members of the coalition to either fight alongside Israel against an Arab nation – or to split off to join their Iraqi brothers in a jihad or holy war that would engulf the entire region.

To produce either political victory, Saddam chose a political weapon: the *Al-Hussein* . Saddam had attacked Tehran with Scuds in the Iran-Iraq War. He used them then as political weapons with a dual purpose: to terrify the people of Tehran and to show them that their government could not protect them. Many Western observers believe that Saddam's "Scud card" ended that war in his favor.

Unlike the precise, self-guided Tomahawk land-attack cruise missile that can pivot around corners and identify landmarks along its methodical journey to a specific target, a Scud just goes up in a preset direction, arcs, and comes down,

with an accuracy of one or two miles (1.6 to 3.2 km.). What a Scud lacks in accuracy, it makes up for in terror. Like the German V-2s that rained down on London during World War II, Scuds fired against cities were intended to induce urban panic and turn frightened citizens against their government. The Scuds that Saddam fired on Israel carried powerful political explosives. In a war shown live and in color throughout the world, he was displaying his power and was goading Israel to fight.

Eight missiles exploded in Israel on the first night of the air war, two in Tel Aviv, two in Haifa, three on unpopulated areas, and one at a site not disclosed by the government, which was withholding potential targeting information from Iraq. No one knew whether the Scuds carried chemical warheads.

At first all that mesmerized television viewers could see were reporters donning gas masks. ABC's Dean Reynolds struggled to put on a mask while trying to report. "I can't imagine what my mother is thinking," he said. While sirens wailed, CNN's Larry Register in Jerusalem phoned his colleague Richard Roth in Tel Aviv. "Is everyone there okay?" They were. CNN anchorman David French in Washington cut in to ask reporter Linda Scherzer how she would know when to use syringes containing poison-gas antidotes. "When it comes time to use this injection, you will know it," she said, and viewers winced in shared horror.

Masks and transparent shrouds shield a Tel Aviv family (left) during a Scud attack. In Saudi Arabia, CNN's Charles Jaco dons his mask. Iraq's previous use of chemical weapons inspired fear that Scuds carried poison gas.
LEFT: G. MENDEL / MAGNUM
ABOVE: CNN

Then came the report from NBC in Tel Aviv: The missiles had chemical warheads. . . . Ambulances were rushing poison-gas victims to hospitals. NBC anchorman Tom Brokaw, his face mirroring incredulity and rage, condemned Saddam, ". . . .a man who portrays himself as a pious defender of the faith. And yet he will stoop to anything." More than 30 minutes passed before NBC and the other networks reported that the missiles had not contained gas.

The United States, mindful of Israel's months-old pledge to retaliate if attacked by Iraq, reacted swiftly. President George Bush expressed his outrage. Secretary of State James Baker telephoned Israeli Prime Minister Yitzak Shamir to assure him that "the United States is continuing its efforts to eliminate this threat."

For several hours the U.S.-led coalition expected Israel to respond. U.S. intelligence officials knew that Israeli Air Force pilots had been preparing for such a mission by bombing mockups of Scud missile launchers at test ranges in the Negev desert. Israeli intelligence had updated their target lists in Iraq to include the latest data they could obtain on the missile situation. At a meeting with Bush in Washington in December, Shamir had said that he would not make a preemptive strike on missile sites.

Live From Baghdad...

On January 28, 1991, a canvas-covered truck arrived in Baghdad after a 520-mile (837 km.) journey from Amman, Jordan. Painted on its top in big red letters was CNN – so that coalition aircraft would not mistake the truck for a Scud missile carrier. In the truck were the components of a portable television transmitter, known in the trade as a fly-away unit (satellite-uplink).

The transmitter would allow CNN correspondent Peter Arnett, the only American journalist in Iraq, to broadcast live rather than onto tapes sent out overland through Amman, Jordan. On the day the transmitter arrived, Arnett was in a "private bungalow" elsewhere in Baghdad, waiting to be ushered into the presence of Saddam Hussein for the first interview by a Western journalist since the war began. (For a behind-the-scenes look at CNN coverage of the war, see page 232.)

The two events coincided to produce both another journalistic coup and another controversy in CNN's coverage of the war from Baghdad. Hovering over the coverage had been the question of whether Arnett was a reporter or a propaganda puppet for Saddam. "Any reports coming out of Baghdad are, in effect, coming from the Iraqi government," presidential press secretary Marlin Fitzwater had remarked about Arnett's reporting. Fitzwater and Pentagon critics failed to note that news was being censored by both sides.

Warnings about censorship appeared on television screens whether a report came from "military-escorted" news pools in Saudi Arabia or from Arnett in Baghdad. But this was the first U.S. war with an American reporter filing stories from the enemy capital, and there were no rules or precedents "Let's face it," Arnett said later, "I was tap dancing."

Arnett often found a way to get around the censorship. "We heard heavy bombing outside the city," he reported one day. Later in the report he noted that he had seen "no civilian damage." Intelligence officers in Washington and Saudi Arabia taped every minute of his reports and scrutinized them for information.

"His reports contained invaluable material," a high-ranking U.S. intelligence officer said. For example, damage assessors compared aerial and satellite imagery of a bombed Baghdad power station with Arnett's televised report from the bombed sites. "Looking down on damage often isn't enough," the officer said. "With the TV images we could look at the rubble on the ground and get a three-dimensional view," the officer said. "We could see enough of the damage to write off the power station without another strike."

Arnett's interview with Saddam began with a question containing raid-damage disclosures that slipped past the "minders" (security people) in the room: "I was driven to this meeting tonight through the dark streets of Baghdad, streets darkened by attacks by American aircraft and others on your power plants. There have been many air strikes against your country and in Kuwait, and the U.S. military command is saying that it is winning this first round of the war. But what do you say to that?"

Saddam, speaking through an interpreter, did not deny the damage Arnett had adroitly described. Saddam's rambling answer began with "What we say is that light comes through the dark . . . ."

Arnett next asked Saddam how he would compare the eight-year Iran-Iraq War with this one – again slipping in a report about battered Baghdad: During "all that time, your country was not affected as badly as it is now. The power is down. Water supplies are scarce."

Again, Saddam waxed into rhetoric. Again, Arnett responded by linking a question with information. He asked about the "large numbers of Iraqi planes" that had gone to Iran. Saddam admitted that the planes were in Iran. When asked whether the planes would "be used in the current conflict," Saddam evaded with, "Each case has its own circumstances."

Arnett focussed on Saddam's propaganda war: coalition airmen, captured by Iraqis, brought before Iraqi television cameras; Iraqis opening valves to cause a massive oil spill in the Persian Gulf; Scud attacks on Israel and Saudi Arabia.

In reply, Saddam compared the prisoners of war to unnamed "Iraqi students," supposedly imprisoned in the West. Of the oil spill, he said his officers used oil as a weapon "of legitimate self-defense." As to the Scud attacks, he dismissed "Scud" as a name, saying the missiles were Iraqi-made *Al-Husseins*, named after "our grandfather who fought injustice." Pressed by Arnett, Saddam said the missile "is capable of carrying nuclear, chemical, and biological warheads."

It was an interview of admissions, of information that Arnett would never have been able to extract from any other source. Nor would Arnett have been able to get such information out of Iraq without the satellite-uplink Saddam allowed into the country. Through it, CNN transmitted Saddam's admissions to the more than 100 countries that receive CNN.

In Iraq and other countries that restrict television, only key officials see CNN. But, whatever the restrictions, throughout the world ordinary citizens and high officials could see and evaluate the Saddam interview and other events that Arnett reported out of Baghdad.

U.S. officials were particularly sensitive about Arnett's reporting on matters that could be used as propaganda. One such incident was the bombing of a Baghdad

structure that was either a command and control center, according to coalition officers, or an air raid shelter, according to Iraqi officials (see page 140). Another involved the bombing of a Baghdad structure that was either a factory for manufacturing baby milk-formula, according to Iraqi officials, or a factory that produced lethal ingredients for biological weapons, according to coalition officers.

Ironically, the CNN video of the controversial "air-raid shelter" substantiated intelligence information that had labeled it a command and control center. "There was the wire fence around the structure," an intelligence officer said. "You don't put that kind of fence around a shelter. And, for us a great tipoff, there were the computer conduits exposed in the busted ceiling. You don't put high-tech computer networks in air-raid shelters."

Arnett stuck to his original report on both bomb sites. Of the command center-shelter issue: "We reported exactly what we saw there." To the baby-milk-or-germ-warfare issue: "Whatever else it did, it did produce infant formula." And, in answer to questions from distant observers: "I was there and they weren't." Backing for Arnett came from a French contractor who oversaw the building of the baby-formula factory in the 1970s as well as from New Zealand technicians, who said they had seen it producing canned milk powder in May 1990. A White House official, however, said the factory had been converted to germ-warfare use in the fall of 1990. U.S. officials also noted what they saw as clumsy propaganda: A sign at the factory entrance said "Baby Milk Plant" in Arabic and English; a worker walking around wearing a shirt with a label that said, in English, "Baby Milk Plant Iraq."

The skirmishes in the propaganda war did not disturb the professionally unflappable Arnett. "I was not thinking of the interests of the [United States], but what would interest viewers," he said, speaking after the war. "The way I see it, the world took sides when they moved against Saddam Hussein. I wondered whether my presence would interfere with the war. Would I influence the war?" His answer: "No way."

CNN correspondent Peter Arnett interviews Saddam Hussein with the aid of an Iraqi interpreter. Arnett transmitting by satellite link (opposite).
BOTH: CNN

But he had said he would retaliate if attacked.

If the missile-hunting Israeli pilots did attempt a retaliatory raid, they would risk being shot down by coalition pilots. Allied aircraft were equipped with IFF (Identification Friend or Foe) codes. Lacking them, the Israelis could be mistaken as foes in high-speed aerial encounters. Baghdad Radio had already tried to enflame Arabs with the claim that 140 Israeli aircraft were flying in the war with U.S. markings. Arab military officers at the coalition headquarters in Riyadh and at various Saudis air bases knew this was a lie. Moreover, they would be among the first to know if the United States did anything to accommodate an Israeli strike. Almost certainly, any U.S. assistance towards an Israel strike on Iraq would mark the beginning of the coalition's breakup.

Bush called Shamir to appeal for Israeli restraint. Shamir met with his cabinet and won a 48-hour reprieve on when to avenge the Scud attacks. When three more Scuds struck in and around Tel Aviv, he cut the deadline by 24 hours. As this new deadline approached, two U.S. responses were on their way to Israel: from Washington came Deputy Secretary of State Lawrence S. Eagleburger and from bases in Germany came Patriot air-defense missile batteries manned by U.S. soldiers. The United States considered both Eagleburger and the Patriots to be diplomatic responses. As presidential press secretary Marlin Fitzwater later said, a Patriot hitting a Scud missile moves a lot faster than a diplomatic pouch.

At the beginning of the Gulf War, the Israeli government had distributed gas masks to all of its citizens – Jewish, Muslim, and Christian – and ordered every household, hotel, and business to prepare one or more rooms that could be quickly sealed to protect against chemical attacks. There were runs on stores selling tape and sheets of plastic. Some Israelis had relatives in Europe mail them boxes of tape for sealing their protective rooms.

No masks were issued to the Palestinians in the occupied West Bank. When the Palestinians clamored for masks, the Israeli government still refused, saying that the missiles were aimed at Israel, not at the Palestinians. Government spokesmen also said that if the Palestinians did get masks they would use them later to defend against the tear gas used by the police in quelling intifada rioting. Finally, yielding to internal as well as U.S. pressure, the protective masks were finally issued to all on the West Bank – with a small cost being charged to the Palestinians.

As the missiles of the first attack hurtled into Tel Aviv, supporters of the Palestine Liberation Front were reported standing on the roofs of houses in the West Bank and cheering. West Bank Palestinians got their view of the war from Jordanian television, which favored the Iraqis. Yasir Arafat, leader of the Palestine Liberation Organization (PLO), was frequently seen hugging Saddam and telling Arabs that the "real aim" of the war was to create a homeland for "three million Russian Jews in a Greater Israel from the Nile to the Euphrates."

After the first attack, Israel hunkered down. Schools were closed. Thousands of wealthy residents of Tel Aviv fled to the homes of friends or relatives in the country or to hotels in Jerusalem, thought to be immune from Scud attacks because Muslims, like Jews and Christians, consider it a holy city.

The Gulf War had virtually wiped out Israel's $1.8 billion tourist industry. As Scud refugees from Tel Aviv and Haifa began to pour into Jerusalem, a hotel manager said, "First, Saddam Hussein chased away our tourists. Now he is bringing them back."

School children disliked carrying gas masks, instinctively feared them, and hated to put them on during alerts or raids. One father finally told his eight-year-old son he would pay him five shekels each time the boy had to put on a mask. The boy eventually made 200 shekels, for there were 40 alerts before the Scuds stopped.

Almost simultaneously with the Scud attack on Israel came the first Scud strike on Saudi Arabia, horrifying television viewers for a second time in one night. CNN reporter Charles Jaco, reporting from the coalition air base at

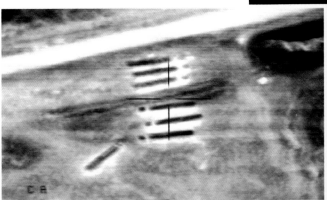

Electro-optical image from an attacking plane shows doomed Scud loading site as a bomb nears it. One Patriot streaks off in search of a Scud (right)as another Patriot scores a spectacular direct hit.

LEFT: U.S. AIR FORCE
RIGHT: CNN VIA ITN

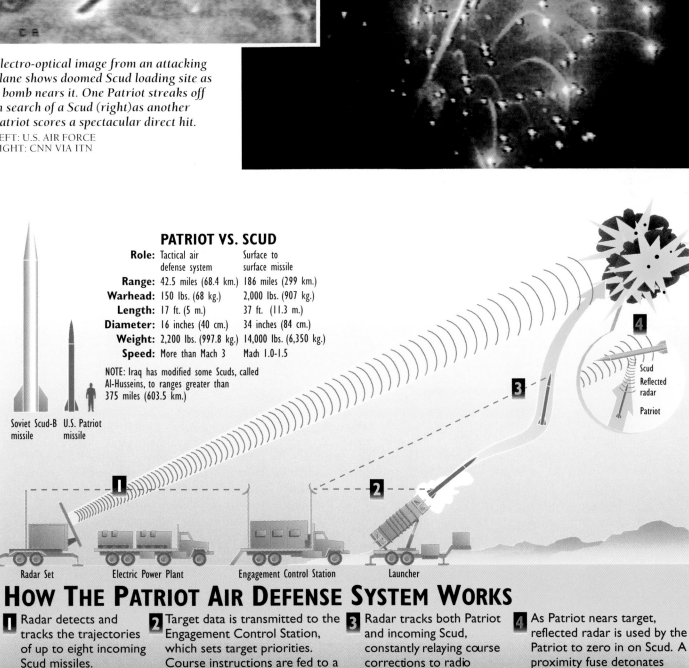

PATRIOT VS. SCUD

Role:	Tactical air defense system	Surface to surface missile
Range:	42.5 miles (68.4 km.)	186 miles (299 km.)
Warhead:	150 lbs. (68 kg.)	2,000 lbs. (907 kg.)
Length:	17 ft. (5 m.)	37 ft. (11.3 m.)
Diameter:	16 inches (40 cm.)	34 inches (84 cm.)
Weight:	2,200 lbs. (997.8 kg.)	14,000 lbs. (6,350 kg.)
Speed:	More than Mach 3	Mach 1.0-1.5

NOTE: Iraq has modified some Scuds, called Al-Husseins, to ranges greater than 375 miles (603.5 km.)

Soviet Scud-B missile   U.S. Patriot missile

Scud
Reflected radar
Patriot

Radar Set   Electric Power Plant   Engagement Control Station   Launcher

HOW THE PATRIOT AIR DEFENSE SYSTEM WORKS

1 Radar detects and tracks the trajectories of up to eight incoming Scud missiles.

2 Target data is transmitted to the Engagement Control Station, which sets target priorities. Course instructions are fed to a Patriot missile and launched.

3 Radar tracks both Patriot and incoming Scud, constantly relaying course corrections to radio receiver in Patriot.

4 As Patriot nears target, reflected radar is used by the Patriot to zero in on Scud. A proximity fuse detonates warhead once within range.

SOURCE: KNIGHT-RIDDER TRIBUNE NEWS

Dhahran, said there had been a warning of missiles. Then— "There was an explosion in the direction of the air base. We can hear sounds overhead."

"Fold it up and go, Charles Jaco!" said a voice from the CNN control room in Atlanta. "Fold it up and go!"

Jaco, ducking, shouted, "Okay, guys. Break it down. Outta here. Let's go."

The screen went blank.

Viewers feared the worst for a few hollow moments until transmission resumed. There was a new war going on, but not the one that Saddam had expected. With his prime-time fusillade, he had started a war of imagery: the gas masks, the rubble, the frantic reporters. The coalition soon countered with its own captivating imagery: the Patriot in action. NBC correspondent Arthur Kent, broadcasting atop a roof in Dhahran with a microphone in one hand and a gas mask in the other, shouted over the sound of a siren. He pointed to a streak of

light in the sky. An explosion erupted. The streak of light was a Patriot missile racing toward an oncoming Scud. The death of that Scud marked the Patriot's spectacular television debut.

Saddam had lost his third gamble. Israel did not retaliate; the coalition held firm. And throughout the world, viewers—including national leaders—saw his vaunted Scuds shot down again and again by U.S. Patriot missiles. As for Saddam's attacks on Saudi Arabia, they stiffened Arab resistance to him and, in unfathomable ways, drew Israelis and Arabs together.

Israeli novelist A.B. Yehoshua, in his home in Haifa, was donning his gas mask when he heard on the radio that people in Saudi Arabia and Bahrain were putting on theirs. Writing of "this strange community of fate with Saudis and Bahrainis," he predicted that the "one-dimensional Arab world, monolithic and menacing, has been destroyed."

Saddam would fire a total of 86 Scuds, 40 at Israel and 46 at Saudi Arabia. Most were blown up by Patriots. In Israel, one person was killed and 239 wounded; an estimated 9,000 apartments and homes were damaged in and around Tel Aviv. In Saudi Arabia, the most lethal Scud attack occurred when the missile exploded over Dhahran and fell onto a barracks housing the newly arrived 14th Quartermaster Company, an Army Reserve unit from Greensburg, Pennsylvania. The explosion and fire killed 28 soldiers and wounded 80.

Attacks with Saddam's chemical and biological weapons never materialized. U.S. intelligence sources say that Saddam was informed that the use of weapons in his chemical arsenal would trigger massive retaliation. The most likely retaliation would have been the eradication of Baghdad by an Israeli nuclear strike if such weapons were used against Israel, and by allied conventional weapons if a chemical strike were made against coalition forces. Israelis spoke freely about the need for such retaliation if Saddam used his chemical or biological weapons.

Warnings were presumably relayed through neutral diplomats, although some sources do not rule out a direct warning from the United States, which, in a break with age-old tradition, did not break off diplomatic relations with Iraq during the war.

Iraq's chemical weapons plants were struck in the early raids of the air war. But Saddam had, by one estimate, some 2,000 to 4,000 tons (2,032 to 4,064 metric tons) of poison gases in stockpiles whose locations may not have been known to coalition targeting officers. On hand were three kinds of gas: mustard gas, which can blind, burn, and kill; nerve gases, which, by disrupting the nervous system, makes breathing impossible; and hydrogen cyanide gas, which causes suffocation by preventing the transfer of oxygen from lungs to blood. The gases could be delivered by artillery, aerial bombs, and rockets.

The Scud wielded more for the television screen than for the battlefield, and established the pattern for Saddam's response to the air war – and his anticipation of a ground war. In the weeks that followed the initial attacks on Baghdad, Saddam chose to react with words and images rather than with his military weapons, such as the Iraqi Air Force.

Except for a few aircraft that flew in the opening days of the air war, most of his war planes had remained on the ground, hidden away or destroyed. Those that did take off from Iraqi air fields were flown by pilots who would rather flee than fight. The aircraft flew to Iran, where they were impounded. By February 4, nearly 150 planes had flown to Iran. Iraq's "white-feather squadron," U.S. military officials believed, included both supersonic deserters and pilots authorized to flee.

The only airmen Saddam deployed were captured coalition air crews he forced to appear on television, where, in stilted, implausible phrases, they denounced their nations' actions. The display of the airmen, in violation of the Geneva Conventions for the treatment of prisoners of war, backfired.

Instead of winning sympathy for his people. Saddam inspired sympathy for the pilots. The puffy, bruised, scabbed face of U.S. Navy Lieutenant Jeffrey Zaun was particularly unforgettable. Zaun, flight officer (bombardier-navigator) on board an A-6E Intruder off the USS *Saratoga* (CV-60), suffered facial injuries when he ejected from his damaged aircraft over southwestern Iraq. Beaten and mistreated by his captors, he banged up his nose, hoping that would keep him off Iraqi television. But the Iraqis forced Zaun to make a videotaped statement. He spoke slowly, haltingly: "I think our leaders and our people have wrongly attacked the peaceful people of Iraq."

President Bush immediately condemned the Iraqi mistreatment of allied prisoners. He said of Saddam Hussein, "If he thought this brutal treatment of pilots is a way to muster world support, he is dead wrong, and I think everybody's upset about it."

Still trying to win the propaganda war, Saddam allowed CNN correspondent Peter Arnett to walk around a badly battered Baghdad neighborhood. A well dressed woman, her face contorted in rage, ran up to the camera and, shaking her finger, screamed in English: "We are human beings!" CNN ran the emotional scene along with an image of another woman: an Israeli, faced streaked with blood, being borne on a stretcher out of the rubble caused by a Scud attack on Tel Aviv.

A week later, CNN showed the outraged Baghdad woman again, this time to identify her as not just another passerby but an assistant to Deputy Foreign Minister Niazar Hamdoon, a former Iraqi ambassador to the United States. Another bit of staged TV had boomeranged on Saddam.

The use of CNN as a conduit of information and misinformation was practiced by both sides, though more subtly and successfully by the coalition. The air war had so shattered Saddam's communications that, as a high-ranking U.S. intelligence officer said, "CNN may have been the only accurate source of information that he had. So we knew what he was getting. We were able to pass information to him." (Although Iraqi television was knocked out, Saddam and chosen officials could pick up CNN transmissions with equipment powered by gasoline-powered generators.)

Much of Saddam's information about the war reached him the way it reached most television viewers: through the coalition's military briefings, by the U.S. military leadership in the Pentagon and allied commanders in Riyadh. The briefing system, set up by the Pentagon and General Schwarzkopf, guaranteed military control of the news. The system broke with Vietnam traditions. In that war, colonels and lieutenant colonels briefed the press in Saigon at what came to be called the "Five O'Clock Follies." In the Gulf War the briefings were given and questions fielded by general officers directly involved with the direction of the war.

Given the eight-hour time difference between Saudi Arabia and Washington,

A Jordanian asks for bids in an auction of bits of wreckage reputed to be from U.S. aircraft downed in Iraq. Fund raisers said the proceeds went to Iraqi refugees who fled to Jordan when the war began.
BOTH: CNN

159

the Central Command briefings were presented usually at 6 P.M. Saudi time (10 A.M. Eastern Standard Time [EST]). The Pentagon briefings usually began at 3 P.M. EST (11 P.M. in Saudi Arabia). U.S. Assistant Secretary of Defense for Public Affairs Louis A. (Pete) Williams usually opened the Pentagon briefings and provided context for the session. Williams worked in radio and television news in Wyoming before coming to Washington to be Representative Dick Cheney's press secretary and legislative assistant. When Cheney became Secretary of Defense, Williams moved with him to the Pentagon.

After opening the Pentagon session, Williams usually gave the stand to Army Lieutenant General Thomas W. Kelly, Director of Operations for the Joint Chiefs of Staff under General Colin Powell. Kelly was factual, unflappable, and used the right touch to keep the briefings professional. Often by his side was Rear Admiral Michael McConnell, head of intelligence for the joint staff, ready to take on questions related to Saddam's forces.

In Riyadh the briefers changed regularly during the first few days of the war, but then Marine Brigadier General Richard (Butch) Neal, the command's chief of operations, took total control of the podium. Neal was a shrewd choice. As operations chief, he had a clear picture of current events and planned actions. Since he was required to stay abreast of the situation in his operations job, he did not need to be briefed or to rehearse before meeting with the media. And, in 1985-1988, Neal had served on the Central Command staff and had developed a good dialogue with military leaders in several Middle East countries.

Officers from other coalition nations, namely, Saudi Arabia, Great Britian and France, also gave briefings, usually about the performance of their own forces.

Through radio and television broadcasting of these briefings, worldwide audiences received information unfiltered by the media. As a result, many journalists were forced to speculate on various facets of the war. (Because audiences were hearing the information first hand, they could form their own impressions of the journalists doing the reporting.) Press coverage of the Vietnam War cast doubts on the credibility of the military. Desert Storm briefings tended to diminish the credibility of the press while strengthening the public's esteem for the military.

The briefings, coupled with "backgrounders" for the press in both the Pentagon and Riyadh, gave the impression of open coverage of the war. But there was in fact heavy censorship of reporting. Reporters were pooled, with movement of journalists and photographers in Saudi Arabia being restricted and requiring military escort. (CBS reporter Bob Simon and crew were captured by Iraqi troops while searching for a story unescorted. Later, after several weeks of captivity, the CBS team was released.) While television viewers were treated to aircraft and smart-bomb films of direct hits on bridges, bunkers, and command structures, views of the misses were never shown, even after those films had been requested by the press.

Similarly, for more than two months after the end of the war, Army censors would not release the thousands of battlefield photos, mystifying those editors and publishers who wished to use them. The Pentagon also held back on making public the thousands of Iraqi prisoner of war interviews.

In Washington, as the war progressed the briefers at the State Department and at the White House used the information and questions from the earlier military briefings at the Pentagon and Riyadh to prepare their own statements for the press. As a consequence, the U.S. government spoke with a well controlled, consistent voice.

Thus, when Saddam heard Lieutenant General Kelly say that coalition aircraft

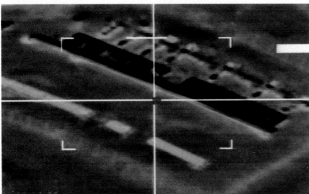

A mammoth oil slick flows from an offshore pipeline opened by Iraqi invaders (opposite) intending to destroy Kuwaiti oil industry. Satellite imagry shows oil in red. Responding to the environmental warfare, U.S. pilots zeroed in on smoking breach (top) and put key valve assembly in cross-hairs of a 2,000-pound laser-guided bomb (above). The blast sealed off the flow.
OPPOSITE: EOSAT
ABOVE, BOTH: U.S. AIR FORCE

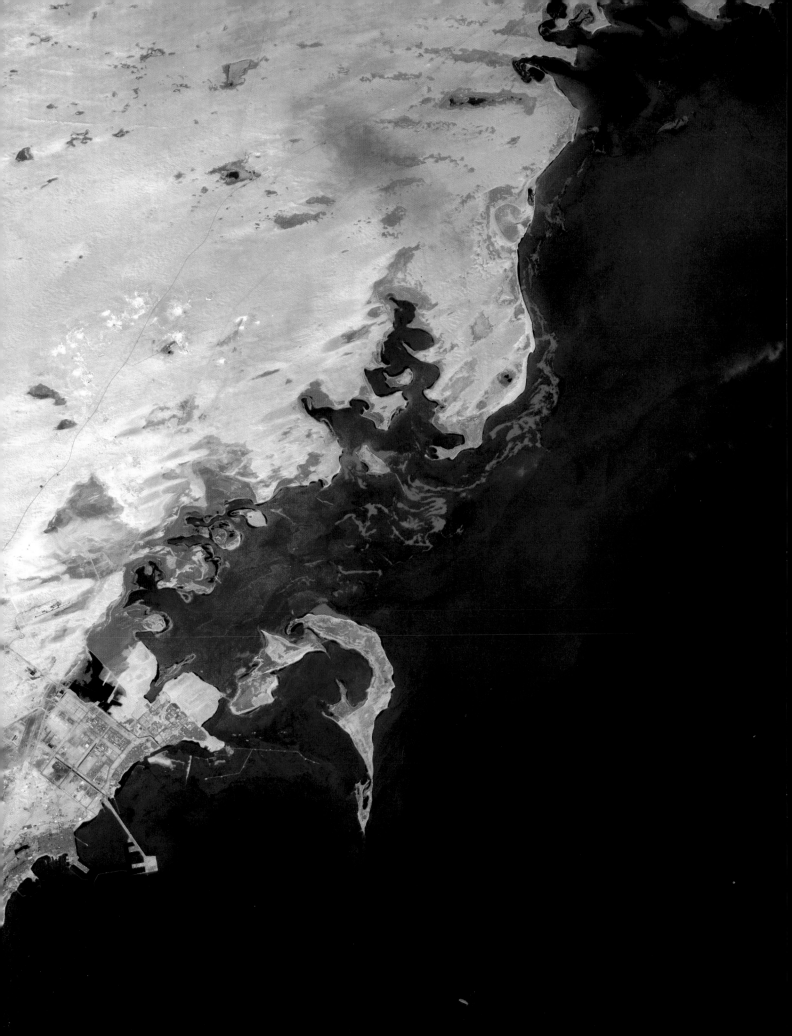

An oil-encrusted cormorant struggles along a Persian Gulf beach blackened by an environmental catastrophe. A message lettered in oil (opposite) names the Iraqi leader who ordered the oil spill. Saddam Hussein's victims called the deliberate spill an act of "ecological terrorism."
GEORGES MERILLON / GAMMA-LIAISON
OPPOSITE: JIM LUKOSKI / BLACK STAR

were targeting all of his command and control facilities, Saddam was hearing the official word. "We had him convinced that we had every single command and control (facility) targeted and had the weapons to hit them," a high-ranking U.S. intelligence officer said. "We didn't know where they all were. But we squashed enough of them for him to think we knew where everyone was.

"We interviewed a captured Iraqi general who said he couldn't walk to the latrine without wondering if a B-52 would bomb him. He believed we were watching him, targeting him. Saddam caught this, too. He didn't dare go to a major command facility. We reduced him to running the war out of the back of a jeep in a Baghdad residential neighborhood."

Hyperbole aside, Saddam, in fact, operated out of Winnebago-style vehicles that served as mobile headquarters. The Pentagon's disinformation denied him access to his best facilities for controlling the war.

The biggest allied deception – the threatened amphibious assault against Iraqi forces in Kuwait – produced the biggest Iraqi reaction and undoubtedly saved the lives of many coalition troops. For weeks, beginning soon after the arrival of U.S. Marines in the Persian Gulf, television cameras recorded the "rehearsals" of a Marine assault on the beaches of Kuwait.

During these exercises, telegenic U.S. Navy battleships pounded the prospective beachheads and impressive air-cushion landing craft skimmed across the waves. Seeing these images on television, Saddam built up Kuwaiti coastal defenses and reinforced his troops. He was wrong again. An assault would come from the sea, but not in the form of a Marine landing.

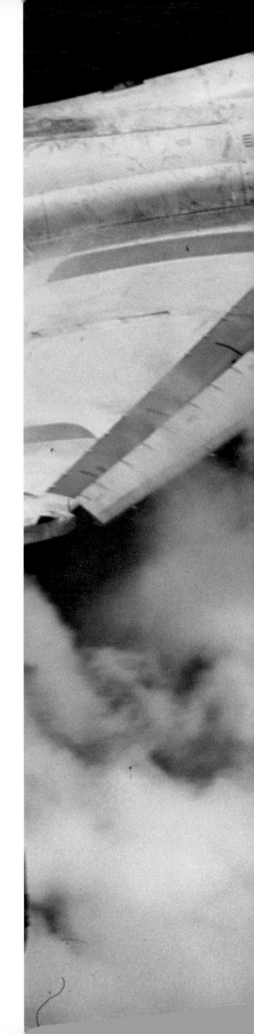

THUNDER FROM THE SEA

The naval buildup in the Gulf area was massive – the largest since World War II. By the start of Desert Storm, the U.S. Navy had more than 100 ships in the Persian Gulf, Arabian Sea, Red Sea, and eastern Mediterranean. Fifty ships from coalition navies also steamed in those waters. The use of naval forces in Desert Shield permitted nations that were unable or unwilling to commit ground forces to be active participants in opposing Saddam Hussein's invasion of Kuwait.

From the early days of August 1990, warships had been enforcing the embargo of Iraq ordered by the United Nations. But they were also preparing for war. Had Saddam Hussein invaded Saudi Arabia immediately after his conquest of Kuwait, while U.S. air and ground forces were only beginning to arrive in the area, planes from U.S. carrier decks would have been a principal means of defense against attacking Iraqi planes and troops. In addition to the cruisers, destroyers, and frigates which protected the carriers and helped to enforce the embargo, the U.S. naval forces in the Gulf included the world's only operational battleships, the USS *Missouri* (BB-63) and *Wisconsin* (BB-64). These dreadnoughts, launched almost 50 years earlier, were still impressive with their long, graceful lines, and tall superstructures, with each ship having nine 16-inch (406-mm.) guns projecting ominously from three massive turrets. Those guns could each send a 1,900-pound (862 kg.) high-explosive projectile against targets 23 miles (37 km.) away with great accuracy.

"There's a lot of years left in these old gals," sighed Captain David Bill, commanding officer of the *Wisconsin*. "They may be old chronologically, but

Steam escapes from the catapult tracks in the steel deck of the carrier America *(CV-66) as she maneuvers in Middle East waters to launch A-6E Intruders.*

PASCAL MAITRE / GAMMA-LIAISON

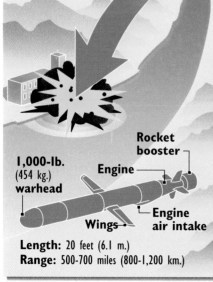

TOMAHAWK MISSILE

The Tomahawk missile is essentially an aircraft with a computer for a pilot. It can be launched from the ground or sea. This weapon is small but potent, able to topple a reinforced concrete building.

1 LAUNCH: Rocket booster punches missile out of launcher, fins deploy, wings extend, engine's air intake pops down.

2 FLIGHT: Engine starts after booster motor burns out.

3 FOLLOWS TERRAIN: Missile's computer uses altitude-sensing radar to reach target. Computer compares terrain with maps programmed in its memory; missile flies at very low altitudes on way to target.

1,000-lb. (454 kg.) warhead

Rocket booster

Engine

Engine air intake

Wings

Length: 20 feet (6.1 m.)
Range: 500-700 miles (800-1,200 km.)

SOURCE: KNIGHT-RIDDER TRIBUNE NEWS

they're really teenagers, and they're still ready to go to work." Bill's views were in reality the epitaph for the two battleships; their two sister ships had recently been retired from service. The "Mighty Mo," on whose deck the Japanese surrendered at the end of World War II, and the *Wisconsin* were scheduled to follow them into "mothballs" immediately after the Gulf crisis. Although impressive, the battleships were too expensive to operate (each was manned by some 1,600 men) and their capabilities were limited in comparison with new missile-armed ships. Still, for the brief war in the Gulf, the battleships would be impressive and would help to mislead Saddam.

Also coming into the Gulf were Navy amphibious ships carrying Marines and the helicopters, amphibious tractors, and air-cushion landing craft to put them ashore. By mid-January, 31 amphibious ships were cruising in the Gulf with more than 17,000 Marines on board. At the peak of Desert Storm, almost one-half of the active-duty strength of the Corps – 93,000 Marines – were ashore and afloat in the Gulf area, with another 5,000 Marines afloat in ships in the Mediterranean, (The Marines called up 24,324 reservists during the war.)

General A.M. (Al) Gray, Commandant of the Marine Corps, declared: "There are four kinds of Marines: those in Saudi Arabia, those going to Saudi Arabia, those who want to go to Saudi Arabia, and those who don't want to go to Saudi Arabia but are going anyway."

Upon arrival in the Gulf, Marines aboard amphibious ships conducted landing exercises along the Oman and Saudi coasts. The message to Saddam was becoming clear: Marines, supported by battleship guns and carrier planes, were planing to assault the coast of Kuwait or, possibly, Iraq. One of these exercises had the provocative code name Imminent Thunder.

Other U.S. and coalition ships in the Gulf included store and ammunition ships and oilers, to keep the fleet supplied with "beans, bullets, and black oil," enabling them to stay at sea indefinitely. The hospital ships *Mercy* (T-AH-19) and *Comfort* (T-AH-20) stood ready in the Gulf to handle coalition casualties. These rebuilt tankers each displace almost 70,000 tons (71,120 metric tons) fully loaded, as much as an aircraft carrier. These ships each have 12 operating rooms, extensive X-ray facilities, an 80-bed intensive care facility, beds for another 1,000 patients, and a complete pharmacy. Normally laid up with a partial crew, the ships took on-board additional civilian seamen and more than 1,000 Navy personnel – doctors, nurses, pharmacists, technicians, and corpsmen quickly ordered to the ships from naval hospitals in the United States. In Desert Shield/Desert Storm, they would treat thousands of U.S., coalition, and Iraqi troops, most for non-combat injuries and illness. (The Navy also set up a large field hospital ashore to support the Marines, who rely on the Navy for medical support.)

Also in the Gulf were mine countermeasure ships, small, wood or fiberglass vessels that hunted the mines being laid at night by Iraqi ships. The mine countermeasure ships were supplemented by large MH-53E Sea Dragon helicopters carried on the U.S. helicopter carrier *Tripoli* (LPH-10). These helicopters towed a variety of devices that could simulate the passage of a ship to detonate mines.

During the more than five months of the Desert Shield buildup, the coalition ships in the Gulf were hard at work, examining ships in the area for contraband, searching for mines, and carrying out landing exercises. Planes from U.S. aircraft carriers in the area flew search and reconnaissance flights over the Gulf, with missile-armed fighters always at the ready should Iraqi aircraft threaten the fleet or eastern Saudi Arabia.

By mid-January, three carrier battle groups were in the Gulf and three more in the Red Sea. These represented half the active carrier strength of the U.S. Navy. The air wings aboard the carriers varied in size, with about 85 planes on each ship. Most ships had two squadrons of F-14A Tomcat fighters; two squadrons of F/A-18 Hornet strike-fighters, a dual-mission aircraft; and one or two squadrons of *Continued on page 170*

A Tomahawk cruise missile climbs skyward from the battleship Wisconsin in the Persian Gulf and (left) a Tomahawk streaks over Baghdad (trees in foreground) as it heads for a predetermined target.
ABOVE: DAN YOUNG / CNN
LEFT: ALI YURTSEVER / GAMMA-LIAISON

A CH-53E Sea Stallion heavy-lift helicopter lands on an amphibious ship in the Persian Gulf. More "amphibs" steam behind her as the Navy and Marines stood ready for a major landing – that never came.

A-6E Intruder all-weather attack aircraft. Each carrier also had several anti-submarine, radar surveillance, and electronic jamming aircraft. The carrier-based aircraft were supplemented by shore-based maritime patrol and electronic surveillance aircraft. Navy HH-60H Seahawk combat rescue helicopters were based in Saudi Arabia. (Those "hawks" joined with Air Force HH-60G Pave Hawk helicopters in flying rescue missions throughout the area – some into Iraq – to pick up downed coalition fliers.) It was an impressive array of maritime aircraft that supported the build-up and war.

On the afternoon of January 16, the coalition warships were getting ready to go to war. In the U.S. Navy's missile ships, target information was fed into the guidance systems of the Tomahawk missiles. On the carrier decks, aircraft were being fueled and armed. Their pilots, like their land-based colleagues at Saudi airfields, were issued target folders that described their targets, approach routes, identification codes, and other information needed for the coordinated air war.

Late on the night of January 16, the carriers began turning into the wind and catapulting their strike planes and fighters into the air. Round-trip flights for planes flying from the Red Sea carriers, including time for in-flight refuelings, were some five hours for those planes attacking targets deep in Iraq. A short time later the Tomahawks began flying from their steel boxes and vertical launching cells on the warships. During the air campaign 16 battleships, cruisers, and destroyers would launch Tomahawks against targets in Iraq. Two U.S. nuclear-propelled submarines, the *Pittsburgh* (SSN-720) and *Louisville* (SSN-724), would also shoot Tomahawks, the first "war shots" fired by U.S. submarines since the end of World War II.

Vice Admiral Stanley R. Arthur, the Central Command naval commander, called the Tomahawks the "reach out and touch someone" weapon that, "During periods of bad weather when you needed to keep the pressure on Baghdad, you could continue to keep their eyes (as well as the cameras of CNN) open. The pinpoint accuracy and resulting low risk of collateral damage were what kept this system in the air when others were diverted to secondary targets."

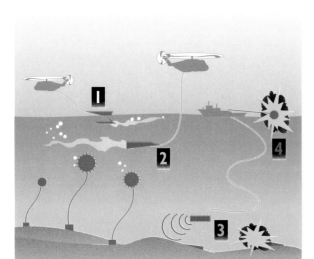

COUNTERING IRAQI MINES

Coalition helicopters and minehunters search for and destroy Iraqi mines in the Persian Gulf.

1 MH-53 Sea Dragon helicopters tow a hydrofoil sled fitted with devices to detonate magnetic and acoustic mines.

2 Sea Dragons tow a Magnetic Orange Pipe (MOP) to detonate shallow-water mines.

3 Non-magnetic minehunters operate cable-controlled remote vehicles to examine objects on the sea floor with close-range sonar and TV cameras. Bottom mines are difficult to distinguish from wrecks and "junk" on the sea floor; if a mine is found, a small explosive charge is placed next to it and detonated by a timer.

4 Moored mines are detonated by helicopter-towed devices; they sometimes break loose and float; when sighted, they are detonated by ship or helicopter gunfire.

SOURCE: THE SHIPS AND AIRCRAFT OF THE U.S. FLEET

The 500 aircraft on the six carrier decks were joined in the air war by Marine aircraft based ashore and on amphibious ships. Marine helicopters and AV-8B Harrier "jump jet" attack planes, which could take-off and land vertically or with a short run, flew strikes into Kuwait from helicopter carriers in the Gulf. And, in one of many instances of inter-service cooperation in the war, U.S. Army gun-toting OH-58D helicopters flew from the frigate *Nicholas* (FFG-47) in the Gulf to attack offshore oil platforms occupied by Iraqi troops that were firing on coalition aircraft.

Attacking on the night of January 16-17, the Army-Navy team and a Kuwaiti patrol ship used naval gunfire and helicopter fire to sweep the nine platforms. Guns, radios, and documents were then removed from the platforms and 23 Iraqi prisoners were taken. Another frigate, the *Curts* (FFG-38), sent in Navy commandos, called SEALs (Sea-Air-Land team), to assault Jazirat Qurah Island, about 16 miles (26 km.) off the Kuwaiti coast on the afternoon of January 24. Coming ashore by helicopters and small boats, the SEALs captured a variety of weapons and night-vision devices before abandoning the small piece of Kuwaiti territory. Twenty-nine Iraqis were captured on the island, and the *Curts* got another 22 from a minelayer that naval aircraft and surface ships destroyed.

When U.S. Navy helicopters investigated reports of Iraqis offering to surrender on the nearby island of Umm al Maradim, they were fired upon by a score of

Iraqi small craft. The helicopters returned fire from their machine guns, sinking four and damaging several others. Carrier-based A-6E Intruders were called in to attack the fleeing boats. On January 29, Marines in helicopters from the USS Okinawa (LPH-3) assaulted and captured the island, which is 12 miles (19 km.) off the Kuwaiti coast.

On January 30, about 20 Iraqi naval ships and small craft attempted to flee to Iran. Naval aircraft attacked and destroyed all but one of the vessels, a Soviet-built Osa II missile craft, which escaped to Iran. Those craft armed with Exocet or Styx anti-ship missiles made no attempt to attack U.S. ships in the Gulf.

The Navy's SEALs as well as other U.S. and British special forces were invaluable in gleaning intelligence during raids into Iraqi territory. The SEALs, however, had the doubly dangerous assignment of making their presence known to the Iraqi forces in Kuwait, to make it appear as if an amphibious landing was imminent. The issue of an amphibious landing became one of the most controversial of the Gulf War. Amphibious landings are the forte of the U.S. Marine Corps, and large numbers of ships, aircraft, helicopters, and specialized equipment had been developed and procured to carry out assaults from the sea. But there was no amphibious landing in the Gulf War.

Although two Marine brigades and a separate battalion were embarked in the amphibious ships in the Gulf, it was not until January that the Marines sent a senior officer, Major General John J. Sheehan, to coordinate amphibious operations. General Gray later said that from the outset, the intimations of a landing on the Kuwaiti coast were part of a deception plan. He explained to the authors that plans were drawn up for other, real landings: to capture islands off the Kuwaiti and Iraqi coasts as a diplomatic move; at Al Faw, on the Kuwait-Iraq border, which could block the Iraqi port city of Basra; at the Kuwaiti port of Umm Qasr, which would permit the Marines and follow-up coalition troops to drive inland if there was a slowdown in the main allied thrusts into southern Kuwait and Iraq. The amphibious assault option was a flexible one.

The fast sealift ship Regulus *(T-AKR-292) refuels from an oiler in the Gulf; replenishment underway enabled some coalition ships to stay at sea for the duration of the operation.*
SCOTT M. ALLEN / U.S. NAVY

171

Carrier operations were conducted around the clock throughout Desert Shield and Desert Storm; (above) an F-14 Tomcat fighter is catapulted from a carrier. One of hundreds of flight deck crewmen who move, rearm, refuel, and launch aircraft (right), awaits a taxiing aircraft; the chains are used to tie down planes on the deck.
BOTH: SCOTT M. ALLEN / U.S. NAVY

The threat of landings forced Saddam to keep several divisions along the coast and to reinforce his coastal defenses with guns, barbed wire, and mines. The Department of Defense said that four Iraqi divisions were set to defend the coast of Kuwait; other estimates said as many as ten of the Iraqi divisions in the area were preparing to counter the anticipated amphibious landings. The only combat landings in the Kuwaiti theater were by SEALs. Marines did land elsewhere during Desert Shield/Desert Storm. On January 3, the U.S. Embassy in Mogadishu, Somalia, asked for immediate evacuation as the two-week-old civil war was threatening all Westerners in the east African country. Armed looters were already in the embassy compound.

Operation Sharp Edge was started immediately. A Navy amphibious ship in the Indian Ocean flew off two large CH-53E Sea Stallion helicopters loaded with 70 Marines. The ship was 460 nautical miles (852 km.) from Mogadishu and the helicopters needed a night aerial refueling by Marine C-130 cargo planes flying from Bahrain. The two helicopters arrived over Mogadishu early on January 4 and landed on the embassy grounds. Some of the Marines were brought in to protect the embassy, while others went into the corpse-littered streets to rescue Americans and other foreigners, including the Soviet ambassador and his staff. That same day, even as the embassy was being fired on, the CH-53Es took off with 62 evacuees. They landed on the helicopter carrier *Guam* (LPH-9), which had steamed to a position 350 nautical miles (648 km.) offshore, with 63 passengers. During the flight a Navy hospital corpsman had delivered a pregnant passenger's baby. The next day, other helicopters from the carrier began airlifting more evacuees, with a total of 260 men, women, and children from ten countries being successfully lifted out of the besieged capital.

The media were encouraged to concentrate on showing the world the high-tempo carrier operations, which accounted for about a quarter of the coalition air sorties and Tomahawk launches. However, every day of Desert Storm the ships of the coalition navies continued to enforce the U.N. embargo. During Desert Storm, U.S. warships on several occasions had to fire warning shots at Iraqi ships in the Gulf to force them to stop. *Continued on page 176*

One ship, the *Amuriyah*, had refused to allow a boarding party on board even after the frigate *Reasoner* (FF-1063) fired warning shots with machine guns and her 3-inch (76.2-mm.) gun. Navy F-14 Tomcat and F/A-18 Hornet aircraft were called in to make low-level passes, screaming over the ship but not firing at her. Still, the *Amuriyah's* master would not stop. Finally, two Marine helicopters entered the fray. While one hovered over the ship to provide covering fire if needed, the second landed an assault team that quickly seized control of the ship, without bloodshed.

The *Amuriyah* was then boarded by Australian and U.S. Navy search teams accompanied by a Coast Guard law enforcement detachment. She was not carrying prohibited cargo and was allowed to proceed. The master's actions were never fully explained.

After the initial boardings in the Persian Gulf, it became evident that no ships would be allowed to carry war materiel or other specified cargo to Iraq, and Iraqi oil could not be shipped out of the country (although Saddam Hussein offered it free to any country that would call for it). As a result, few vessels were found inbound for or outbound from Iraq and Kuwait. Instead, the coalition warships sought cargoes that were going to Iraq through third-party ports. Consequently, some 93 percent of all boardings took place in the Red Sea, with the remaining activity taking place when Iraqi ships were sighted in the North Arabian Sea and Persian Gulf. By the end of hostilities on February 27, the coalition's warships had carried out almost 7,000 interceptions of merchant ships in the Gulf area, with nearly 1,000 boardings having taken place. The interceptions continued, with Iraq losing an estimated $30 million every day because of the naval stranglehold on its economy.

The Navy continuously had to be prepared to defend against the threat of Iraqi attacks on coalition warships in the Gulf as well as against the stream of merchant ships bringing in weapons, munitions, and supplies for the coalition, and tankers carrying crude oil from the Gulf. Mines and missiles were

the two threats feared most by Vice Admiral Arthur. The U.S. frigate *Stark* (FFG-31) was victim of a missile attack in 1987 and the frigate *Samuel B. Roberts* (FFG-58) was severely damaged by a mine in 1988, both in the Persian Gulf.

Iraq had the air-launched French Exocet anti-ship missiles, which had been used by the Argentines against British ships in the 1982 war in the Falklands, and also the land-based Silkworm missiles that had been purchased from China. To counter these threats, U.S. Navy and coalition aircraft struck at Iraqi ships and small craft continuously, sinking several. Within two weeks of the start of the air campaign, some 35 Iraqi naval craft had been sunk or severely damaged by U.S. and coalition aircraft and ships; all Iraqi missile craft had been destroyed. None had come out to attack allied ships in the Gulf. Two Iraqi Mirage F1 aircraft seen flying with Exocet anti-ship missiles were shot down by a Saudi F-15C fighter.

The Iraqis did attack U.S. naval forces with missiles: On February 25, an Iraqi-launched Silkworm missile streaked from shore toward the *Missouri*. A Navy electronic surveillance aircraft had detected the missile and gave warning to the British destroyer *Gloucester*, riding "shotgun" for the battleship. The *Gloucester* fired two Sea Dart interceptor missiles that destroyed the incoming Silkworm. A second Silkworm was fired but fell into the Gulf. U.S. Navy strike aircraft immediately attacked the missile launch site.

Low-cost, easy-to-plant, and hard-to-find mines were also used by Iraq. About 1,000 were used, most laid on the seafloor of the Gulf. U.S. helicopters and minesweepers and coalition minehunters searched continuously for them. On February 18 the cruiser *Princeton* (CG-59) and the helicopter carrier *Tripoli* struck mines in waters off the Kuwaiti coast that had been previously swept. Ironically, the *Tripoli* was operating MH-53E minesweeping helicopters at the time. Both ships were damaged, the *Princeton* more so and had to be towed to port. Several men were injured in both ships, but neither was in danger of sinking. None of the other coalition ships struck mines despite the large number in the Gulf. Vice Admiral Arthur, however, would conclude from the Gulf operations that "Our mine countermeasures capability is inadequate." Many of his colleagues would probably have added, "and we were lucky, this time."

The battleships had to steam relatively close to shore to strike targets with their 16-inch (406-mm.) guns. While naval aircraft searched out and attacked possible Silkworm missile sites that could threaten the dreadnoughts, coalition minesweepers concentrated on clearing paths for the battleships. Mines and the missiles were not the only problems faced by the coalition navies.

The Gulf is a relatively restricted area and there were many doubts whether carriers would have enough sea room to launch and recover aircraft in those waters. By the end of the war, four carriers were operating in the Gulf, the fourth having entered on February 14 in anticipation of the coming ground war. Also in the relatively restricted waters of the Gulf were the two battleships and scores of other naval ships, numerous super tankers, and countless merchant ships. Careful planning and navigation prevented collisions; but the Gulf was still a crowded body of water.

In some respects the most difficult problem for naval forces in the Gulf was communications. The computers in Navy carriers were not compatible with those at Central Command headquarters and every day aircraft had to fly computer disks out to the carriers. Beyond these problems with communication systems there was too much paperwork in running the war. "If Iraq had perfected a paper-seeking missile, we would have been in deep trouble," wrote Vice Admiral Arthur. "Trees were big losers in Desert Storm—not trees in the Middle East, but trees in the United States that supplied all the paper we went through."

When the allied ground offensive began early on February 24, the carriers and battleships stepped up their strikes against targets in occupied Kuwait and eastern Iraq. Through February 27, Navy and Marine pilots had flown 26,000 combat and support sorties in Desert Storm. By the time the allied offensive halted the *Missouri* had fired more than 750 rounds of 16-inch (406-mm.) ammunition and the *Wisconsin* more than 320 rounds. Most of their firings were made with Marine-controlled Pioneer drones identifying targets and spotting the fall of shot.

The Pioneers are small, unmanned aircraft that carry television cameras which transmit their images back to the fire control consoles of the battleships; gunfire is called down on targets sighted by the Pioneers. Marines on board the battleships control the drones by radio signals.

The Israeli-developed Pioneers were also flown by Marines and Army troops ashore with more than 1,000 Pioneer flights being recorded during the Gulf operations. Each battleship went into action with five Pioneers; all but two were lost through accidents and enemy fire during Desert Storm.

Their use was considered a complete success. In addition to gunfire spotting, the Pioneers carried out general surveillance work, including scouting missions for coalition troops ashore. On February 27, a drone detected two small boats fleeing Faylaka Island. Navy attack planes were called in and destroyed the craft, believed to be carrying Iraqi secret police. Subsequently, hundreds of Iraqi soldiers on Faylaka Island surrendered to the drone from the *Missouri*, which was circling over the island after a bombardment of Iraqi positions.

But heavy ground fighting was expected before there would be mass surrenders by the Iraqi forces.

PRECEDING PAGE
A momentary pause in flight deck operations catches an F-14 Tomcat being readied for a catapult launch; inset shows part of a carrier's combat direction center.
THOMAS HARTWELL / TIME MAGAZINE
INSET: BARRY IVERSON / TIME MAGAZINE

Unmanned Pioneer aircraft – called drones and Remotely Piloted Vehicles (RPVs) – were used by the Marines ashore and from battleships for reconnaissance and gunfire spotting. The Israeli-designed Pioneer RPVs are shown being launched from a ship and, after a mission, "landing" into an arresting net. The Army also flew Pioneers from Saudi Arabia.
BOTH: U.S. NAVY

PRELUDE TO BATTLE

General Norman Schwarzkopf, U.S.commander of coalition forces, awoke each morning with the same question: Has Saddam moved his forces? Schwarzkopf went directly to a map showing the latest deployment of Iraqi troops on the coming battlefield. He wanted to see whether Saddam Hussein had begun shifting forces to defend his exposed right (western) flank. Schwarzkopf, a massive prototype of the professional soldier, was trained to think in terms of enemy forces. But he thought of his enemy as a man, Saddam Hussein.

"Someone once asked me what is the difference between me and Saddam Hussein," Schwarzkopf told television interviewer David Frost in a long and enlightening recollection of the war. "The answer is I have a conscience and he doesn't . . . In my mind, he is an evil man."

What Schwarzkopf saw on the map was Saddam Hussein "building very, very heavy obstacles and barriers in front of his forces, which could have given us a lot of problems. But, the more you watched his deployment of forces, the more he was stuffing forces into a bag, for all intents and purposes, called Kuwait. And he was not defending that [western] flank."

When Schwarzkopf looked at his battle maps, he was looking at the work of thousands of intelligence specialists gleaning from hundreds of sources a detailed picture of Iraqi strength, locations, and movements. The sources ranged from KH-11 spy satellites that overflew the Middle East to U.S. and British reconnaissance teams that trekked or flew by helicopter into Iraq and Kuwait seeking information on the enemy. The KH-11 satellites, flying some 120 to 300 miles (193 to 483 km.) above the earth, were electro-optical imaging craft that could instantly transmit views of Iraq to U.S. ground facilities. Because clouds and darkness could reduce the KH-11's vision, Lacrosse radar imaging and Magnum and Vortex electronic eavesdropping satellites were also used.

U.S. Marines churn desert sands as they train for war in M60A1 tanks. They rehearse for Desert Storm by day; they will go to the real battle by night.

FRED MAYER / MAGNUM

In Saudi Arabia, a U.S. soldier carries
two vital objects for war in the desert, a
bottle of water and a rifle.

STEVE BENT / KATZ / WOODFIN CAMP

Also overflying the Middle East were U.S. global-positioning, meteorological, and launch-warning satellites. Positioning satellites permitted U.S. troops on the ground to use hand-held receiving devices to determine their exact position without reference to any ground features. Meteorological satellites produced weather pictures, highlighting sandstorms and other phenomena that could affect air and ground operations. And, warning satellites had infrared sensors to detect and track missile launches, including Scuds, and could immediately alert allied commanders.

At lower levels, coalition photo and electronic reconnaissance aircraft streaked across Iraqi and Kuwaiti skies day and night. Radar planes gave detailed radar pictures of Iraqi movements – day or night – and provided continuous radar pictures of the air space. Schwarzkopf was getting a more detailed view of their battlefield than any previous commander in history.

Schwarzkopf's plan was built upon a military textbook formula: METTT, mission, enemy, terrain, troops available, and time. Schwarzkopf knew his mission, knew his enemy, and on November 8, 1990, he knew what troops would be available; that was the day President Bush ordered 200,000 more U.S.

troops added to the 230,000 already in and en route to Saudi Arabia. As for time, that depended upon Schwarzkopf's commander in chief, President Bush.

Schwarzkopf was a soldier who had been wounded in Vietnam, where his valor won him three Silver Stars. He knew what war was. "Casualties were his greatest concern," a general in Central Command headquarters told the authors. "He always wanted to know how many pilots were downed, and when he was planning the ground war, he wondered how many young kids are going to have to be hung up on the wire of those obstacles." Avoiding a frontal assault on the obstacles was the key aspect of his battle plan.

Schwarzkopf was planning an offensive war like no other in modern times. Electronics had given him eyes for watching the battlefield and had also blinded the eyes of his enemy. The blinding had begun on the first night of the air campaign, when coalition aircraft began to destroy Iraqi communications, radar, and reconnaissance aircraft. After that, every Iraqi radar that was switched on was quickly detected by U.S. Wild Weasel and Prowler aircraft and attacked with anti-radiation missiles.

Coalition forces were also aided by intelligence from Israel, whose agents are

Alone in the desert night, an airman totes up a day's cargo. Batteries of computers did not cut back war's endless paperwork.

PERRY HEIMER / U.S. AIR FORCE

181

British soldiers leap from a Puma helicopter during a training exercise in the Saudi desert.

PATRICK BAZ / AFP

highly knowledgeable of the region, and who had kept abreast of Iraqi military and technological developments. There was a continuous exchange of information between Israeli and U.S. intelligence agencies. One U.S. official noted, "We gave them much more intelligence, but they gave us key material."

With his aircraft destroyed, grounded or in Iran, Saddam had no aerial reconnaissance or fire power. "I could move the forces without him being able to see them," Schwarzkopf told Frost, "and, more importantly, even if he saw them, he couldn't do anything about it because we were going to control the air."

The blueprint for Schwarzkopf's version of the mother of battles was laid out in the U.S. Army's AirLand Battle Manual: "Envelopment avoids the enemy's

front, where his forces are most protected and his fires most easily concentrated. Instead, while fixing the defender's attention forward by supporting or diversionary attacks, the attacker maneuvers his main effort around or over the enemy's defenses to strike at his flanks and rear." The strategy was proven in Schwarzkopf's lifetime by Rommel, Patton, MacArthur, and other battlefield commanders.

Desert warfare added another element to the AirLand strategy. Troops initially had to live with heat, lack of cover, and a scarcity of water. Taking their cue from the nocturnal scorpions, troops made the cooler night their environment. Nighttime training was practical, for it kept down cases of sunstroke and heat exhaustion. And the training was a rehearsal for the real battle would be launched in the dark. Troops learned to prowl at night along routes marked by cyalume light sticks, the kind that American children carry around on Halloween night.

Morale remained high through the long months of waiting for the ground war. But by February, after months in the desert, some soldiers were getting restless. CNN correspondent Greg LaMotte overheard one soldier say to another, "If I don't get to kill somebody soon, I'm going to kill somebody."

For many U.S. forces, life in the desert was not a new experience. U.S. soldiers and Egyptian forces join together every year in maneuvers called Operation Bright Star. And U.S. Army troops regularly serve in U.N. peace-keeping deployments to the Sinai desert. But such a large scale U.S. military presence in the Middle East was unprecedented.

Saudi Arabia, guardian of the sacred Islamic cities of Mecca and Medina, had maintained an image of Muslim orthodoxy. The Saudis had been able to keep predominately Christian Westerners out of sight. The oil industry cooperated by putting employees in compounds, advising Western women not to drive, and overtly obeying anti-alcohol laws.

Confronted with the possibility of invasion and inevitable conquest by Saddam, King Fahd did not hesitate to accept the U.S. offer of aid. The coalition was born. By the time Schwarzkopf was ready to start the ground war, his army had troops and airmen from 21 countries. His men and women included 200 Czech chemical-warfare specialists who had trained with the Warsaw Pact to fight the armies of the West and some 300 Afghan *mujaheddin* rebels taking leave from their fight against Afghanistan's Continued on page 186

FOLLOWING PAGE
From "somewhere in Saudi Arabia," an 8-inch self-propelled howitzer of the 2nd Marine Division fires at Iraqi positions in Kuwait.

SADAYUKI MIKAMI / AP WIDE WORLD PHOTOS

Mrs. Gayle Edwards, widow of Marine Captain Jonathan Edwards, clutches the hands of their sons, (left) Bennett (in his father's flying jacket) and Spencer, at Arlington National Cemetery. He also left a daughter, Adriane, 8. Captain Edwards was killed in action while piloting a Cobra helicopter that was escorting a medivac helicopter.

DOUG MILLS / AP WIDE WORLD PHOTOS

government. Saudi Arabia provided some 45,000 troops and the other Gulf states sent about 10,000 more; Egypt sent 38,500. Other troops came from Syria, which had harbored anti-Western terrorists, and Bangladesh, one of the world's poorest countries.

Among the United Kingdom forces were such illustrious units as the Queen's Dragoon Guards, the Queen's Royal Irish Hussars, the Scots Guard, the Queen's Own Highlanders, and the Royal Green Jackets, an especially fraternal and witty choice: The unit had been a refuge for Tories during the American Revolutionary War; and prior to America's entry into World War II, Americans who went to England to fight were assigned to the Green Jackets.

Another touch of World War II nostalgia came from the French, whose Rapid Action Force established a close rapport with the U.S. 82nd Airborne Division. The 82nd is legendary in France because it liberated Saint-More-l'Eglise on D-Day, 1944. It was the first town in France freed by Americans.

Scattered through the Arabian forces in the polyglot coalition army were detachments of U.S. Special Operations Forces. These commands had a job classification new to the military: "facilitators." The special-forces troops lived

with Arab units, learned their ways, and some knew their language. They provided a reliable linguistic link between the Arab units and Central Command during training, as they would in combat. Speaking of the facilitators' role, an officer familiar with secret missions of the Special Forces, said, "Although many of the other actions were more dramatic – and will remain obscure for a while – few, if any, were more important."

Iraq was losing about 100 tanks and numerous troops a day to coalition air power when Iran, then the Soviet Union, made diplomatic moves to stop the war before the coalition ground attack began. On February 10, Iran offered to mediate. U.S. Secretary of State Baker asked, "Mediate? Mediate what?" and Iran's peace offer vanished.

The Soviet diplomatic moves were complex and more deeply rooted than U.S. actions. Foreign Minister Eduard Shevardnadze had helped draft the U.N. resolution authorizing the use of arms to force Iraq from Kuwait. This had guaranteed that President Bush would be able to assemble the coalition. If the Soviets had blocked the resolution, the war against Iraq would have been not a U.N. war, but an American one. An earlier Soviet contribution had been the end of the Cold War. As a Soviet official in Washington remarked to one of the authors, "Don't forget. If it weren't for us, you couldn't do what you did."

Shevardnadze never lost an opportunity to show his sympathy for the coalition. Prince Bandar bin Sultan, the Saudi ambassador to the United States (and an ex-fighter pilot, U.S.-trained), was in Moscow speaking to him soon after the invasion. "Shevardnadze looked at me," the prince recalled, "and he said, 'Prince Bandar, I am sad because those tanks that rolled over Kuwait were Russian tanks.' I looked him straight in the eye and I said, 'Mr. Minister, you're sad? I am sad because we paid for those tanks.'"

Shevardnadze's pro-American, anti-Iraqi stand may have led to his resignation. Soviet President Mikhail Gorbachev was playing the Mideast diplomacy game in two arenas. He wanted to side with the United States and to maintain ties with Iraq, long a customer for Soviet arms and in the 1970s a client state. For Gorbachev to play that side of the game, Shevardnadze had to go.

Soviet military officers, derided by Shevardnadze as "boys in colonel stripes," claimed he was so under·American influence that he planned to have Soviet troops join the coalition forces. The rising hard-liners kept up the pressure against him, and he resigned on December 20, warning that a dictatorship loomed in the Soviet Union's future.

Soviet President Mikhail Gorbachev took over the Persian Gulf diplomacy on February 10, saying he was sending a personal envoy Yevgeny Primakov, to

President Bush and Secretary of State Baker (above) huddle in the White House over a peace proposal from Soviet President Gorbachev.

DIRCK HALSTEAD / TIME MAGAZINE

Baghdad. "The . . . character of the military actions is creating a threat of going beyond the limits of the [U.N.] mandate," Gorbachev said. ". . . The flywheel is spinning faster and faster." He appealed to Saddam to leave Kuwait "and show realism."

After meeting with Saddam, Primakov told Gorbachev there was some hope, and Gorbachev passed this information to Bush. To maintain post-Cold War cordiality, Bush had to accept the Soviet initiative while Schwarzkopf was positioning forces for the ground war which was to begin February 21; Schwarzkopf later changed it to Sunday, February 24.

On Friday, February 15, as Gorbachev's vague peace plan stalled, the Iraqi Revolutionary Command Council announced that Iraq would "deal with" U.N. Resolution 660. Americans waking up to television news shows on Friday morning heard excited talk about an imminent end to the war. CNN's Peter Arnett, standing amid smiling, shouting Iraqis firing guns in the air, reported from Baghdad: "There's a celebration here."

After seeing how many strings were attached to the Iraqi announcement, President Bush denounced it as a "cruel hoax" and British Prime Minister John Major called it "something of a bogus sham." That would have been the end of the proposal if Gorbachev had not folded it into his own evolving plan. On February 21, the Soviets said the Iraqis had accepted a phased withdrawal to begin one day after a cease-fire. Bush publicly thanked Gorbachev for his help. Then, standing in the White House Rose Garden on Friday, February 22, he denounced Saddam's "scorched-earth policy against Kuwait" and gave him an ultimatum: Get out of Iraq, unconditionally, by Saturday noon, February 23.

For some coalition soldiers, the ground war had already begun. On the night of January 31 Iraqi tanks rolled into Khafji, six miles (9.6 km.) within Saudi Arabia. It was deserted except for several U.S. Marines there for reconnaissance and artillery spotting. The Marines managed to elude the invaders for 36 hours, some hiding in a building occupied by Iraqis.

In a battle punctuated by air strikes and close-support artillery fire, U.S. Marines fought side by side with Saudis and other Arab troops, driving the Iraqis from the town. Some 50 Saudis were killed or wounded and 11 Marines were killed - the first U.S. combat deaths on the ground.

Schwarzkopf, looking back on Khafji 24 days later, saw it as a sign that he had nothing to fear. His army of many nations would fight well. When the air war had begun he had told his troop, "I have seen in your eyes a fire of determination to get this war job done quickly." On February 24, as the ground war began, his confidence was higher than before.

Troops of the 82nd Airborne Division (top, opposite) train under live fire as they prepare for the ground war. Even before it began, a battle in the Saudi town of Khafji tested coalition soldiers. An armored personnel carrier (opposite, lower) burns outside Khafji's gates.

OPPOSITE TOP:
RUDI FREY / TIME MAGAZINE

OPPOSITE LOWER:
GEORGES MERILLON / GAMMA-LIAISON

THE 100-HOUR WAR

The battle for Khafji on January 31 was not the beginning of the ground phase of Desert Storm. But the intense, 12-hour firefight, in which U.S. Marines and Saudi and Qatari soldiers repulsed the Iraqi invaders, was a precursor of the battle to come. General Norman Schwarzkopf and his commanders were being patient, refusing to be drawn into a ground campaign ahead of their schedule. Armed with this initial victory to encourage his troops, Schwarzkopf pressed on with the air campaign while preparing to execute the coalition's opening moves of the ground war.

Inside Iraq and occupied Kuwait, elite coalition Special Forces teams carried out dangerous, long-range reconnaissance missions, locating Iraqi troops and relaying information concerning their numbers and their weapons. Teams positioned along the highway connecting Baghdad and Basra moved by night and burrowed into the desert by day to report on Iraqi troop movements. Other teams marked high-priority targets, such as Scud missile launchers, with lasers. On call from an inbound strike aircraft, they projected a laser beam onto the target, making it easier for a laser-guided "smart" weapon to home in and make the kill. This clandestine work, said General Schwarzkopf, "let us know what was going on out there." (Special Forces also carried out search-and-rescue missions for coalition pilots downed in Iraqi-controlled territory.)

By mid-February 1991, the allied air campaign had severed the supply lines from Baghdad to the more than 40 Iraqi divisions in the Kuwaiti area. Coalition forces had achieved undisputed air supremacy, and they used it to pound away at the defensive barriers erected by Iraqi troops along the southern border of Kuwait. Also targeted were the tanks, guns, short-range missiles, and troops defending those barriers. No army in history had ever been subjected to such a relentless, around-the-clock pounding. *Continued on page 196*

Continued on page 196

Performing cavalry's traditional fast-moving screening role, M1A1 tanks of U.S. Army's 3d Armored Cavalry Regiment dash across the rugged Iraqi desert. Sergeant Pat Armijo commands the closest tank.

LUCIAN PERKINS / THE WASHINGTON POST

PRECEDING PAGES

A Multiple Launch Rocket System (MLRS) of the U.S. Army's 1st Cavalry Division fires into Iraqi positions in preparation for the ground campaign. The MLRS can fire up to 12 rockets in a single load out to a distance of 20 miles (32 km.).

STEVE ELFERS / ARMY TIMES

U.S. Army AH-64 Apache attack helicopters gather to refuel and rearm near the burning Al Burgan oil field in Kuwait. Apaches opened the war by knocking out Iraqi early-warning radar stations. Throughout the campaign they were potent tank-killers.

ABBAS / MAGNUM

Many units in these front-line positions and in the formations behind them soon became captives in their own bunkers as it became too dangerous for them to leave their protection.

On the eve of the ground campaign, allied forces implemented a new bombing strategy designed to inflict heavy casualties and encourage Iraqi troops to surrender. The B-52s attacked the Iraqi positions with salvoes of 750-pound (340-kg.) bombs. Then, as the land campaign approached, specifically modified MC-130 Hercules cargo planes dropped 15,000-pound (6,818-kg.) "daisy-cutter" bombs off of their rear loading ramps to smash Iraqi positions. These bombs exploded above ground, compressing the earth and generating shock waves that collapsed bunkers. In addition, fuel-air-explosive bombs were used. These also inflicted severe damage, killing troops and detonating the minefields that were interlaced with Iraqi defensive belts. Fuel-air-exlosives release a mist of fuel that is then ignited and explodes, creating severe over-pressures and shock waves. It has been nicknamed "the poor man's nuke," because of its devastating effects. Aircraft also dropped napalm to ignite the oil pools or "fire trenches" that formed part of the defensive belts.

Between the bombings, other aircraft would release thousands of propaganda leaflets written in Arabic that encouraged Iraqi troops to give themselves up. The leaflets emphasized Arab hospitality, and offered the hope of continued life, instead of death in the sand. Saddam Hussein and his subordinate commanders took the leaflets seriously. So-called "morale squads" of Iraqi thugs searched bunkers and troop positions for evidence that troops were keeping the leaflets. Iraqi soldiers found with leaflets were, reportedly, punished and, in some instances, executed.

Despite the air, rocket, and artillery bombardments, several hundred thousand Iraqis remained huddled in bunkers under tons of sand in the Kuwaiti area. Iraq still had about 40 divisions in the region, including several Republican Guard divisions positioned in reserve behind the front lines. However, with each passing day the loss of men and equipment reduced the combat effectiveness of those divisions until some were impotent. While some troops were being killed and injured in the bombings, more were being demoralized as they were forced to cower in their fortifications and bunkers; desertions increased.

There was absolutely no Iraqi aircraft interference with the allied air efforts. However, Iraqi anti-aircraft guns and ground-launched missiles were still taking a toll of coalition aircraft, but the losses were extremely light in view of the number of sorties being flown and the size of the Iraqi air-defense forces.

During the week of February 17, coalition forces stepped up their short-range reconnaissance missions across the Kuwaiti and Iraqi borders. The coalition ground offensive was now scheduled to begin on February 21, "G-Day." But last-minute Soviet attempts at diplomatic negotiations put the plan on hold for another three days.

As a consequence of the air campaign, Saddam Hussein and his commanders were operating in the blind, ignorant of General Schwarzkopf's plans. Saddam's best glimpse at the coalition's strategy for the ground phases of Desert Storm had come a month earlier, during a news conference at the Pentagon in Washington, D.C., General Colin Powell, the Chairman of the Joint Chiefs of Staff, summarized how the campaign would develop: "Our strategy to go after this enemy is very, very simple," he said. "First we're going to cut it off and then we're going to kill it."

Before midnight on February 22, two U.S. Marine task forces, each of two-battalion size with several hundred troops—nicknamed "Grizzly" and "Taro"—slipped across the border into Kuwait to prepare paths through layered Iraqi defensive obstacle belts and minefields. Iraqi forces counterattacked, but the Marines defeated them and retained positions 12.5 miles (20 km.) inside Kuwait. The Marines' intrusion into Kuwait, and the raids and probes nearby, were intended to convince Iraqi field commanders that an attack across the border into Kuwait was imminent. A massive amphibious and air assault by U.S. Marine forces appeared likely as well, with 31 amphibious force ships carrying 17,000 Marines steaming off the Kuwaiti coast. Nearly a month earlier, Marines had captured Faylakah Island, located 15 miles (24 km.) east of Kuwait City. Faylakah commands the entrance to Kuwait Bay, and Iraqi commanders viewed its seizure as a necessary prelude to an amphibious operation against Kuwait.

These actions and the air campaign that blinded Iraqi reconnaissance enabled General Schwarzkopf to pull off a monumental deception. This is how he described it: "When we took out his air force, for all intents and purposes, we took out his ability to see what we were doing down here in Saudi Arabia. Once we had taken out his eyes, we did what could best be described as the 'Hail Mary play' in football. I think you recall when the quarterback is desperate for a touchdown at the very end, what he does is he sets up behind the center, and all of a sudden, every single one of his receivers goes way out to one flank, and they all run down the field as fast as they possibly can and into the end zone, and he lobs the ball. In essence, that's what we did.

"When we knew that he couldn't see us anymore, we did a massive movement of troops all the way out to the west, to the extreme west, because at that time we knew that he was still fixed in this area with the vast majority of his forces, and once the air campaign started, he would be incapable of moving out to counter this move, even if he knew we made it. There were some additional Iraqi troops out in this [western] area, but they did not have the capability nor the time to put

A wounded U.S. soldier (opposite) being evacuated by helicopter to the 5th Mobile Army Surgical Hospital, learns that one of his friends has been killed.

DAVID TURNLEY / BLACK STAR / DETROIT FREE PRESS

in the barrier that had been described by Saddam Hussein as an absolutely impenetrable tank barrier that no one would ever get through. I believe those were his words."

Despite his characterization of the operation as a Hail Mary play, General Schwarzkopf was far from desperate. There was no way in which the Iraqis could intercept the ball or even stop the play. The only issue was how many casualties the coalition force would suffer in achieving victory. Schwarzkopf sent two corps—the armor-heavy VII Corps and the XVIII Airborne Corps—secretly moving westward, south of the weakly defended Saudi-Iraqi border. So far as Iraqi commanders were concerned, the heavy concentration of allied forces along the Kuwaiti border had not budged. Near the border, the Iraqis monitored radio communications and daily activity of coalition forces that never changed, while the artillery and rocket duels across the border continued. But two of the allied corps were no longer there.

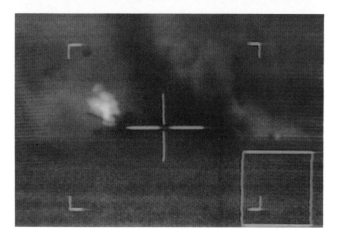

More than 250,000 troops in the two corps, among them the British 1st Armoured Division and French 6th Light Armored Division, were gone. Behind the allies' cloak of deception, the forces had shifted more than 200 miles (320 km.) westward, taking along thousands of tank and armored vehicles, several hundred heavy guns, and enough fuel, ammunition, and other supplies to fight for 60 days. That is like moving the entire population of Akron, Ohio, and all of their vehicles and worldly goods westward to Fort Wayne, Indiana, while the neighbors in Cleveland, a few miles to the north, think they are still at home.

General Schwarzkopf placed the move in perspective: "I can't recall any time in the annals of military history when this number of forces have moved over this distance to put themselves in a position to be able to attack. But what's more important, and I think it's very important, very important that I make this point, and that's these logistic bases. Not only did we move the troops out there, but we literally moved thousands and thousands of tons of fuel, of ammunition, of spare parts, of water, and of food out here in this area, because we wanted to have enough supplies on hand so if we launched this, if we got into a slugfest battle, which we very easily could have gotten into, we'd have enough supplies to last for 60 days. It was an absolute gigantic accomplishment, and I can't give credit enough to the logisticians and the transporters who were able to pull this off, for the superb support we had from the Saudi government, the literally thousands and thousands of drivers of every national origin who helped us in this move out here. And, of course, great credit goes to the commanders of those units who were also able to maneuver their forces out here and put them in this position."

The night of February 23-24 was cold, clear, and dark, the quarter-moon having set earlier that day. After periods of overcast skies and showers early in the week, the weather for the previous two days had been cool and partly cloudy. By contrast with the 110-degree Fahrenheit (43-degree Centigrade) days of August and September, nighttime temperatures dropped into the low 40s and upper 30s. Instead of dry sand blowing in their faces, now the troops endured rain and thunderstorms, and slogged through mud. Besides the sweaters, scarves, gloves, and field jackets that kept them warm, the troops also wore protective suits and rubber boots, to shield them during a chemical attack. "We fully expected them to use chemical weapons," said Marine Brigadier General Richard Neal, General Schwarzkopf's director of operations.

For the coalition forces, the waiting was nearly over. G-Day was here: At 4 A.M. Saudi time (8 P.M. in Washington), the allies launched the ground

offensive to liberate Kuwait.

Allied aircraft and helicopters crisscrossed the night sky, while naval and land-based artillery and rockets rained down on Iraqi positions. Along a more than 250-mile (402-km.) line, stretching westward from the seacoast, coalition forces were poised to strike northward on schedule. The allied troops had night-vision goggles and other devices to enable them to see the Iraqi lines clearly in darkness and mist, and in some areas smoke from burning oil wells.

The coalition assault line from the Persian Gulf coast began with the Joint Forces Command East, Saudi units reinforced with other Islamic units. Further west in the line was the I Marine Expeditionary Force, and adjacent on its western side was the other Islamic corps, called Joint Forces Command North. The Islamic forces were commanded by Saudi Lieutenant General Khalid bin Sultan. All Islamic units were accompanied by U.S. special forces to coordinate supporting artillery and naval gunfire, and to ensure close liaison among the advancing units. Continuing westward, the VII Corps was next, and on the far western end of the line was the XVIII Airborne Corps.

Allied forces punched into Kuwait in four thrusts. The first push was made across the border into occupied Kuwait by the I Marine Expeditionary Force, commanded by Lieutenant General Walter   *Continued on page 202*

Bombs, Maverick missiles, and 30-mm. cannon rounds are loaded on a U.S. Air Force A-10 Warthog. The A-10 flew low and slow to kill Iraqi Scud missile launchers and armored vehicles. Two A-10s from the Air Force Reserve 926th Tactical Fighter Group shot down two Iraqi helicopters.

DENNIS BRACK / BLACK STAR

The copilot/gunner of this U.S. Army AH-64 Apache sees a Republican Guard armored column at night on the cockpit display generated by his infrared sensors (opposite). Flames and smoke from burning vehicles create lighter images on the screen.

U.S. DEPARTMENT OF DEFENSE

Iraqi soldiers waving white flags and clutching coalition surrender leaflets give themselves up. More than 65,000 Iraqi soldiers surrendered to coalition forces during the liberation of Kuwait and campaign in Iraq.

ERIC BOUVET / ODYSSEY / MATRIX

PRECEDING PAGE

U.S. troops check Iraqi stragglers during the liberation of Kuwait City.

ERIC BOUVET / ODYSSEY / MATRIX

E. Boomer. Its striking power was in the 1st and 2d Marine Divisions and the 1st Brigade of the Army's 2nd Armored Division, nicknamed the "Tiger Brigade." These troops cut through sand berms and minefields of the first Iraqi defensive belt. The move was made easier by the earlier penetrations of task forces Grizzly and Taro. The 1st Marine Division ripped through the Iraqi breaches without meeting heavy resistance and battled through the Al Burgan oil field south of Kuwait City en route to the Al Jabr airfield. The airfield was an intermediate objective on their march to Kuwait City. Once secured, Al Jabr would serve as a forward refueling position for attack helicopters and for medical evacuation of wounded troops by air. To the left of the 1st Division, the 2d Marine Division faced the most challenging series of minefields and obstacle belts of the Iraqi defenses. These Marines, with the Army's Tiger Brigade, cleared the hazards by the second day of fighting.

The surviving Iraqi artillery fired several hundred rounds at the Marines, but those guns were soon silenced by coalition artillery and air attacks. A U.S. Air Force pilot returning from a mission over Kuwait in that early-morning darkness described the scene lit up by the explosions of battle and by the flames of hundreds of oil well fires. Colonel Hal Hornburg said, "It looks like what I envision hell would look like. . . the country of Kuwait is burning."

As the liberation of Kuwait entered its final phase, President Bush asked the world to pray for the coalition forces and for "God's blessing on the United States

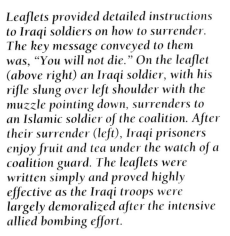

Leaflets provided detailed instructions to Iraqi soldiers on how to surrender. The key message conveyed to them was, "You will not die." On the leaflet (above right) an Iraqi soldier, with his rifle slung over left shoulder with the muzzle pointing down, surrenders to an Islamic soldier of the coalition. After their surrender (left), Iraqi prisoners enjoy fruit and tea under the watch of a coalition guard. The leaflets were written simply and proved highly effective as the Iraqi troops were largely demoralized after the intensive allied bombing effort.

اوقف القتال الان، حافظ على حياتك

من الملجأ، يجب على حامله التقيد بالخطوات التالية:
للبحث بالسلام.

١. اسحب مخزن الذخيرة من سلاحك.
سلاحك على كتفك الايسر مع توجيه الماسورة الى الاسفل.
٢. احمل
٣. ارفع يديك فوق راسك.
من مواقع القوات المتعددة الجنسيات ببطء، وي فرد في
٤. اقترب
المقدمة يرفع هذه الوثيقة فوق رأسه.
٥. اذا عملت هذا تنجو من الموت.

CEASE RESISTANCE - BE SAFE

To seek refuge safely, the bearer must strictly adhere to the following procedures:

1. Remove the magazine from your weapon.

2. Sling your weapon over your left shoulder, muzzle down.

3. Have both arms raised above your head.

4. Approach the Multi - National Forces' positions slowly, with the lead soldier holding this document above his head.

5. If you do this, you will not die.

of America." In Baghdad, Saddam took to the air waves as well, and broadcast a message to his troops: "Fight them, Iraqis! O' Iraqis, fight them with all the power you have and all struggle for everything and all the faith you have in a people that believes in God and in his dignity and his rights to choose and select and make its own decisions. Fight them, brave Iraqis! The men of the Mother of Battles, fight them of your faith in God! Fight them!"

While exhorting his troops "to fight and show no mercy," Saddam also declared that the American-led coalition had "stabbed us in the back" by the ground attack. Saddam had patiently waited out the allied air campaign, planning to apply the tactics he had learned in the Iran-Iraq War to destroy the coalition armies in the ground campaign, a victory that he believed would come to Iraq in the Mother of Battles. While the allied armies attempted to smash through the double belt of defensive positions just inside of Kuwait, his vaunted artillery—possibly using chemical warheads—and his tank forces would destroy the coalition armies. He envisioned such heavy casualties being inflicted on the coalition forces that they would have to capitulate, as Iran had been forced to do in 1988.

The coalition's initial attacks across the Saudi-Kuwait border and north along Kuwait's coastal road occurred where Iraq had expected the allied thrusts to come. Unknown to Iraqi commanders, another allied army was on the move more than 200 miles (322 km.) to the west, penetrating into western Iraq.

By early morning on February 24, the XVIII Airborne Corps, commanded by

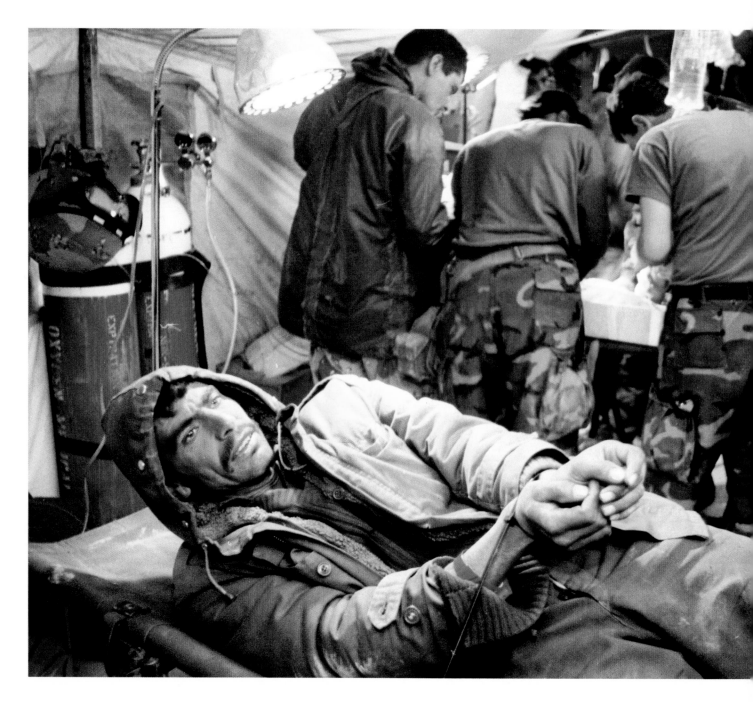

An Iraqi prisoner awaits medical treatment at a forward clearing station while surgeons care for another casualty.

Lieutenant General Gary E. Luck, was moving northward, across the border into Iraq. General Schwarzkopf's plan was to use the mobile XVIII Corps to swing wide to the west and cut off the Iraqi forces, landing a lightning "left hook," and then to close in with the heavy punch of VII Corps to destroy the trapped Iraqi divisions. The farthest left (western) unit of the XVIII Airborne Corps was the French 6th Light Armored Division (under Major General Bernard Janvier) with the 2nd Brigade of the U.S. 82nd Airborne Division.

At 5:30 A.M., the men of the French division and the American paratroopers dashed into Iraq and drove 94 miles (151 km.) north to capture the small junction town of As Salman. Iraq's 45th Infantry Division with 10,000 troops held As Salman. The Franco-American force destroyed the division.

The rest of XVIII Airborne Corps held fast for the moment. Several hours later, after waiting for the weather to improve, some 400 helicopters airlifted the U.S. Army's 101st Airborne Division more than 60 miles (97 km.) northward into

Iraq, where troops established a forward supply and operating base. The operation would be recorded as the largest combat helicopter movement in history as the helicopters airlifted more than 2,000 troops of the "Screaming Eagles" division, 50 of their "Hummer" utility vehicles, several howitzers, and several tons of fuel and ammunition. The helicopters—some with female pilots— never flew more than 100 feet (30 m.) above the ground. One OH-58 Kiowa crashed in the desert while flying through fog; the crew was rescued. The advanced desert base also provided the springboard for later leaps by the 101st Airborne.

But other factors began to influence General Schwarzkopf's execution of his battle plan. "We were worried about the weather. The weather was going to get pretty bad the next day, and we were worried about launching this air assault. We also started to have a huge number of atrocities of really the most unspeakable type committed in downtown Kuwait City. . . . When we heard that,

Seeing the ultimate price of combat, American troops contemplate the charred remains of an Iraqi soldier.

ERIC BOUVET / ODYSSEY / MATRIX

Trophies of war soon to be scrap: stacks of AK-47 assault rifles, rocket launchers, and machine guns taken from Iraqi prisoners.

ERIC BOUVET / ODYSSEY / MATRIX

we were quite concerned about what might be going on. Based upon that, and the situation as it was developing, we made the decision that rather than wait [until] the following morning to launch the remainder of these forces, that we would go ahead and launch these forces that afternoon," he explained.

The remaining forces of the XVIII Airborne Corps, centered on the U.S. Army's 82nd Airborne Division and 24th Infantry Division, began moving north early in the afternoon on February 24.

In the center of the allied line, the VII Corps, led by Lieutenant General Frederick M. Franks, began moving north into Iraq. The VII Corps had the U.S. Army's 1st and 3rd Armored Divisions, and the 1st Infantry Division as well as the British 1st Armoured Division (under Major General Rupert A. Smith).

On the evening of February 24, General Schwarzkopf reported that while coalition casualties were "remarkably light," more than 5,500 Iraqi prisoners had been taken within the first ten hours of battle, and that hundreds more with white flags were waiting to surrender to anyone or anything that moved. Iraqis were even giving up to journalists following the allied armies. Asked "Are you going around or over?" Schwarzkopf replied, "We're going to go around, over, through, on top, underneath, and any other way it takes to get in." Even before Schwarzkopf's briefing ended, the number of prisoners had risen, approaching 10,000. "Some of these Iraqis didn't realize the ground campaign had begun until our tanks rolled over their position," said a coalition general.

Overwhelmed by these numbers and preoccupied with reaching their objectives, some advancing allied units collected the prisoners' weapons, left food, and simply pointed them south before charging ahead. These prisoners were eventually picked up and moved to prisoner-of-war camps in Saudi Arabia.

The fast-moving armored units of VII Corps – centered on the U.S. Army's 1st and 3rd Armored Divisions and the 1st Infantry Division as well as the British 1st Armored – began to squeeze the Iraqi forces within the Kuwaiti area into a pocket. The XVIII Corps' 24th Infantry Division completed its dash into the Tigris-Euphrates Valley by sundown on February 25. By using their night-vision sights, gunners on the M1A1 Abrams tanks were able see through the night, smoke, and dust to locate Iraqi T-72 tanks at far greater ranges than the Iraqis could see them.

The 24th Infantry Division, after overrunning a large supply dump and two airfields, turned eastward, driving the allied left hook toward Basra. The other forces of the XVIII Airborne Corps, on the allies' left flank, picked up momentum as Saddam's divisions crumbled and surrendered. The French 6th Division and U.S. 82nd Division formed a screen to the left of the allied assault, extending north to the Euphrates River, guarding a flank that was nearly 200 miles (322 km.) long and trapping Iraqi forces in the Kuwaiti theater.

About this time, swarms of U.S. Army UH-60 Black Hawk helicopters carried more than 1,000 troops of the 101st Airborne into the Euphrates Valley, where they began attacking Iraqi convoys on the road, severing Highway 8, connecting Baghdad and Basra. A communique from Baghdad said all of the U.S. troops that had landed were annihilated and called on Americans to ask President Bush "to tell them about the fate of the forces and the losses they suffered instead of telling lies."

By February 25, the second day of ground fighting, General Schwarzkopf's battle plan had developed a life of its own. Toward the Gulf coast, around 8 A.M., as fighting continued at the Al Jabr airfield just west of Kuwait City, all five of 1st Marine Division's artillery battalions fired simultaneously into Iraqi concentrations

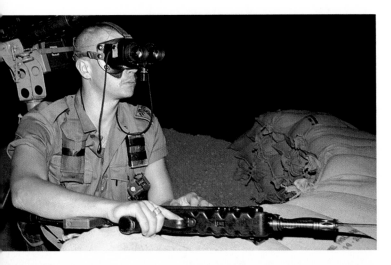

Night watch: a French trooper wearing night vision goggles scans the terrain. The French 6th Light Armored Division was reinforced by a brigade of the U.S. Army's 82d Airborne Division on the far western flank of the coalition attack forces.

GILLES BASSIGNAC / GAMMA-LIAISON

Sailors of a U.S. Navy SEAL team circle the American Embassy compound at Kuwait City in their dune buggy. SEAL teams, along with other U.S. and British special forces, operated behind Iraqi lines before and during the campaign.

CHRISTOPHE SIMON / AFP

TANK KILLERS

U.S. forces used several weapons systems to counter Iraqi tanks. How major anti-tank weapons work:

HELLFIRE MISSILE

Apache AH-64 helicopters engage tanks on their own or with the help of spotters.

1 Helicopter spotter projects laser spot on one target.

2 Soldier projects laser spot on another target from the ground.

3 Standoff AH-64 launches missiles.

4 Missiles steer toward laser spots on targets; enemy tanks are destroyed.

M1A1 ABRAMS

The M1A1 is the U.S. Army's main battle tank. How it attacks:

1 A tank gunner beams a laser onto the target; M1A1 computer interprets data that's beamed back and generates a firing solution.

2 M1A1 keeps moving to avoid being shot by other tanks.

3 Turret and gun adjust on the move, as computer tracks target; gunner squeezes firing trigger.

A-10 THUNDERBOLT

The A-10A "Warthog" is one of the Air Force's chief anti-tank weapons. It is designed to fly slow and low; deliver Maverick missiles or 30mm cannon fire; require little maintenance and survive treacherous anti-aircraft fire. How it typically attacks:

1 Pilot selects target; locks Maverick seeker on target and fires missile.

2 Pilot rolls and banks sharply when using 30mm gun.

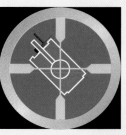

TOW MISSILE

TOW (Tube-launched, Optically-tracked, Wire-guided) missile can be launched from a tripod, Cobra helicopter, or ground vehicle.

1 Gunner acquires target through optical sight.

2 Launches missile.

3 Gunner keeps crosshairs on target until wire-guided missile hits.

ANTI-TANK WARHEADS

APDS (Armor Piercing Discarding Sabot). Warhead's aluminum sabot (outer casing) falls off in flight, leaving one-piece depleted uranium penetrator rod to smash at high velocity through armor. (This is the primary anti-tank round for M1A1 Abrams 120-mm. gun.)

HESH (High Explosive Squash Head) warhead's tip squashes and detonates, causing scab of tank's interior metal to break free and ricochet inside tank.

AIM FOR THE WEAK SPOTS

Though many tanks have layers of reactive armor, tracks and the tops of turrets remain vulnerable.

HEAT (High Explosive Anti-Tank) warhead's base detonates on impact, producing molten metal that sprays into tank.

SOURCE: KNIGHT-RIDDER TRIBUNE NEWS

U.S. Marines clamber down from a UH-60 Blackhawk helicopter onto the roof of the American Embassy in Kuwait City to clear the building and prepare for its reopening. The haze is caused by smoke from burning oil wellheads.

RICHARD ELLIS / REUTERS / BETTMANN

in the Burgan oil field. The Marines hoped to get an idea of Iraqi troop strengths in the area. The salvo drew an immediate Iraqi counterattack, which threatened the division's forward command post. There were reports that Iraqi T-62 tanks were attacking everywhere. By 10 A.M., Marine AH-1W SeaCobra helicopters armed with TOW anti-tank missiles along with the Marines' own artillery, and Air Force and Marine air strikes took a deadly toll on the Iraqi attackers, as allied fire power knocked out 30 tanks and armored personnel carriers.

The helicopters were so close to the Marine ground units during the fight that one Marine officer later recalled that he could reach up and touch the skid of a hovering SeaCobra as hot shell casings from the helicopters' 20-mm. cannon rained down on the Marines. With the Iraqi counterattack repulsed, the Marines continued their advance toward Kuwait City.

After this firefight, the wind shifted and the billowing smoke from an estimated 500 burning oil wells settled over the battlefield. At high noon, troops in the 1st Marine Division could see only ten feet in any direction and had to read their maps with flashlights. The soot and oil covered their clothing and burned their throats.

Finally, after several months of amphibious exercises and publicity in expectation of a Marine amphibious assault, the Marines came ashore. But it was not an assault across the defended beaches; instead, it was a helicopter lift of the 5th Marine Regiment, which was landed behind the advancing Marine divisions to serve as a reserve should Iraqi resistance harden.

Near the end of the ground battle, General Schwarzkopf told the press how things stood. "We were 150 miles (240 km.) from Baghdad, and there was nobody between us and Baghdad. If it had been our intention to take Iraq, if it had been our intention to destroy the country, if it had been our intention to overrun the country, we could have done it unopposed, for all intents and purposes, from this position at that time. That was not our intention, we have never said it was our intention. Our intention was truly to eject the Iraqis out of Kuwait and destroy the military power that had come in here."

The coalition's forces moved with remarkable speed and across unprecedented distances. The campaign was a classic envelopment, involving some 6,000 tanks on both sides, more than were used by German and Soviet forces at the Battle of Kursk in 1943, and many times the numbers that Generals Erwin Rommel and Bernard L. Montgomery had in North Africa in 1941-1942. The movement even out-paced the drive of General George Patton's Third Army during the 1944 Normandy breakout, and was conducted over a much larger area.

Desert Storm commanders and troops rested during breaks lasting a few minutes or, at most a couple of hours. Troops strung hammocks inside their tanks and fighting vehicles, or slept sitting up during brief pauses. While they rested, the engines of their vehicles purred at idle. Armor troops do not shut off their engines in combat; they continue at idle to be ready to move out instantly, and not be killed because a balky engine refused to start. The troopers crunched the Meal, Ready to Eat field ration, or MRE, for hasty nourishment. Rest was secondary to the objective of keeping unrelenting pressure on Iraqi combat units.

The logistic efforts supporting these attacks also set precedents, exceeding the figures in U.S. Army planning manuals. Such manuals reckon that a mechanized division consumes about one million gallons of fuel each day when moving across the country. In 70 hours of operations, the 24th Infantry Division alone burned diesel and aviation fuels at twice that rate. Through rain and mud, and under combat stress, thousands of men and women driving heavy cargo trucks or flying CH-47 Chinook and CH-46 Sea Knight cargo helicopters struggled to transport the fuel, ammunition, food, and water to sustain the offensive's momentum.

A low overcast and cold rain persisted through February 26. Coalition troops rolled over pockets of Iraqi resistance, collecting several thousand additional prisoners. From crowded skies that resembled a civilian air traffic controller's worst nightmare, medevac helicopters swooped low over the muddy terrain to evacuate the wounded while coalition attack aircraft and helicopters responded rapidly to calls for fire support.

On the outskirts of Kuwait City the Iraqi resistance stiffened. After Marines seized the Al Jabr airfield, another armored battle erupted at the Kuwait International Airport. In the early-morning fog, U.S. Marines used their night vision advantage to engage the Iraqi T-55, T-62, and top-line T-72 tanks before their own tanks were within Iraqi sights and ranges. Once the fog cleared and observers could more readily control allied fire, close-air support and naval gunfire added their lethality to the battle. By day's end on February 27, Marine and Arab forces had decimated Iraq's 3d Armored Division, liberated the Kuwait airport, and took control of the access routes to Kuwait City. The city was entered with Arab troops and U.S. Special Forces units in the lead.

In Kuwait City, U.S. forces reoccupied the U.S. Embassy as one of the first orders of business. Iraqi troops had been inside the embassy, but fled before friendly troops arrived. The American flag was still flying over the embassy. For some reason the Iraqis never lowered it during the occupation. After bomb disposal experts checked the building and grounds for mines and booby traps, Ambassador Edward Gnehm arrived by helicopter to reopen the Embassy.

Northwest of Kuwait, by February 27, the tanks and troops of the VII Corps were smashing through the Republican Guard armored divisions outside of Basra. With his laser sights, a U.S. tank gunner in an M1A1 Abrams could "lase" a T-72, wait a moment for the tank's computer to come up with a firing solution, then squeeze off a round in a matter of seconds. *Continued on page 212*

American Ambassador Edward Gnehm, escorted by U.S. Army Colonel Jesse Johnson, arrives to reopen the American Embassy in Kuwait City.

PEARSON / AFP

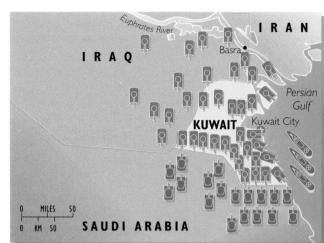

HOW THE WAR UNFOLDED

In one of the largest ground campaigns since World War II, allied forces smashed through Iraqi defenses, destroyed more than 2,000 Iraqi tanks, captured more than 65,000 Iraqi prisoners and ousted all Iraqis from Kuwait in just 100 hours.

JANUARY 17 Allied forces massed south of the Kuwaiti border, deliberately ignoring the weak Iraqi flank to the west.

FEBRUARY 23

With the Iraqis unable to see them, U.S., British and French forces completed a massive flanking movement westward.

FEBRUARY 24-26

While U.S. Marines and Arab troops attacked the Iraqi line in Kuwait, U.S. airborne units and French troops raced into the desert and began setting up supply bases for the tank columns that would follow. As coalition troops pushed into Kuwait, taking thousands of Iraqi prisoners, tank columns wheeled around the Iraqi flank along the Eurphrates River, preventing escape to the north. An estimated 21 Iraqi divisions are knocked out.

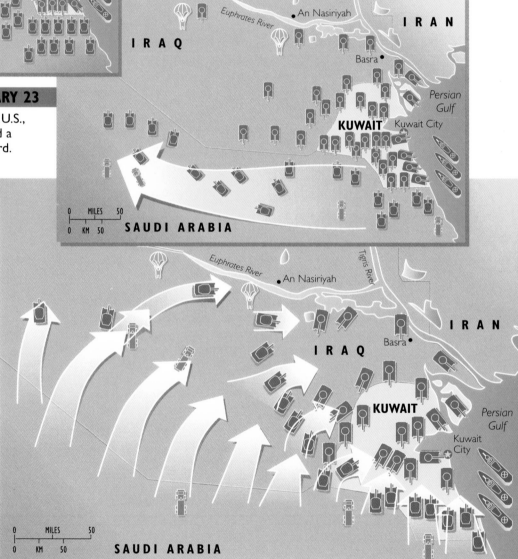

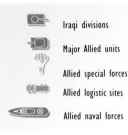

Iraqi divisions

Major Allied units

Allied special forces

Allied logistic sites

Allied naval forces

FEBRUARY 27

Allied troops liberate Kuwait City and surround remaining Republican Guard divisions, fighting intense tank battles. "A solid wall" of coalition forces cuts off remaining Iraqi troops from escape. President Bush stops offensive military action.

Pointer in hand, General Norman Schwarzkopf, U.S. commander of coalition forces (right), begins his classic briefing on the battle that ended the Gulf War. On February 27, 1991 he spent an hour in the ballroom of a Riyadh hotel giving reporters a "complete rundown on what we were doing and, more important, why we were doing it." When he was finished, a reporter asked whether Schwarzkopf thought he had possibly overestimated the hazards of the Iraqi barriers facing his forces, Schwarzkopf lunged forward, using the body language that earned him the nickname The Bear, and asked: "Have you been in a mine field?" The reporter weakly answered, "No."

Schwarzkopf had. In May 1970, during the second of his two tours of duty in Vietnam, Lieutenant Colonel Schwarzkopf, a battalion commander, was in his command helicopter when he received a radio report: two officers had been wounded in a mine field. Their men, trapped amid unseen mines, were near panic. Schwarzkopf ordered his helicopter to land and evacuate the wounded, leaving him behind. He promised the men he would lead them out, telling them to take the same path they took when they had stumbled into the mine field. He ordered them to stay well apart and walk in the footsteps of the man ahead.

But a foot strayed. A mine exploded, throwing a soldier into the air and spewing shrapnel. Fragments hit Schwarzkopf and another officer. The soldier who stepped on the mine began writhing. Fearful that the soldier's movements would set off another mine, Schwarzkopf began crawling toward him. Another movement by another soldier triggered another mine. The explosion killed three and mutilated a third. Schwarzkopf, himself wounded, led the rest of his men out of the mine field. His action won him his third Silver Star.

Schwarzkopf had been in a mine field and he had been a student of war. On the table next to his bed in Saudi Arabia was *Infantry Attacks* by German Field Marshal Erwin Rommel, the Desert Fox of World War II. Rommel had written the book about his experience in World War I. But he was a master of the war of movement, and, whenever or wherever the battle, Rommel's operations taught lessons to the generals who came after him.

"The commander," Rommel once said, "must try, above all, to establish personal and comradely contact with his men, but without giving away an inch of authority." Schwarzkopf followed that rule throughout his career and throughout the Gulf War.

Saddam Hussein, the man who warned his foes they would bleed and die in "The Mother of Battles," was not a military man. But he had won a war against Iran with a brutally simple tactic. His troops fell back before advancing Iranians, pulling the green, lightly armed soldiers into "killing zones." Trapped in front of massive obstacles and flanked by dug-in artillery and tanks, the Iranians were massacred.

That was the mother of battles Saddam had planned. Schwarzkopf planned another. He said so publicly back in September. "A war in the desert," he said in a briefing, "is a war of mobility and lethality. It's not a war of straight lines drawn in the sand, where you dig in and say, I will defend here or die."

Saddam Hussein could have learned a lesson from what Schwarzkopf had said. But it was not Saddam who would set up, fight, and win the Mother of Battles. The winner would be the man who had been in a mine field.

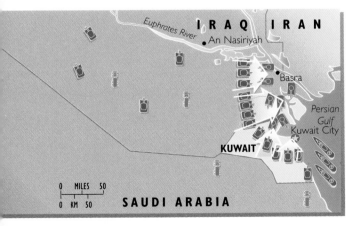

Resident of newly-liberated Kuwait City shows his joy by kissing the American flag.

SANTIAGO LYON / REUTERS / BETTMANN

The high-velocity, 120-mm. tank-killing round, with depleted uranium in the shell's rod that penetrates through enemy armor, could smash through T-72 armor and penetrate into the tank's turret, or knock the turret off its mounting. While hundreds of Iraqi tanks were killed, of the 1,956 M1A1 Abrams that engaged Iraqi forces in battle, only four were disabled and four more were damaged but could be repaired. One M1A1 tank took two direct hits in the turret from a T-72. The Abrams crew was shaken, but their tank was still able to fight. The tank commander slewed his turret around, the gunner lased and fired, and they killed the T-72 that had hit them. (The Marines had some Abrams tanks, but mostly the older M60A1 tanks with a 105-mm. gun.)

To the north and west of Kuwait, now only about 150 miles (240 km.) from Baghdad, the French and American divisions of the XVIII Airborne Corps formed, in General Schwarzkopf's words, a "solid wall" across the north. Next to the XVIII Airborne Corps, another wall consisting of the VII Corps attacked to the east, against other Republican Guard divisions.

Iraqi troops were now fleeing north, pursued by coalition units and attacked

212

relentlessly from the air. In three and one-half days of sharp fighting, more than 29 Iraqi divisions were smashed, with an estimated 3,000 Iraqi tanks destroyed or captured. But some Republican Guard divisions were still capable of combat and disposed to fight. However, the Iraqi army had ceased to exist as a formidable threat.

Addressing the overwhelming defeat of Iraqi forces, General Schwarzkopf made one of the most devastating evaluations ever made by a military leader of his opponent. Addressing Saddam Hussein and his military leadership, Schwarzkopf declared: "As far as Saddam Hussein being a great military strategist, he is neither a strategist, nor is he schooled in the operational arts, nor is he a tactician, nor is he a general, nor is he a soldier. Other than that, he's a great military man. I want you to know that," he told a televised press conference.

President Bush, addressing the American people from the White House on the night of February 27, said that effective "at midnight tonight, Eastern Standard Time, exactly 100 hours since ground operations commenced and six weeks

Jubilant residents of Kuwait City crowd around a U.S. Special Forces soldier as the city is liberated. Special Forces troopers accompanied all Islamic forces of the coalition for liaison and fire support coordination.

LAURENT REBOURS / AP / WIDEWORLD PHOTOS

since the start of Desert Storm, all U.S. and coalition forces will suspend offensive combat operations. It is up to Iraq whether this suspension on the part of the coalition becomes a permanent cease-fire." Thus, despite the dire predictions by many experts of a long and bloody war that would repeat the Vietnam experience, U.S. and coalition forces had won a rapid and stunning victory, with relatively few casualties.

In his television interview with David Frost a few weeks later, General Schwarzkopf recounted the last hours of the war: "After the third day. . . we knew we had them. . . . it was literally about to become the battle of Cannae, a battle of annihilation. . . ." Schwarzkopf, a student of military history, was referring to Hannibal's slaughter of at least 50,000 Romans at Cannae in southern Italy in 216 B.C. Hannibal's smaller army outmaneuvered the Romans, trapping them in a classic double envelopment.

Take that, Saddam! Kuwaiti boy expresses his feelings about Saddam Hussein by stoning his image at Sief Palace after liberation of the city.
F. STEVENS / SIPA PRESS

"I reported the situation to General Powell," Schwarzkopf continued. "And he and I discussed, have we accomplished our military objectives? The campaign objectives? And the answer was yes. . . . We had destroyed the Republican Guard as a militarily effective force."

The decision was then made by President Bush and his advisors to halt offensive action. That decision had stopped the coalition's advance. The decision was a "very courageous decision on the part of the President, said General Schwarzkopf. "Frankly, my recommendation had been. . . continue the march. I mean we had them in a rout and we could have continued to, you know, reap great destruction on them. We could have completely closed the door and made it, in fact, a battle of annihilation. And the President, you know, made the decision that, you know, we should stop at a given time, at a given place that did leave some escape routes open for them to get back out and I think it was a very humane decision and a very courageous decision on his part also. 'Cause it's you know—it's one of those ones that historians are going to second guess forever. Why did we stop when we did, when we had them completely routed? We are already getting the question."

General Schwarzkopf's candid appraisal sparked a debate in Washington, fanned by media anxious to highlight an apparent schism between the Commander-in-Chief and senior field commander. After a brief exchange of telephone calls, both the President and the General made it clear that there was a difference of opinion but no difference of purpose.

General Schwarzkopf, in the first meeting with Iraqi military commanders on March 3, imposed conditions on Iraqi forces to cease resistance. The Iraqi and coalition military commanders met in a field tent in the desert near the town of Safwan, the tent ringed by U.S. tanks and armored fighting vehicles. The Iraqi officers had been told to come to a desolate airfield. There they surrendered their sidearms and were flown by helicopter to the meeting site.

The halt to allied military operations was the first step in a political process that ultimately led to a U.N.-mandated cease-fire in mid-April. For President Bush, repatriation of American and other coalition prisoners of war in Iraq was the top priority. At the same time, coalition forces prepared to begin repatriating the Iraqi prisoners they held.

With offensive operations apparently over, the task of "policing the battlefield" began. The wreckage of thousands of burnt-out vehicles littered the area, as did hundreds of thousands of mines, booby traps, and other explosives. More than

65,000 Iraqi prisoners had to be cared for until they could be sent back to Iraq. The sick and wounded on both sides required medical care.

While the living were being tended to, the task of burying hundreds of Iraqi dead began. During the air campaign, each morning the Iraqis had buried their comrades who were killed the night before. When the ground campaign began, the Central Command required that Saudi graves registration teams accompany advancing coalition units to bury the thousands of Iraqi dead in accordance with Muslim custom. U.S. soldiers and Marines buried another 444 Iraqi soldiers. The total number of Iraqi troops killed in the air and ground campaigns has been unofficially estimated at more than 100,000. But there were no official enemy body counts by the coalition, either during the war or immediately after. General Schwarzkopf had too many frustrating experiences with body counts in the Vietnam War and had decided that there would be none in the Gulf conflict, nor would there be overly optimistic reports about future operations. It is doubtful if the exact number of Iraqi troops killed will ever be known.

When offensive operations were suspended, coalition forces controlled one-fifth of Iraq, about 35,000 square miles (90,671 sq.km.), approximately the size of the state of Indiana. But in a northeast corner of that territory, on March 1, the Hummurabi Armored Division of the Republican Guard attacked the 24th Infantry Division more than 24 hours after hostilities had been suspended. Major General Barry R. McCaffrey, commander of the 24th, said that the attacking Iraqi force consisted of 400 to 500 vehicles, including "a couple of hundred" tanks and personnel carriers. McCaffrey said, "They bumped into us going west, trying to break out across the causeway [leading to the Baghdad highway]."

The 1st Brigade of McCaffrey's division came under fire from the Guards' T-72 tanks, Sagger anti-tank missiles, and rocket-propelled grenades. The 1st Brigade counterattacked, supported by attack helicopters. The helicopters stopped the force. McCaffrey massed his division's entire artillery, more than 200 howitzers, to blast the Iraqi division; then his 1st Brigade attacked on line with their M1A1 tanks and Bradley fighting vehicles. In a battle lasting almost five hours, the entire Iraqi force was destroyed. Enemy killed were estimated at several hundred; the survivors fled or were captured. This was the last major engagement of the war.

American casualties in the air and ground campaign were far lighter than expected. The reckoning of combat casualties was 144 killed in action and 339 wounded in action, plus ten more missing. Two French soldiers were killed, and ten British. Casualties in the attacking Islamic units were equally light. However, 16 of the coalition combat deaths were caused by U.S. Air Force air strikes; seven Marines were killed near Khafji and nine British soldiers were killed in the VII Corps' operations to this "friendly fire." General Schwarzkopf said, "We deeply regret that. There's no excuse for it." The mistaken attacks were made at night, in the confusion of heavy fighting. There were also reports of friendly artillery falling on friendly troops, but deaths were not reported in those instances.

In Washington, General Powell reflected on how well the forces worked together: "It was a textbook joint operation. No service parochialism. No logrolling. Each service doing what it does best to ensure victory. It was a great team effort."

Lieutenant General Tom Kelly, the principal Pentagon briefer during the Gulf War, later recounted one of the sayings going around the Pentagon after hostilities were suspended. "Iraq went from the fourth-largest army in the world to the second-largest army in Iraq in 100 hours." Earlier, General Schwarzkopf had told coalition troops: "I have seen in your eyes a fire of determination to get this war job done quickly. My confidence in you is total, our cause is just. Now you must be the thunder and lightning of Desert Storm."

The thunder and lightning of Desert Storm had smashed the Iraqi forces in the Kuwaiti area. The military victory was undeniable. What remained uncertain was the course of the political and economic consequences created by the triumph on the battlefield.

CHAPTER ELEVEN

SHINING VICTORY, DARK CLOUDS

I n the final hours of the war, a strange motorcade pulled out of Kuwait City. Armored personnel carriers, tanks, private cars, buses, trucks, and ambulances clogged the highway. What looked like a mammoth traffic jam was an army in frantic retreat. Troops of the Iraqi Army had loaded their loot – stereos, children's toys, furniture, seemingly anything that could be lifted – into every vehicle they could steal. And then they had fled northward, toward the sanctuary of their homeland.

Most of the miles-long, bumper-to-bumper column had reached the outskirts of the city when out of the sky came a rain of bombs and bullets from allied aircraft. Unable to move, vehicle after vehicle exploded in flames. Hundreds, perhaps thousands of Iraqis died. Hours later, the war ended with total victory for the coalition. In every country of the coalition, people celebrated their troops' triumph and the remarkably few casualties. The images of charred bodies sprawled on the highway gave grisly proof that the Iraqi Army had been annihilated.

In a televised address, President Bush announced that a cease-fire would go into effect at 8 A.M. on February 28, Iraqi time. "Kuwait is liberated," he said. "Iraq's army is defeated. Our military objectives are met."

The best news for the coalition was about casualties. Losses by U.S. and other forces were much lower than anyone had predicted. As of March 8, when the U.S. Department of Defense issued a detailed report, 144 U.S. service men and six service women had been killed in Operation Desert Storm. During Desert Shield, from the arrival of U.S. forces in Saudi Arabia in August 1990 to the start of Continued on page 220

Home is the warrior from Desert Storm. A soldier of the U.S. Army's 24th Infantry Division hugs the kin who waited and prayed.

CYNTHIA JOHNSON / TIME MAGAZINE

216

A sea of burning oil engulfs a refinery south of Kuwait City. Iraqis methodically set Kuwaiti oil fields afire, producing what scientists called an environmental catastrophe of unprecedented scale.

AMALVY / AFP

the air war on January 16, 1991, there were 108 non-hostile deaths.

During the previous, peaceful year of 1989, a total of 1,684 service men and women died, mostly in automobile accidents. The death rate was 79 per 100,000. The death rate in the Gulf area, based on a force of 540,000 men and women (and including combat deaths), was 68 per 100,000.

"The big killers in peacetime are automobiles," a Pentagon public affairs officer said. "And most automobile accidents involve alcohol." In Saudi Arabia, officially at least, there was no alcohol to drink and no private cars to drive.

On the Iraqi side, casualties remained unknown. Pentagon analysts said that a policy of careful targeting, along with the use of highly accurate missiles and guided bombs, held down civilian casualties. The analysts also believed that Iraqi army units collapsed because of desertions and surrenders rather than battlefield deaths. Desertions probably totaled 100,000; more than 65,000 became prisoners of war. A Republican Guard division of 10,000 men,

according to one report, lost 100 killed in action, had 300 wounded – and lost 5,000 by desertion.

Short-lived postwar revolts against the Baghdad government scattered incredible numbers of Iraqi civilians from their homes. Estimates made in April, two months after the war ended, put 450,000 Iraqi Kurds in Turkey; another 400,000 just south of the Turkish border in the mountains of northern Iraq; 1 million Iraqi Shiite refugees over the border into Iran; another 500,000 in Iraq near the Iranian border.

Ecologically, Kuwait suffered more from the war than Iraq did. Even as grinning, waving liberators rolled into Kuwait City in February, Kuwait was ablaze. Departing Iraqis had set fire to more than 600 oil wells. Some 5 million gallons of oil a day were going up in flames. Black, choking smoke blotted out the sun. Kuwait's oil fires were consuming more oil each day than Kuwait had sold before the invasion. Breathing, said a Kuwaiti, was "like taking the exhaust pipe of a diesel truck in your mouth and breathing that."

The cease-fire that formally ended the war put a large area of southern Iraq under coalition control. In Basra, just north of this zone, units of Saddam Hussein's Republican Guard, unscathed by the war, suddenly appeared a few days after the cease-fire. They sent tanks against dissident troops and Shiite Muslims fighting to overthrow Saddam. On the tanks were printed "No Shiites after today." Refugees fleeing from the Shiite holy city of Najaf said soldiers had massacred thousands of civilians and left their corpses along the sides of a road.

Shiites revere Ali, the son-in-law of the Prophet Mohammed, and the 12 successive Imams esteemed as the descendants of the Prophet. Shiites make up about 55 percent of the Iraqi population, but Sunnis, who consider Shiites blasphemers, support Saddam. Many rebellious Iraqi Shiites give religious and political allegiance to Shiite brethren in Iran. These Iraqi Shiite rebels had always been a problem for Saddam. In Basra and in a dozen Shiite cities he was solving that problem, with military might, just as he had done in the past.

U.S. satellite and aerial photographs showed about 5,000 Iraqi troops fighting rebels in Basra, which refugees called "a dead zone" because of the bodies of rebels lying in the streets.

Shiites streamed out of towns along the edges of the occupied zone and sought help from U.S. troops. American soldiers gave food and bottled water to exhausted, barefoot *Continued on page 224*

PRECEDING PAGE

Wrecked and gutted vehicles litter the "Highway of Doom," the getaway road without an exit. Retreating Iraqi troops stole cars, buses, and trucks to flee Kuwait City. But the motorcade became a lethal trap when coalition aircraft knocked out the lead vehicle and swept down the column, destroying 1,000 vehicles, civilian and military.

ERIC BOUVET / ODYSSEY / MATRIX

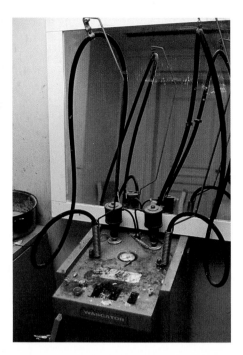

A torture chamber (below) used by Iraqi occupation forces stands as grim proof of interrogation techniques. Victims were strapped to an "electric bed" and doused with water. The bedspring was wired to an apparatus (left) that controlled the intensity of the electricity surging through the victim's body when a question was not answered. Kuwaitis told of being rubbed with sandpaper, hung from hooks, and beaten. Middle East Watch, a human-rights group, estimated that Iraqi occupation forces killed 300 to 600 Kuwaitis. Bodies were found bearing burns made by acetylene torches and wounds inflicted by axes, power drills, meat hooks, and saws.

BOTH: LUKE DELAHAYE /SIPA PRESS

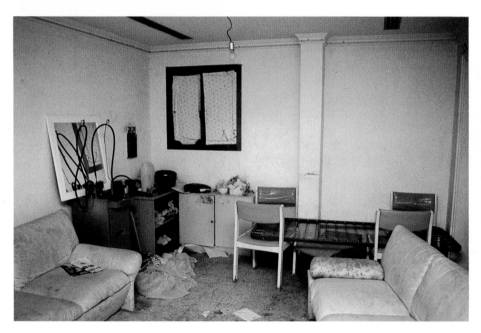

PRECEDING PAGE

A Kuwaiti stands amid the ruins of a market deliberately destroyed by Iraqi troops during their occupation of Kuwait City.

ERIC BOUVET / ODYSSEY / MATRIX

refugees. Women and children wounded by Iraqi guns were cared for by American doctors who had gone to war expecting to treat soldiers. Tens of thousands of Shiites, along with Iraqi Army deserters, fled to the occupied zone or into Iran.

To the north, Iraqi Kurds again rose in revolt against Saddam. Kurds, who are Indo-European Sunni Muslims, make up almost 25 percent of Iraq's population but are powerless. An old adage says, "Kurds have no friends." To crush the rebellious Kurds in 1988, Saddam had killed thousands with poison gas and wiped out about 4,000 Kurdish villages, forcing hundreds of thousands of Kurds to "relocation centers."

In a post-Gulf War revolt, the Kurds briefly held one of their population centers, Kirkuk, site of a major oil field. But within a month after the end of the war, Saddam's troops had quelled the Kurdish revolt. More than 1 million

Kurds, driven from their northern villages by Saddam's forces, fled toward Turkey or Iran.

Coalition officers and spokesmen for the Bush administration seemed stunned by the surge of revolt in the north and south. But President Bush himself had publicly urged the overthrow of Saddam. And for months an Arabic-language clandestine radio station, the "Voice of Free Iraq," had urged armed revolt.

In an "appeal to the Iraqi Army" on January 3, 1991, for example, the Voice of Free Iraq urged "a revolution against corruption, aggression, and the rule of the family of crime"—the family of Saddam Hussein. "Let your guns be directed toward criminals instead of the sons of your people or brothers," said the broadcast. On the same day another broadcast said, "The only solution is an uprising." The next day, a broadcast exhorted the Army to "direct your rifles at the regime of the tyrant Saddam Hussein." On February 24 the radio called for

Gun-toting Kuwaiti resistance fighters parade an accused collaborator through the streets of Kuwait City. A fact-finding team from Amnesty International said vengeful Kuwaitis arbitrarily tortured and killed residents believed to have aided Iraqi occupation forces.

CHRISTOPHER MORRIS / BLACK STAR

"a revolution now, before it is too late. . . . Hit the headquarters of the tyrant."

After the war, the Voice of Free Iraq started sounding murderous. On March 16: "As for you, Saddam, you have proved that you are no more than a harmful insect sticking to the body of Iraq, an insect that can be plucked out of it only with a knife. . . . A just bullet will be coming to you soon, very soon. . . ."

Kurdish leaders in exile claimed that the U.S. Central Intelligence Agency had set up the radio station, which broadcast from Jiddah, Saudi Arabia. Such a station could not operate without Saudi approval, but Washington officials declined to comment on reports of U.S. involvement.

Whatever the sponsorship of the Voice of Free Iraq, its words were clearly inspiring armed revolt, by soldiers – who did briefly fight the Republican Guard in Basra – and by civilians, who died by the thousands in the north and south.

Under skies darkened by the smoke of burning oil wells, a Kuwaiti father and son face a future just as dark. Scientists fear that prolonged exposure to soot-filled air will cause a dramatic rise in lung disease. Satellite photographs show the widespread effects of the oil-well fires set by the Iraqis. In February (opposite, left), skies are clear. In April (opposite, right), when Iraqis set some 600 wells afire, smoke blots out hundreds of square miles.

L.VANDERSTOCKT /GAMMA-LIAISON
OPPOSITE: EOSAT

Asked on March 13 about reports that Iraqi Army helicopters were firing on civilians in rebellious cities, President Bush said, "I must confess to some concern about the use of Iraqi helicopters in violation of what our understanding was."

The "understanding" was an oblique reference to an agreement made at the meeting of General Norman Schwarzkopf, commander of U.S. forces in the Persian Gulf, and Iraqi military leaders. At the March 3 meeting, the two sides agreed on the cease-fire and on such matters as prisoner of war exchanges and disclosure of the locations of Iraqi mine fields.

Schwarzkopf shed new light on the helicopter issue in his interview with David Frost broadcast on public television on March 27. Schwarzkopf said he had been "suckered" by the Iraqis when they asked for permission to use helicopters for transporting government officials. "I think they intended – right then, when they asked that question – to use those helicopters against the insurrectionists," Schwarzkopf told Frost.

Had the Bush administration urged a revolt against Saddam and simultaneously kept him strong enough to crush it? A kind of answer – or at least an interpretation of administration policy—had come on March 21.

The day before, a U.S. F-15 had shot down an Iraqi Su-22 Fitter fighter near the Kurd city of Kirkuk. Asked at a Pentagon press conference how U.S. policy differentiated between fighter planes and helicopters, U.S. Assistant Secretary of Defense for Public Affairs Pete Williams struggled to find an answer. He would not say whether U.S. aircraft would shoot down Iraqi helicopters used against insurgents. Then, as if in desperation, Williams said, "Is our policy somewhat ambiguous? Yes." (The next day, a U.S. F-15 shot down another Su-22.)

More than 60,000 of the Iraqi prisoners of war and 25,000 civilian refugees and deserters poured into the American occupation zone in the south. In the north, hundreds of thousands of Kurds fled from villages destroyed or threatened by Saddam's troops in the wake of the smashed Kurdish revolt.

Refugees told of Iraqi helicopters flying low over villages, firing on inhabitants and dropping napalm. They said the Iraqi Army also used artillery against them, blasting villages where ruins still bespoke similar attacks in 1988. During lulls in the bombardment the terrified families, fearful of a resumption of 1988 poison-gas attacks, abandoned their battered homes and villages.

On foot, by mule, and by truck and car, they headed for refuge across the border into Turkey. They followed the footsteps of other Kurds who had escaped to Turkey following Saddam's poison-gas attacks in 1988. The first of the new arrivals got food and help from their brethren in Turkey. But, the stream of refugees grew to a flood – as many as a million men, women, children, and babies. The exodus was threatening to become the worst refugee disaster in modern times.

Throughout the world, television screens that had shown images of war and

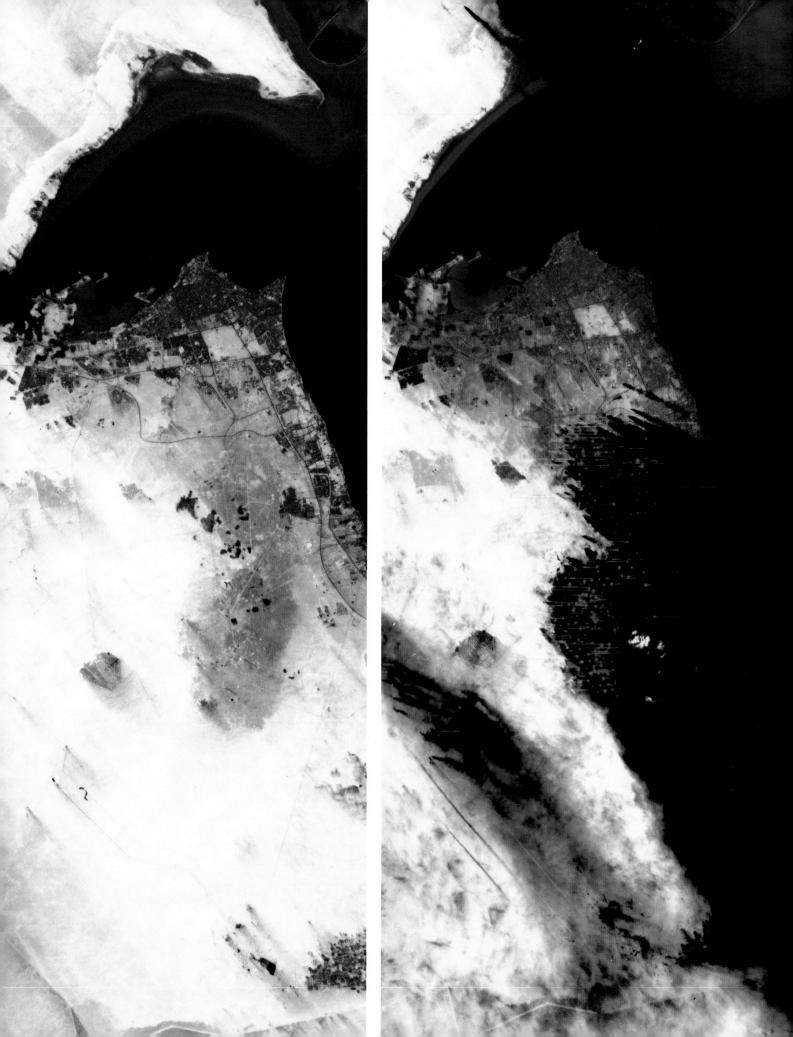

victory now showed images of wretched refugees starving in the mountains along the Turkish-Iraqi border. The very young and the very old were dying at the rate of 1,000 a day. Little bodies wrapped in dirty shrouds were carried past the camera and buried in muddy graves. Mothers wept for the dead and the dying. Gaunt men stared hollow-eyed into television cameras.

Each day brought new, heart-rending images from the slopes where the Kurds were dying. The Bush administration had proclaimed a policy of getting U.S. forces home and crisply ending U.S. involvement in Iraq. But the images from the mountains could not be ignored. Step by step, the administration moved toward the mountains: parachute drops of food and clothing . . . a seven-minute helicopter visit to the refugee camps by Secretary of State Baker . . . financial aid to Turkey . . . and, finally, U.S. troops. They joined with British, French, and Dutch forces giving protection to the refugees, building tent camps, establishing safe havens in Iraq, and urging Kurds to return to their villages.

Some of the Kurds did begin trekking back to their homes and to Saddam's mercies. Perhaps this time, they thought, it would be different. A promise of forgiveness from Saddam had come once before.

In 1989, under international pressure, Saddam had declared amnesty for all Kurds and all political opponents. But at least 11 Kurds who gave themselves up to claim amnesty were executed. And, according to a June, 1990 Amnesty International report on Iraqi human-rights violations, "the situation of 1,900 other Kurds who had returned remained unclear."

To "counter adverse international publicity," the report said, Iraq "announced a major liberalization program" and "extended an invitation to selected journalists to observe the democratic process in the country." One of the journalists was Farzad Bazoft of the London Observer. He was hanged by Iraq as a spy in March 1990.

While instability marked the situation in Iraq, coalition troops, ships, and planes began returning to their home countries. U.S. troops began leaving Saudi Arabia at the rate of several thousand per day, being flown home by the same military and commercial transports that had brought them to the Middle East. By late April 1991, the last U.S. troops were withdrawn from southern Iraq as a U.N. peacekeeping force moved into the coalition-controlled portion of Iraq. American troops did remain in the northern area of iraq, near the Turkish border, to protect Kurdish refugees. Meanwhile, U.S. and other coalition aircraft

Staff Sergeant Daniel Stamaris, taken prisoner by the Iraqis, salutes his freedom while his wife weeps for joy on his arrival at Andrews Air Force Base in Washington. A victory rally in Sandy Hook, New Jersey, (lower, opposite) typifies the flag-waving patriotism that marked civilian support of the Gulf War.

UPPER: BRAD MARKEL / GAMMA-LIAISON
LOWER: LISA QUINONES / BLACK STAR

Desperate Kurdish refugees clamor for food at a refugee camp in Turkey. Camps stretch for miles (opposite) in a Turkish mountain pass. Hundreds of thousands of Kurds fled the guns of Saddam Hussein, whose army struck Kurdish areas as the Gulf War ended. As many as 1,000 died each day on the Iraqi-Turkey border.Coalition forces set up havens (see map opposite) to protect the Kurdish refugees.

ABOVE: CHIP HIRES /GAMMA-LIAISON
OPPOSITE: MARC DEVILLE /GAMMA-LIASON

were flying Kurdish refugees from western Iran into areas of Iraq under the protection of U.S. or U.N. forces.

For those troops returning to the United States there were celebrations, parades, and honors reminiscent of the end of World War II. General Schwarzkopf returned to a "quiet" welcome at MacDill Air Force Base in Florida—only a few thousand troops, friends, and his immediate family were on hand. But parades and honors were in the offing. On April 23, Schwarzkopf lunched at the White House with President Bush.

Wearing a dress green uniform in lieu of the camouflage or "cammies" combat outfit made famous in the Gulf War, Schwarzkopf politely and laughingly brushed aside the issue of whether or not coalition troops should have continued to destroy Iraqi military forces beyond the 100-hour ground war. He told a press group at the White House: "What I'd really like to say is, if the

President's not going to answer any questions, I damn sure am not going to answer any."

President Bush praised the conquering general and—as did the country—praised the performance of the thousands of American and coalition men and women who had fought the Gulf War.

On April 28, 1991, exactly two months after a cease-fire ended the Persian Gulf War with a coalition victory, the oil wells that Saddam Hussein had set afire still burned in Kuwait. The oil that Saddam Hussein had spewed into the Gulf still blackened the shores of Saudi Arabia. The Shiite Iraqis whom Saddam Hussein had driven to Iran still huddled in their border camps. The Kurds whom Saddam had driven to the mountains still wandered and still died. And Iraq once more celebrated its April 28 national holiday, the birthday of Saddam Hussein. He still ruled.

CNN Covers The War

In Washington, D.C., on the night of January 17, 1991, as the War in the Gulf began, a senior intelligence official walked into his boss's office to brief him on the situation. "I'm 15 minutes ahead of what CNN has. . . ," he began.

"I couldn't compete with CNN," the official later recalled. The television set in his office, in the offices of his colleagues throughout Washington, in the White House, in other allied capitals, in Saddam Hussein's capital of Baghdad, and millions of private homes around the world were all tuned to the Cable News Network. As bombs and missiles began to fall on Baghdad, three CNN newsmen in that besieged city gave a blow-by-blow description of the attack: veteran war correspondent Peter Arnett, reporter John Holliman, and anchorman Bernard Shaw.

Moments after the attack on Baghdad began, CNN lost its television signal from Iraq; but around the world viewers still watched their screens, which most of the time showed a map of Iraq and photos of the three journalists. The world was riveted to television sets as — for the first time in history — a live account of the start of a war was broadcast from inside an enemy country. The broadcast was descriptive and dramatic.

"The undisputed star of the initial coverage was CNN, the 24-hour-news channel, which affirmed its credibility and world-wide clout with new authority," wrote Richard Zoglin in *Time* magazine of January 28. "Though ABC, NBC and CNN managed to air telephone reports with their correspondents in Baghdad during the initial shelling. . . ABC and NBC lost contact after a few minutes. Only CNN was able to keep its line open and broadcast continuously throughout the attack," noted Zoglin.

While several CNN staffers cite luck as being a key factor in their successful coverage, hard planning and hard work were also vital. Ed Turner, CNN executive vice president, said, from CNN's viewpoint, the war started on August 2. Although Americans were not yet involved, he knew it would be a big story. At that point CNN began "educating itself," he said, as well as sending men and equipment to the Gulf area. The equipment included the "four-wire," a device that provided an open circuit, hard-wired to avoid switching circuits that were vulnerable to power loss. The four-wire provided reliability and two-way communications for broadcasters in the field. (The reports over the four-wire went by phone line from Baghdad to Amman, Jordan, for satellite relay to CNN's headquarters in Atlanta, Georgia.)

The four-wire and the lightweight fly-away transmission unit brought into Baghdad on January 28 would provide – through satellite relay – real-time transmissions to CNN subscribers throughout the world. Initially, the Iraqis objected to installation of the four-wire. "Bob Weiner went door to door," recalled Ed Turner, discussing how Robert Weiner, CNN bureau chief from Berlin, sought permission from the Iraqis to install the four-wire in Baghdad. "We became the biggest nuisances the Iraqi government ever saw until the arrival of the U.S. Air Force." The Iraqis gave permission in September 1990.

The CNN leadership decided before the shooting started to devote the entire CNN news schedule to the war when the fighting began. "The war," Turner explained, "will have a foothold around the globe and somewhere people will be awake." When not actually covering the war, CNN would go to locations around the world to see how its impact was being felt, and would put experts on camera.

According to Turner, the Gulf situation was "the most important story of a generation. It's almost impossible to do too much on it, particularly since all we do is news and because of the global audience we have. People are hungry worldwide for information, opinion, analysis, and commentary." By mid-January,

CNN photographer William Walker being lowered onto a destroyer in the Red Sea (opposite). Ed Turner makes a point in the newsroom at CNN headquarters in Atlanta (top). In Baghdad's Al Rashid Hotel, (lower) John Holliman types notes as Mr. Alla – a "minder" – translates a Saddam speech; at left are CNN producer Ingrid Formanek and Berlin bureau chief Robert Weiner.
OPPOSITE : U.S. NAVY
ABOVE TOP: KELLY MILLS/CNN
ABOVE: MARK BIELLOW/CNN

CNN had a crew of 20 in Baghdad. And, newly arrived CNN President Tom Johnson in Atlanta was adding his long-time, worldwide contacts to the network's scope and effectiveness.

CNN was appreciated: "I Love CNN" was the message whitewashed on the seawall of Kuwait City when liberated. Troopers of the U.S. Army's 82nd Airborne Division painted a CNN logo on one of their satellite antennas set up in the Iraqi desert when they encountered CNN's Brian Haefeli.
TOP: DAVID LEESON/JB PICTURES/DALLAS MORNING NEWS
RIGHT: BOB FRANKEN/CNN

Although the television picture was lost soon after the initial air attacks began, the CNN reporters in Baghdad continued their dramatic reporting using only audio links. CNN finally lost all direct contact with its Baghdad team 17 hours after the war began when Iraqi officials, citing security reasons, shut down the four-wire. Shaw, Holliman, and most other American television people left Baghdad the next day. In particular, Shaw was wanted back in Washington to anchor CNN's broadcasts from the capital city. For more than two weeks Arnett was the only American broadcasting from Baghdad.

The U.S. government wanted to debrief Shaw, a former Marine, when he came out of Iraq, but the newsman refused. To have talked in private to military intelligence about what he saw, said a CNN official, would have put him in danger the next time he was in a crisis area, as well as endangering CNN people still in Baghdad.

Arnett had gone to Baghdad to stay: "When I left Israel for Iraq it was with the understanding that I would stay there even if war broke out." Would he leave if ordered to by CNN: "No," was his definite reply. Said Ed Turner: "There is no doubt that Arnett could not have been driven out of there short of an Iraqi tractor pulling him down the road to Jordan."

CNN had kept an aircraft under charter for $10,000 a day at an airstrip in Jordan to fly people out of Iraq in the event things got too hot in Baghdad or Saddam ordered newsmen out of the country. The other networks used the plane on several occasions;

CNN used it once. However, Holliman and Shaw came out of Iraq into Jordan by truck because of the air war.

From the 14-story Al Rashid Hotel in downtown Baghdad, a mecca for foreign newsmen and diplomats during the war, Arnett used a satellite telephone from the hotel to continue his reports to the world. A CNN generator powered the satellite link after allied bombing knocked out electrical power in the city.

While Arnett's reports were censored prior to broadcast, the question-and-answers were relatively free-ranging and quite informative. For example, when CNN Atlanta asked if there was much military traffic on the highway to Basra after Arnett said that he had been to the road, he replied "There is not much civilian traffic," thus, telling that there was military traffic on the highway while not violating Iraqi censorship.

Arnett and others at the Al Rashid were always in danger of an errant bomb or missile striking the hotel. (A British television correspondent on a sixth-floor balcony reported looking down to see a Tomahawk cruise missile come streaking by.) There was an "exchange of information" with the U.S. government over the possible bombing of the Al Rashid, said a CNN executive. The Al Rashid was not a target because of the diplomats and journalists housed there. Arnett told the authors that he was certain that General Norman Schwarzkopf, whom he had known in Vietnam, "owed me one," and would have gotten a message to Arnett if coalition aircraft were going to hit the hotel. Still, the possibility of an accidental strike on the hotel was very real.

At the peak of the war, CNN had some 150 broadcasters, technicians, and support people in the Gulf area. World-wide another 1,500 were working on the Gulf War story. Camera crews visited scores of military bases in the United States and abroad to report on troops, ships, and aircraft departing for the Gulf. National leaders were interviewed by CNN in every major capital. And hundreds of experts on every phase of the Gulf War and its implications appeared daily on the network.

In addition, an average of some 60 experts per day appeared on camera to address military, political, economic, religious, and cultural aspects of the crisis and then war. Gale Evans, CNN vice president of guest booking, and her staff maintained a vast, computerized index of experts and pundits located throughout the world. Once identified, their qualifications were checked, they were contacted, and then scheduled into the programs. About 2,500 interviews related to the Gulf were aired on CNN

during the war.

"It was like a dance," recalled Evans as she described working with the news staff during the war. "We had been working together for years—everyone knows how much of a product they have to produce." (Evans joined CNN in 1980, the year the network began; longevity is a hallmark of the operation.)

The only competition CNN had for obtaining top-level guests were the Sunday interview shows of the major networks. Otherwise, said Evans, "What we did yesterday, they were doing today." Indeed, the other networks were soon calling CNN for names and phone numbers.

During the war CNN maintained two permanent specialists, Perry McCoy Smith, a retired Air Force major general, who was in Atlanta, and Dr. James A. Blackwell, a strategy expert at the Center for Strategic and International Studies in Washington. They provided the continuity to CNN's expert commentary on the war. (They were the only experts appearing on CNN who were paid for their services.)

As Peter Arnett became an "icon" in Baghdad for television viewers, so did Charles Jaco broadcasting from Dhahran, Saudi Arabia, and Wolf Blitzer, CNN's Pentagon reporter, in Washington. Minutes after the war began, CNN had switched to Blitzer at the Pentagon, who for the next 43 days would report on events at the nation's military command center. Usually shown with a world map as the background, Blitzer also took viewers to the daily press briefings at the Pentagon. CNN gave full coverage to those briefings as well as the military briefings in Riydah.

Politics were covered from Washington by CNN White House correspondents Frank Sesno and Charles Bierbauer, while Mary Tillotson covered Capitol Hill. These reporters and others in Washington were joined by hundreds overseas and in the field, reporting on reserve units being called up, on Gorbachev supporting the U.N. resolutions, and innumerable news stories in between.

What were the effects of the Gulf War on CNN? Ed Turner responds to the question with the story of how Chinese leader Chou En Lai was asked what the effects on China were of the French Revolution. "He said it's too early to tell," relates Turner. It's too early to tell. . . but CNN is a hell of a lot better known than it was before the war."

Many at CNN take pride in pointing out the multitude of problems that cropped up in covering the Gulf War and how they were resolved. "The next time we'll be better prepared," said Charles Hoff, managing director of Newsbeam, CNN's satellite hookup. But he quickly acknowledged that there will always be

Doonesbury

surprises.

Planning, hard work, and luck were the keys to CNN's unprecedented success in covering the war. Planning was meticulous. Before the war began, detailed schedules, plans for backup coverage, equipment replacement, and numerous other aspects of covering the war were worked out. The day-to-day planning was the responsibility of Eason Jordan, CNN's vice president for international coverage, and every minute of the day had to be planned. Initially the newsroom and technical staffs simply remained around the clock, with CNN's 24-hour cafeteria serving food to the newsroom and offices.

After about two days the planned 12-on-12-off schedule was implemented, although in reality it was 14-on because of the need for overlap. The Omni Hotel, adjacent to CNN headquarters, became the refuge for the few hours off-duty.

The comprehensive CNN coverage of the war brought unending controversy. An official of the Palestine Liberation Army (PLO) complained that CNN was giving disproportionate time on the air to Israeli Deputy Foreign Minister Benjamin Netanyahu. Eason Jordan responded, "Look, the day the war broke out, I called you to get reaction from Chairman Arafat and you told me he couldn't be interrupted, that he was in the situation room watching CNN."

More controversial was the interruption of Jordan's King Hussein just as he was saying why he was not objecting to Iraq firing modified Scud missiles across his country toward Israel. When CNN switched to another story, it brought down the wrath of the Israelis, who wanted the world to hear the king's statement, while Arab callers also objected to CNN cutting off the king. (The entire press conference was broadcast later in the day.)

Many American viewers criticized CNN and, especially, Peter Arnett for broadcasting Iraqi-censored "news" – which they said was propaganda.

To some degree it was. Opinions varied greatly. Senator Alan Simpson (R-Wyo.) called Arnett an Iraqi "sympathizer" and described his reporting as repugnant and harmful to the United States." Simpson later gave a qualified apology. But a U.S. intelligence official told the authors: "On a daily basis I was pissed off at Arnett. On a singular basis he was an invaluable source to me in bomb damage assessment. . . satellites and aircraft gave me a 'straight-down' view"; Arnett, he said, "gave me a street view of what had happened and what the people were doing and thinking."

But 56-year-old, New Zealand-born Arnett, who became an American citizen a few years ago, still believes without qualification that the structure claimed by U.S. military intelligence to have been a command bunker was an air raid shelter for civilians, and the so-called baby milk factory was just that, and not a chemical warfare plant.

Indeed, the use of CNN as a conduit of information and misinformation was practiced by both sides, though more subtly and successfully by the coalition. Allied air attacks had so shattered Saddam's communications that, as a high-ranking U.S. military officer said, "CNN may have been the only accurate source of information that he had. So we knew what he was getting. We were able to pass information to him."

Even at the tactical level Arnett was often lauded. According to *Aviation Week* magazine, Colonel Al Whitley, commander of the 37th Tactical fighter Wing, which flew the F-117 Stealth attack plane, observed: "It certainly was interesting for us to come back and land and watch the [television] replays of what it's looking like from another perspective. Knowing where some of the broadcasts were coming from, and seeing the skyline. . . we could actually pick out who some of the bombs belonged to. . . . There was some good in having good old Peter Arnett on the ground."

A large number of individuals and organizations assisted the authors in the research and writing of this book. Several, however, have asked that their assistance not be publicly acknowledged because of their positions at the time of the Gulf War. The authors are in debt to those individuals as well as to the following persons:

Peter Arnett, journalist, CNN; Laurent Aublin, Press and Information Counselor, French Embassy, Washington; Rear Adm. Brent Baker, USN, Chief of Navy Information; Maj. James Bates, USAF, Military Airlift Command; Wolf Blitzer, Pentagon correspondent, CNN; Robert Bockman, Department of Defense (Public Affairs); Brig. Gen. P.L. Bolte,USA (Ret.), former armor commander, Rear Adm. Thomas A. Brooks, USN, Director of Naval Intelligence; Bill Caldwell, Department of Defense (Public Affairs); Kenneth Carter, Department of Defense (Public Affairs); Lt. Col. Jim (Snake) Clark, USAF, U.S. Air Forces in Europe; J.H. Crerar, Betac Corp.; Lt. Col. Mike Cox, USAF, Military Airlift Command; Linda Cullen, Photographic Library, U.S. Naval Institute; Vice Adm. Francis R. Donovan, USN, Commander, Military Sealift Command; Russell Egnor, Office of Navy Information; 1st Lt. Karen Finn, USAF, 1st Tactical Fighter Wing; Lt. Gen. Howard M. Fish, USAF (Ret.); Maj. Gen. Thomas Foley, USA, Commadant U.S. Army Armor School; William Funk, Public Affairs Office, Military Sealift Command; CWO Randy Gaddo, USMC, Public Affairs Office, Headquarters, Marine Corps; Lt. Col. Mike Gallagher, USAF, Air Force Electronics Systems Division; Lt. Col. Mike Gannon, USAF, Office of the Secretary of the Air Force(Public Affairs); John Gilleland, General Dynamics Land Systems; Lu Gregg, Vice President, Hughes Aircraft; Larry Hamilton, Grumman Corp.; Capt. Uri Har, Israeli Navy (Ret.), General Manager, Association of Israeli Electronic Industries; Marge Holtz, Public Affairs Officer, Military Sealift Command; Gen. H.T. Johnson, USAF, Commander-in-Chief U.S. Transportation Command and Military Airlift Command; Charles Krohn, CAK, Inc.; Lt.Col. Phil Lacombe, USAF, Joint Information Bureau, U.S. Central Command; Dave LaForte, Hughes Aircraft Training Systems Division; Tim Laur, Editorial Director, USNI Military Database; Comdr. John Leenhouts, USN, attack pilot, Navy Attack Squadron 72; Lt. Comdr. Andrea Licci, Italian Navy, Assistant Naval Attache, Italian Embassy, Washington; Peter Mersky, Assistant Editor, *Approach Magazine*; Col. Miguel Monteverde, USA, Department of Defense (Public Affairs); Capt. Michael Murray, USA, Army Armor School; Brig. Gen Richard I. Neal, USMC, Director of Operations, U.S. Central Command; Maj. H. Nickerson, USA, Joint Information Bureau, Central Command; Col. Bob Pastusek, USAF, Director of Requirements, USAF Tactical Air Command; Brig. Gen. H.E. Robertson, USAF, Director, Office of the Secretary of the Air Force (Public Affairs); Comdr. Rudy Rudolph, USN, fighter pilot, Defense Systems Management College; Tony Salame, Middle East expert; Lt. Comdr. Kenneth Satterfield, USN, Department of Defense (Public Affairs); Dave Shea, Hughes Aircraft; Kiane Smigel, LTV Corp.; Capt. Asher Sofrin, Israeli Air Force (Res.), Manager, Teldan Information Systems; Bettie Sprigg; Department of Defense (Public Affairs); Mary Beth Straight, Photographic Library, U.S. Naval Institute; Joe Sutherland, General Dynamics Corp.; Capt. Steven Tate, USAF, fighter pilot, 71st Tactical Fighter Squadron; Capt. Kris Thompson, USA, Army Armor School; Patricia Toombs, Office of Navy Information; Hal Watkins, Hughes Aircraft Missile Systems Group; and Maj. Gen. Frank Willis, USAF, Director of Requirements, Military Airlift Command.

Editorial assistance was provided by Carol Swartz and Scott C. Truver, research assistance by Christopher Henley, Estelle Tarica, and Connie Allen Witte; and design assistance by Elizabeth Doherty and Susan Stenquist.

The authors made use of numerous official and public reports and other documents, published articles, and transcripts of radio and television programs related to the Gulf War. Three documents merit special citation for their value to the authors: The U.S. Army War College reports, <u>Iraqi Power and U.S. Security in the Middle East</u> (1990) by Stephen C. Pelletiere, Douglas V. Johnson II, and Leif R. Rosenberger, <u>Lessons Learned: The Iran-Iraq War</u> (1991) by Pelletiere and Johnson; and "Crisis in the Gulf," chronology compiled by Judith Walters of the U.S. Naval Historical Center.

Appreciation is also expressed to those individuals at CNN whose superb work led to unprecedented achievements in broadcast journalism during the War in the Gulf, making this book possible; led by Tom Johnson and Ed Turner, they were: Todd Baxter, Kathy Christensen, Tyronne Edwards, Mike Epstein, Gail Evans, Ingrid Formanek, Dave Haberlin, Brian Haefeli, Steve Haworth, Charlie Hoff, John Holliman, Stacy Jolna, Eason Jordan, Tom Knotts, Kris Krismanich, Bernard Shaw, Mike Simon, Kit Swartz, Steve Tallent, Dick Tauber, William Walker, Bob Weiner, Ann Williams, and Dan Young.

The publishers would also like to thank; Mary Jane Batson, John Bavier, Todd Baxter, Katherine Bird, Chuck Brock, James Burns, Gordon Castle, Ann Coningsby, Pat Costello, Susannah Dance, Fredic De Wulf, Marta Donovan, Marcia Dworetz, Mike Gordon, Anna Griffin, Laura M. Heald, Beth Hoffman, Larry Johnson, Vivian Lawand, Nina Marson, Craig McMahon, Scott Mikus, Kelly Mills, Ira Miskin, Stephen Neely, Lisa Oliver, George Puckhaber, Molly Roberts, Dan Rosen, Karl Schnellinger, Suzanne Volkman-Skloot, Bonnie Stewart, Jim Taylor, Debbie Turoff, Preston Walklet, Michael Walsh, Pam Wedding, and Donna Wheeler.

CNN wishes to express its gratitude to the men and women of print, radio, and television journalism who put their lives at risk to report on the soldiers, sailors, Marines, and airmen of the coalition, some of whom did not return - all of whom met the enemy with courage.

Video images converted for print by Editel, New York, N.Y. Color separations by Color Response, Inc., Charlotte, N.C. Pages, type, and graphics composed on Macintosh computers with Quark XPress and Aldus FreeHand software. Graphics data courtesy Knight Ridder Tribune News, Washington, D.C. Printed and bound by R.R. Donnelley & Sons, Inc., Chicago, Ill. Paper by Westvaco, New York, N.Y.